The Comprehensive Guide To Pairpoint Glass

Shapes and Patterns

Sandra and Marion Frost

Schiffer Publishing Ltd
4880 Lower Valley Road, Atglen, PA 19310 USA

Dedication

We dedicate this book to the memory of the craftsmen and artisans at "the Pairpoint."

'Tho' the work you did
is your legacy,
Your spirit lives on
in our memories.

...And to Myldred Costa, *Memory Keeper Extraordinaire*

Library of Congress Cataloging-in-Publication Data

Frost, Marion.
The comprehensive guide to Pairpoint glass : shapes and patterns / Marion and Sandra Frost.
p. cm.
ISBN 0-7643-2417-9 (hardcover)
1. Pairpoint Glass Works. 2. Glassware—Massachusetts—History. I. Frost, Sandra. II. Title.

NK5198.P3A4 2006
748.209744'85—dc22

2006000350

Designed by "Sue"
Type set in Seagull Hv BT/Souvenir Lt BT

ISBN: 0-7643-2417-9
Printed in China

Published by Schiffer Publishing Ltd.
4880 Lower Valley Road
Atglen, PA 19310
Phone: (610) 593-1777; Fax: (610) 593-2002
E-mail: Info@schifferbooks.com

Contents

Acknowledgements

We have no illusions about who should receive credit for the existence of this book. Without the people who cleared the paths, providing direction to our research, there would be nothing between these covers. We have been little more than technicians assembling the puzzle pieces provided by others.

These people must have had a sense of something important and grander than themselves when, so many years ago, they acquired and preserved the invaluable Pairpoint documents and artifacts that were so generously made available to us. There could be no better tribute to several generations of incredibly gifted artisans and craftsmen than to recognize their greatness through the preservation of the document trail that would ensure the immortality of their life's work.

And so, to these kind, unselfish, and important individuals, we salute you, and extend our sincerest gratitude and profound thanks. This is your book.

Myldred Costa of North Dartmouth, Massachusetts
Kauko Kahila of East Falmouth, Massachusetts
Charles and Barbara Coulter of South Easton, Massachusetts

We would also like to extend our appreciation to the Schiffer Publishing Company for their continuing interest in our work.

Foreword

Pairpoint glass has certainly earned its rightful place in history, but most people don't think about how it got that way. They don't stop and think that it took a lot of very talented people to come together and join their many different skills to make products of such beauty. It would only be fitting to acknowledge some of the great men who helped make Pairpoint one of the most popular glass companies in the United States. Anders Thoen, whose skills as a stemware maker were unmatched, came from Norway. Hjalmar Gerhard "Gilly" Gulbranson, considered one of the best glassmakers in the country, started training under his father's eye at the age of 6-1/2. Brothers John and Sture Bjorgen, heavy glass cutters and engravers, were very talented, and were responsible for teaching their craft to many of our New Bedford men, many of whom became well recognized in the industry. Tony DeCosta and Carl Silva, Ollie Cayton, Billy Frates, Joseph Cambra, and so many more that escape my memory today, were responsible for the magnificent cutting and engraving work that came out of Pairpoint during the 1920s, 1930s, and 1940s. And let's not forget one of the best glass decorators that ever lived, Frank Guba. An incredibly gifted artist, Mr. Guba was known for his beautiful paintings on Pairpoint lampshades and other art glass objects. He is perhaps best known for his painting of a wrecked sailing ship named the "Wanderer," which is currently on display at The New Bedford Whaling Museum.

Had these men not left other companies to join Pairpoint and share their gifted talents, we can only speculate whether Pairpoint would have ever achieved its level of success. We want to remember them always. As each one of these men joined and became a part of this glass company, they made the foundation of Pairpoint stronger. Their skills and expertise made Pairpoint glass desirable in every household then and now, 75 years later.

Today, as I was thinking of what I wanted to say here, I walked through my living room and noticed the sun shining brightly through a window onto some of the Pairpoint glass I have displayed on a bookcase. It was like seeing a rainbow; the beautiful heavy cut glass was picking up the reflections from the colored pieces sitting nearby. I realized then that when New Bedford lost Pairpoint, so did the whole country. Those beautiful engraved pieces can never be replaced or reproduced again, nor can the heavy cut lead crystal. Being so close to all this glass for so long and to realize that whatever is still in homes like mine, or museums, is the end of it. I've learned to appreciate and enjoy what I have and feel sad for those who never got to own even one piece. To see how talented these men were, many of whom came from foreign countries to teach and share their gift of glassworking with us. What we had and took for granted then was destroyed in that terrible fire. But what we, and I, have left are precious treasures and memories of what made Pairpoint the finest glass factory in our country.

Myldred Costa
North Dartmouth, Massachusetts
August 2003

Author's Note:

It is with profound sadness that Sandy and I acknowledge the passing of Myldred Costa during the wee hours of the morning on Thanksgiving Day, November 24, 2005.

Assisting us with this book has been one of the most important things in Myldred's life for the past couple of years, but we know, wherever she is, a great smile will cross her face each time a collector picks up this book and reads about her recollections of the glory days at the Pairpoint.

May you rest in peace, Myldred, and keep those old-timers in line up there.

Preface

When Sandy and I became interested in Pairpoint glass more than fourteen years ago, little did we know that good fortune would allow us to become one of the relatively few custodians of some of the few remaining Pairpoint historical documents. We started our Pairpoint adventure in 1990, as collectors, and remain that way today…just the same as most of you who are reading this book.

One thing we have learned over the years, and have tried to remain focused upon, is that the possession of documents and the accumulation of knowledge does not grant anyone the license to self-proclaimed "expert" status. Just as an historian can take no credit for the great historical events he may chronicle, we can take no credit for Pairpoint's greatness, even though the authorship of books on the subject spotlights us a little in the public eye. Public recognition, "expertness," and celebrity status are all fleeting in nature, and have nothing to do with the one true fact…Pairpoint was a great company and represented an era when American craftsmanship was the best in the world.

When the time came for us to consider compiling information into book form, our mission was very simple, and it still is. We recognized the existence of an information and awareness gap among other Pairpoint collectors, a gap that frustrated us from the beginning as we attempted to find and identify Pairpoint glass. We decided to take on the responsibility of providing as much documented information and observational commentary to the collecting public as we could. We wanted other collectors to be able to recognize, identify, evaluate and converse about the Pairpoint glass they would come upon in their searches. Simple in concept. Harder in implementation. Our work, upon occasion, has been criticized as being shallow, non-scholarly, and, while well-intentioned, not well-informed. Our published work was never intended to be an in-depth historical discourse; you would have to rely upon a first class researcher and historian such as Kenneth Wilson for that. Nor have we chosen to showcase through photographs only those most rare and unique examples of Pairpoint products that most of us will never see; we show the ordinary with the extraordinary. Only by showing it all can we achieve our goal. Our efforts have always been to preserve documentation and make it available to the general collecting public in a useful and practical way. We have made errors in the past, and we will certainly make more in the future, but we will remain true to our mission as we determined it to be.

It's hard for us to believe that we are putting together another book on the topic of Pairpoint glass. Sitting and writing at the craziest times, when the mood and the ideas strike, how lucky (or unlucky) can someone be? When asked four years ago by Peter and Nancy Schiffer, our publishers, if we could write another book on the subject, we emphatically said "No;" there just wasn't any new material to be found. If ever we have been wrong about something, that statement was it! Our steadfast belief that there are no true experts in the field of collecting was about to be validated again. Just when you think you are on top of your subject, and there is nothing more to learn, WHAM!!…your ego legs get knocked right out from under you. So, here we are again, hoping that our work will meet with your approval and satisfy your needs.

About five years ago, Sandy and I had the remarkably good fortune of meeting Charles and Barbara Coulter, antique dealers from Easton, Massachusetts. They were setup at the semi-annual glass show in Harrisburg, Pennsylvania, and sold us our first piece of documentation, a Gundersen-Pairpoint Franchise Catalog. We thought it to be unusual and something of a novelty, but our aspirations to acquire more documentation remained unformed.

Our friendship with the Coulters appeared to take a foothold right from the start, and we eagerly anticipated seeing them twice each year at Harrisburg. As time passed it became apparent to us that these were "tell it like it is" people of great integrity and honesty, the kind of people with whom we could feel very comfortable. Coupled with their long-term knowledge of Pairpoint glass, we knew there would be none better suited than Charlie and Barbara to review and critique the new book on Pairpoint glass we were putting together at the time. We sent them an early draft of *The Essence of Pairpoint*.

During the summer of the year 2000, Sandy and I visited New Bedford, Massachusetts, the home of The Pairpoint Corporation, to determine whether there was any last minute information available prior to submitting our manuscript to the publisher. While on that trip, the Coulters graciously invited us to supper at their home. Not only did we get the chance to visit with friends, but we had the opportunity to discuss the book draft "face to face." As our evening drew to a close, Charlie said to me, "Wait a minute. I've got something for you. I'll never have any use for it." You could have pushed us over with a feather when Charlie returned to the kitchen with a couple boxes of old Pairpoint factory documents. Our search for Pairpoint documents was launched at that moment.

Months later, after having had the opportunity to sort and examine the papers from Charlie and Barbara, we realized that we had the beginning of enough documentation to consider the possibility of putting together a second book covering a different, and little documented, Pairpoint era. This was a genuinely exciting realization for us, especially when contemplating the significance that such a book would mean to other collectors and dealers in the future, not to mention the preservation of archival material. Another short period of time passed and Lady Luck dealt us another winning hand. We were able to purchase another large cache of documents on the Internet. This purchase dovetailed with that which we already had and put us within striking distance of turning the possibility of a second book into a probability. The paper chase was on!

Caught up in the frenzy of searching for more and more documents, we decided to place an advertisement in the local New Bedford newspaper. We were asking anyone having old factory documents or catalogs to contact us, and many did. With one exception, everyone that was kind enough to respond had the same information we already had in our possession. Myldred Costa, from North Dartmouth, Massachusetts, did not have a large quantity of material, but what she had was akin to tapping into the mother lode. Myldred sent us everything she had without any financial expectation or condition. We were quite surprised at her generosity. Like the Coulters, her motivation was that the importance of preserving the history of Pairpoint and the memory of its workers transcended all other considerations; she thought that we would better ensure that result.

During the same time frame that our newspaper advertisement was running, we had the additional good fortune of being invited to the current Pairpoint Glass factory in Sagamore, Massachusetts, on Cape Cod. We spent several hours with Valerie Kelly, the owner of Pairpoint Glass, and John Kennan, the General Manager, touring the factory and discussing Pairpoint, then and now. There is no question that Pairpoint's legacy is in good hands. Valerie cherishes and is committed to the Pairpoint heritage, and recognizes the importance of her role in the perpetuation of Pairpoint for future generations.

While visiting the Pairpoint factory, John Kennan made it possible for us to meet a very distinguished gentleman who is probably more responsible for the preservation of Pairpoint's history than any other person. Mr. Kauko Kahila, or "KoKo," as he prefers to be called, became the curator of The New Bedford Glass Museum in 1976, when he retired as a trombonist with the Boston Symphony Orchestra. KoKo now visits Pairpoint regularly to make glass paperweights, a skill he learned later in his life. His paperweights, individually signed "KoKo," are relatively few in number and are sold in Pairpoint's factory store in Sagamore. As before, Sandy and I were blessed with good fortune when KoKo allowed us to borrow the large box of factory documents he brought for us to examine. We struck the mother lode again!

We now had a very large quantity of Pairpoint archival material, more than we had ever expected to obtain.

The obvious question began to emerge. Did we have enough material to put together the second book? We reviewed what we had and realized we were still short of our goal; we still needed more information from the 1940s. We were disappointed and pondered whether we would ever find what we needed. Then, a glimmer of light penetrated our mental fog. We realized that with the information we had obtained from Myldred Costa and KoKo Kahila, we had enough material for a third book, the preface to which, you are now reading.

The search for information has been an exercise of frustration, elation, humility, and enlightenment, all occurring simultaneously. The frustration of not finding material easily was soothed by the sense of elation upon discovering a tiny fragment of information that pulled many things together. And the humility of realizing that the search process results were totally beyond your control ultimately led to the enlightened understanding that the material we had discovered could never really belong to us. It is of more value to society as a whole than it could, or should, ever be to any one person.

This book is the result of our search and is our attempt to place as much information about Pairpoint glass identification within the reach of collectors, dealers, and enthusiasts as possible. It is more data-specific than one would normally expect to find in the collectible book market today, and is primarily an information extension of *The Essence of Pairpoint*. Although we include in the next chapter a glimpse of the human side of Pairpoint, by way of an interview with Myldred Costa, the focus of this book is upon shape and pattern identification. Over 300 new, and never before published, blank shapes are included as well as almost 50 new engraving patterns. Whenever possible we have included dimensional information. In addition to the new shapes and patterns, we have included a significant amount of updated information with regard to the patterns and shapes shown in *The Essence of Pairpoint*. Never before has so much comprehensive information about Pairpoint glass shapes and engraving patterns been assembled in one source book. We know the search is not yet over, but it is unlikely that it ever will be. So, here is our humble offering to serious Pairpoint collectors and dealers everywhere. Our hope is that this helps expand your knowledge of Pairpoint products so that you can play a role in educating other enthusiasts who may look to you for guidance in the future.

Sandy and I are keenly and anxiously aware of our responsibility regarding the stewardship of the many thousands of pages of original factory documents in our possession. Some of the original notebooks, sketches, and product sheets are one-of-a-kind and absolutely irreplaceable. Had we not been at the right place at the right time, most of this material would have become lost forever. Although we have compiled most of the pertinent information from the documents into our book projects, we feel a great responsibility that this material not be lost in the future; we are constantly discussing the best disposition of the documentation but we have reached no final conclusion. In the meantime, all we can do is to ensure that this material be available to the interested public without reservation. We may own the physical documents at this moment in time, but the material really belongs to the future.

In closing we would like to extend our sincerest gratitude to those who have purchased our book. Also a warm "Hello and Thank You" to our new friends who have taken the time to contact us to share their thoughts about Pairpoint or to ask questions...we really appreciate your comments and interest. And, finally, we would like to extend our invitation to anyone desiring to share their thoughts, provide new information, or ask questions, to contact us through Schiffer Publishing, Ltd.

Chapter 1

Pairpoint Personalized

The inclusion of this chapter may seem inconsistent when you consider that this book is, essentially, a technical reference book. Is it a Pairpoint shape, or isn't it? Did Pairpoint engrave that pattern, or didn't they? But, to those of you who are familiar with our style of collecting and presenting Pairpoint information (*The Essence of Pairpoint*, Schiffer Publishing, 2001), you are aware of the importance we attach to the human side of the glassmaking process. To know more about the human dynamics of producing such objects of beauty can only serve to heighten one's appreciation of those objects.

Pairpoint employed many people during the 75 years they were producing fine silver plate and glassware in New Bedford, Massachusetts. Certainly not all were engaged in the higher profile duties such as glassblowing or decorating, but everyone's contribution was necessary and they all shared similar experiences. Most are gone now, and many years have passed since the last handcrafted item left the New Bedford factory in the 1950s. Those folks that remain today were children when Pairpoint was in its glory days and young adults when the factory closed for good. But they have recollections and memories of those days when their fathers, or uncles, or neighbors would come home with stories from the workplace. Some stories were happy and many were sad, but it was the reality of the times. We rely upon those second hand stories, and the experiences of those sons and daughters, to give us a glimpse into the past, and to appreciate the dedication, hard work, and personal sacrifice that went into making Pairpoint such a success.

During the summer of 2003, Sandy and I met one of those daughters for the first time. Myldred Costa had answered an advertisement that we had placed in the New Bedford Standard-Times Newspaper. She had some old Pairpoint documents and sent them to us. On a trip to New Bedford, we visited Myldred at her home in North Dartmouth. We have kept in close contact with her and consider her to be like one of the family. The more we got to know Myldred, the more we learned of her many and various connections to Pairpoint. Her mother had worked there during the beginning years of the great depression, Myldred had carried messages between departments as a teenager, and after graduating from high school she worked fulltime in the office in the early 1950s. She grew up in the same neighborhoods that housed many of the workers; she seemed to know everyone, in one way or another. The most intriguing connection for us, however, was her friendship with her Godfather, engraver Carl Silva.

Myldred Costa. *Courtesy of Myldred Costa., North Dartmouth, Massachusetts.*

Carl Silva went to work for Pairpoint in 1928, setting aside his aspirations of becoming a Catholic priest to help support his family. He entered the Pairpoint engraving department as an apprentice to master engraver, Olympio "Ollie" Cayton. Carl graduated from his apprenticeship in 1931, and later was promoted to Journeyman status in 1933. He also became the union secretary. Carl stayed with Pairpoint through their shutdown in 1938, and continued working under Robert Gundersen until 1943. That was the year he accepted a foreman's position at the Morse Twist Drill Company, from which he retired in the middle 1970s, to care for his ailing wife. It wasn't until 1979, when Myldred lost her husband in an accident, that their paths really crossed again. Myldred built an addition onto her home, and Carl moved out to the country, where he lived until he passed away in 1988. With his passing, the Pairpoint era of Myldred's life, which had been so impor-

Carl Silva, Pairpoint Engraver. *Courtesy of Myldred Costa, North Dartmouth, Massachusetts.*

tant to her, went dormant. And so it remained until she answered our ad in the newspaper. Her voice and eyes light up when you talk to her about Pairpoint glass. The human side of Pairpoint still lives in the hearts and minds of people like her.

We are not attempting to tell the story of a glass engraver, although the centerpoint of our discussion may lead one to that conclusion. Nor are we trying to tell the story of a very kind lady from North Dartmouth. We think the saying goes, "Time waits for no man," and time is certainly passing for those who can still recall the stories of almost a lifetime ago. Time passes, memories dim, and then, seemingly overnight, voices go silent; the only chronicle of times past is the written word.

We are fortunate to know Myldred Costa and benefit from her experiences with the people from Pairpoint. She has been gracious enough to allow us to interview her, so that her insight and memories may become words for future generations of Pairpoint enthusiasts. This is not her story, or even Carl Silva's story, although they play the starring roles. We believe that generalizations can be made from their individual viewpoints as recounted to us. Carl, as quiet and reserved as he was, was not unique in his attitudes and behaviors at Pairpoint. He was just another man doing what he was paid to do. His thoughts and experiences were the thoughts and experiences of just one man out of many. It was the everyday human side of Pairpoint. And every time you hold a vase, or a bowl, or a candlestick in your hands, look beyond the color, the shape, and the decoration, and you may be lucky enough to see what Carl and his friends saw everyday.

An Interview with Myldred Costa

North Dartmouth, Massachusetts
August 2003

QUESTION: Can you share any stories or philosophies that Carl shared with you over the years that would give someone a better appreciation of what it was like to be a Pairpoint employee during their finest years?

ANSWER: Most of the men with the greatest knowledge of glassworking eventually came to work at Pairpoint, leaving other glass companies for better wages. Most of the experienced glass men had originally come from Sweden or Norway where they learned the trade from their fathers. Pairpoint was willing to pay them more money because of their high skills and their ability and willingness to teach the local men who had hidden talent and wanted to take up the trade. Carl wasn't a man who was impressed easily, but he greatly respected the talent these men had, and appreciated the fact that they were so willing to share their knowledge and teach the apprentices. Carl always thought that part of Pairpoint's greatness came from these unselfish attitudes. And Carl always was grateful for the inspiration these men gave to him to make him work twice as hard to achieve his goal

Anders Thoen, Pairpoint Glass Blower, who continued working until the early 1950s. *Courtesy of Kauko Kahila.*

William (Billy) Frates, Pairpoint Glass Worker. *Courtesy of Kauko Kahila.*

Ollie Cayton, Pairpoint Engraver, in 1980, at Carl Silva's engraving bench. *Courtesy of Myldred Costa, North Dartmouth, Massachusetts*

of becoming an engraver. He had to produce the best or he wasn't satisfied. Carl used to reflect on the fact that when he was six years old, he was in first grade; when Gilly Gulbranson was six years old, he was already working in the factory starting to learn his trade. He really admired those men, and had the insight to know what it took to be one of the "greats."

QUESTION: While working as an engraver at Pairpoint from 1928 to 1943, did Carl ever think of himself and his fellow engravers as "artists"?

ANSWER: Yes. While serving his apprenticeship under Olympio "Ollie" Cayton, he developed the highest respect for him and the natural talent he had. He remained a life-long friend and visited Ollie's home many times after Ollie retired from Pairpoint. They would talk about the "good ol' days" and who was still doing what. Carl also kept in touch with Gilly Gulbranson and Tony DeCosta, two very talented men in their own departments. Gilly was the most recognized glass blower in the country, and Tony was known for his skills in the heavy cutting department. These people, among others, had talents that were special and above normal. They had a gift, so I think Carl always saw their abilities as artistic. As for himself, Carl remained humble and knew he would have never been able to achieve what he had if he had not had the good fortune to have Ollie Cayton as his instructor.

QUESTION: Was Pairpoint a busy place? What was the general attitude of the workers toward the company and its management? Were most of the people "company people"?

ANSWER: I believe most everyone worked together in harmony. Mr. Gundersen was very well liked by the workers, as were the department foremen. This contributed greatly to the men's happiness and certainly helped to keep things running smoothly. Pairpoint maintained a sales force on the road and sales were doing well. This led to the ability of Pairpoint to pay good wages and expand their workforce. Sales were so good that Pairpoint had to add a second shift. Pairpoint's management tried to keep many of the workers living close by, on South Second Street, so they would get to work on time. Even with the second shift, it was difficult and very hectic trying to fill the orders from the different districts all over the country. In spite of the hard work, Pairpoint kept a good environment for the workers. People tended back then to look out for the company that was looking out for them. It wasn't like it is today where people take their company and their job for granted.

An Employee's Identification Badge. The name of the gentleman shown is not known.

QUESTION: What did the employees at Pairpoint think about the quality of their products as compared to the other glass companies of their day? Was there a friendly competitiveness or a hostile competitiveness?

ANSWER: They must have thought Pairpoint made a product to be proud to be associated with. Because, many of our best employees left other glass companies located in Trenton, New York, and other well-known glass centers to come to New Bedford to work for Pairpoint. As far as cooperation between the glass companies went, it must have been somewhat friendly. After all they would sell to one another, and occasionally help each other out if their production load was too big, or if someone had labor problems.

QUESTION: Did Carl have a particular admiration or respect for any other engravers at Pairpoint?

ANSWER: I think I answered this question before. When Carl went to work at Pairpoint in 1928, he was apprenticed under the great Ollie Cayton, who saw his potential and kept him going through the tedious learning process. Carl probably respected Ollie more than any other, not just for his engraving talent, but for his qualities as a man and a teacher. Carl wasn't one to make friends easily, but he really admired Ollie. He would never let Ollie down or make him sorry he had invested so much of his time and energy into Carl's success.

QUESTION: Did each engraver cut every design, or did they specialize in just a few?

ANSWER: Each engraver when hired was taught one special pattern to learn. When Carl Silva started his career, he was assigned to learn the Daisy pattern under the direction of Ollie Cayton. For three years, day after day, he engraved that pattern until Ollie was satisfied that Carl's work was perfect and that he had learned his craft. Then, and only then, Carl was allowed to work on a new pattern, which he mastered quickly, due to his training on the Daisy pattern. The engravers were expected to be able to engrave any pattern, but some did better than others on certain patterns.

QUESTION: Pairpoint required that their engraving patterns be very consistent with regard to the inclusion of specific design features. Do you know if Carl or any of the other engravers had a personal feature that they included on the pieces they engraved?

ANSWER: Pairpoint strived for perfection; that's a fact! Carl told me that he was the only engraver who ever put a pattern on the foot of his stemware. He couldn't stand seeing an engraved piece with a plain foot. This pattern was a continuous wreath. Some engravers put their initials. Ollie Cayton only signed one piece of glassware that I know of; I wish I knew what became of the piece. Most of the other workers engraved their lots without personalizing them. Today, I think everything coming from the Pairpoint factory in Sagamore is signed.

Carl Silva's working sketch of his continuous wreath engraving. *Courtesy of Myldred Costa, North Dartmouth, Massachusetts.*

QUESTION: Pairpoint's workmanship was closer to consistent perfection than that of most other glass houses of the time. Why do you think they were able to maintain that level of quality for so long?

ANSWER: I think management's attitude had a lot to do with the quality of the work; the workers were happy there. Mr. Gundersen, then a manager at Pairpoint, had a way with the workers. He learned by listening and wasn't quick to give them a reply unless he knew it would satisfy them. You never heard about strikes at Pairpoint, or unhappy working conditions. Back then people needed the money badly; they knew that if they produced quality, as opposed to quantity, the company would be satisfied.

QUESTION: It appears that very few new engraving patterns were created after the early 1920s. Did Carl or any of his contemporaries ever create engraving designs that resulted in commercial use at Pairpoint? Did they ever create engraving designs that they used on their own?

ANSWER: Carl did a pattern on 250 mugs for Robert Bryden, but he never named it. My cat broke the one mug I had, but it was beautiful. Then he did the "Wheat" pattern…Pairpoint never had that. We started doing this when Carl came to live with me. People seemed to like it. They would order sets of wine glasses, flutes, and Vodka

Carl Silva's working sketch of his Wheat engraving. *Courtesy of Myldred Costa, North Dartmouth, Massachusetts.*

glasses, and give them as wedding gifts. But I don't know of any designs he created while he was at Pairpoint. I know Ollie Cayton would create his own designs when he was working for himself after leaving Pairpoint. The only other engraver that was working in the later years was Carl Schweidenback, who lived in Sandwich. He went to work as a foreman for Princess House, but he retired in the late 1970s. Princess House used to call Carl to ask if he would engrave for them, but the drive was too far. Besides, Carl was doing very good engraving at home for his local customers, so he declined.

QUESTION: Were there a lot of mistakes when engraving glass that sent the blank to the scrap pile?

ANSWER: If there were mistakes made, the engraver did his best to salvage the piece he was working on. If he was successful, the item was usually put on a "seconds" shelf with the price marked down. Hence, there was very little waste. Molds were kept clean, as well as the tools; this helped shrinkage in the company and kept the scrap pile small.

After the factory closed for the last time in the middle 1950s, Robert Bryden and his wife Cynthia opened a small retail store on William Street where the seconds and other odd pieces of glass were sold. I think it only stayed open for about five years. That's when Mr. Bryden started his factory in Sandwich.

QUESTION: Were the engraving patterns applied freehand, or were they laid out first? How was this done?

ANSWER: After graduating from his apprenticeship, every engraver was given his own small box of "cutouts," which were cardboard patterns. When he was assigned a lot with a specific pattern to engrave, he would take the appropriate cutout from his box to make sure he spaced everything correctly on the blank. They would mark layout lines with red crayon. Sometimes, they would practice with the pattern on pieces of window glass they kept around. It was better to make a mistake on window glass than to ruin a valuable blank.

This trumpet form vase or epergne component was an invaluable find for us, because it shows an engraving pattern laid out in black grease pencil. Whether the pattern was experimental or actually put into production is unknown at this time; we have never seen this pattern in its fully executed form.

QUESTION: Did many of the engravers do private work at home after working hours? After retirement? Did they ever cut Pairpoint designs privately on glass blanks that were not of Pairpoint origin?

ANSWER: Yes. One would think that after sitting some days for ten hours, an engraver would have had enough, but not so for some of the men. Ollie Cayton, Carl's mentor, lived on Borden Street in New Bedford. He had turned his cellar into an engraving shop, and did custom engraving for private customers. He also did a lot of glass repair to salvage items for people who appreciated the quality and beauty of Pairpoint glass for their own enjoyment and that of generations to come.

Carl Silva left Pairpoint in 1943 for a higher paying foreman position at Morse Twist Drill. He retired from there in the middle 1970s to care for his ailing wife. However, he still continued to engrave glass from his home during all those years. After his wife passed away in 1977, Carl kept on with his private engraving work at his New Bedford home for another three or four years. I was Carl's Godchild, but we had lost contact over the years. It was only after I had suddenly lost my husband in 1979, in an accident, that Carl and I became reacquainted. We talked many times about Carl coming to live in the country with me and my daughter Carolyn. By 1981, I had built an addition onto my home, Carl had moved in, and he was set-up and back into the engraving business.

Carl Silva, Pairpoint engraver, working at home in 1980. *Courtesy of Myldred Costa, North Dartmouth, Massachusetts.*

While living in my home, Carl did endless work for Mr. Bryden, who by now had opened a small glassmaking factory in Sandwich, Massachusetts. Mr. Bryden had no one to do glass repair or engraving at the time, so he sent the work to Carl. Carl made good money doing home engraving for Mr. Bryden, special orders, and repair work. All of this retirement income was a result of what he had learned at Pairpoint during his younger years, and he always appreciated that fact.

After coming to live with me, Carl and I started going around to yard sales and auctions. It amazed us to find how many people did not know what they had. You just sort of figured that New Bedford people would be able to recognize Pairpoint glass. We were able to buy things for so little back then. Actually, I still can sometimes. We bought every undecorated Pairpoint blank we could find. When we got it home, Carl would engrave one of the Pairpoint patterns on it and buff the piece up just like it came from the plant. If I didn't keep it, we sold it. That's the only time he engraved a Pairpoint pattern…it had to be on an old Pairpoint blank. If he was engraving on anything else, he would make up his own pattern. He never felt right about doing it any other way. Carl was like that.

QUESTION: Did Carl enjoy his work or did he see himself as just a part of a manufacturing process?

ANSWER: You have to remember that things were different back when Carl went to work at Pairpoint. Times were hard and the men needed to work to take care of their families. I think men may have been more serious about their responsibilities, because they were the sole provider for the family. Carl had to abandon his own personal dream of becoming a priest, and go to work at Pairpoint, because the family needed his help. He continued his studies for the priesthood while working at Pairpoint, but eventually gave it up. He continued to help his family, even after he married. I think men accepted the fact that they were just part of a process, but there wasn't a stigma attached to that reality back then. Carl enjoyed his work very much, but was a person who was never quite satisfied with what he had worked on. I think if he hadn't gotten satisfaction from the work, he wouldn't have continued doing it privately until he passed away.

Carl Silva's sketch of his boyhood home at 209 Allen Street, New Bedford, Massachusetts. *Courtesy of Myldred Costa, North Dartmouth, Massachusetts.*

QUESTION: Did Carl ever think that the quality and artistry of the Pairpoint products would pass the test of time and be so appreciated by future generations? Do you know of any others that foresaw the future desirability of Pairpoint products?

ANSWER: Carl enjoyed working at Pairpoint and really appreciated watching the men who made Pairpoint a name that would long be remembered. He didn't collect a lot of pieces, and regretted it later on as he saw how it never lost its value, becoming more and more desirable and collectible as the years passed. But, some others must have been different.

I remember, back when Carl was living with me, that I would occasionally go with Carl when he visited a few of his old friends from his Pairpoint days. This one particular house we were invited into took me by surprise. When I walked into their living room, I just stood there and looked up at large shelves that completely surrounded the room two feet from the ceiling. On these shelves was every glass animal that Pairpoint ever made along with perfume bottles, plates, and an example of just about everything Pairpoint made. It looked like a showroom with everything on display. Kept well out of reach for anyone to touch, and out of sight for the normal eye, who would expect to look up at a twelve-foot high ceiling and see a wonderful four-wall museum display? I had to promise to never talk about what I saw or where I had seen it.

You asked about the glass passing the test of time; I don't know if this explains it right, or not. But I think it does. Carl was a very quiet, reserved, and particular man; he rarely displayed his emotions. But I used to watch him, when we would go to shows or auctions, as he picked up a well-done piece of glass. You could see him disappearing into his own world, and revisit the old days in his mind. The emotion you could see, as he delicately traced the engraving pattern with his fingers, was very moving. As he slowly, and reverently, placed the piece back on the table, he would mutter, "A lot of work went into that." So, I think if it passed Carl's test of time, it would pass anyone's test of time.

QUESTION: From a community perspective, was the job of glass engraver a respected one? If you could compare the job of engraver to other professions that we may be familiar with today, on a status level, what would it have been equivalent to?

ANSWER: An experienced Pairpoint engraver was more than respected. Do you realize the time and talent it took to learn the trade? It took three years to teach each man to become an engraver. For three years he was getting paid to sit there day after day engraving the same pattern, over and over again. That cost the company money. Pairpoint surely must have had to reject a lot of men whose patience, endurance, and talent ran out be fore the training period was finished. Only the chosen few who were really talented stayed with it. Carl Silva was one of those. Yes, these men were well regarded in the community.

I can't think of a profession today that would be equivalent to being an engraver; everything is so different with so much being automated. An engraver was able to take a blank piece of glass and turn it into a beautiful piece of art...so, maybe...an artist. Frank Guba, a famous Pairpoint decorator, took a blank sheet of paper applied his brush or pencil, and created a beautiful piece of art. Just the same as Carl did on glass. Yes, an artist.

QUESTION: Was there a "snobbery" between the two main departments, the glassmakers and the engravers?

ANSWER: No, none that I ever saw or was aware of. You have to remember that times were hard; we were moving into a depression. Men needed money and Pairpoint always paid good wages. They did have thoughts and discussions about who was better at doing what, but I think that was very normal, not snobby. They worked long hours, and were happy for the work. Strikes in hard times were unheard of, food on the table and bills being paid were more important.

Pairpoint was the largest factory in New Bedford, making a product that was selling well and making money. The only other place the men could turn to to make a living was the sea. I think the women were happier with husbands working in a factory than being out to sea for weeks at a time. Pairpoint made New Bedford famous for glass as well as being known as the Whaling City. The men all got along with one another pretty well. At lunch time all the departments came outside and mixed together. When the whistle blew, they all just went about their individual duties...no whining about who made what or who earned how much. The glassmakers did their job, and after the pontil was buffed and cleaned up, the blank just moved along to inventory, or to the engravers, like Carl or Ollie, or to the heavy cutters, like Tony DeCosta, just another step along the way.

QUESTION: Which tradecraft would have been held in higher esteem at Pairpoint, the gaffer or the engraver?

ANSWER: I suppose if you have to draw a distinction, which I'm not sure would be proper, I would say the Gaffer was the single most important person in each department. It was up to him to see that every piece of glass he worked on was in perfect shape before it left his department. More than once before he separated a vase, for example, he would put it back into the furnace and rework it to make the sizing and shape as correct as possible. Only after he was satisfied would he separate it from the rod. Haljmer "Gilly" Gulbranson was a perfectionist and was called the best Gaffer in the country. In 1939, Pairpoint sent him to the New York World's Fair to demonstrate his skills at the Pairpoint exhibit. Yes, I'd say the Gaffer was the backbone of the process.

Haljmer "Gilly" Gulbranson, Pairpoint Gaffer. *Courtesy of Kauko Kahila*

QUESTION: After Carl left Pairpoint in 1943, to take a job with Morse Twist Drill, he continued to engrave glass at home for private customers. Did he ever engrave Pairpoint patterns again? Do you know which Pairpoint patterns he engraved while at Pairpoint?

ANSWER: Yes, he engraved whatever people brought to him. He would match Pairpoint patterns on plain blanks for people who had broken theirs. Or, as I mentioned before, he would engrave Pairpoint patterns on plain blanks we would find at yard sales and auctions. His favorite pattern was the Grape Design; he always had the correct amount of grapes. After learning his trade at Pairpoint by engraving the Daisy Pattern, he mostly engraved the Grape pattern.

He had built himself a nice little business, and was doing engraving work for many people. He had put some engraved glasses on consignment at the Sea Witch, an expensive shop in New Bedford, and regularly filled special orders. We constantly had people from all over coming to the house with glass they needed repaired or matched. He got so busy that we started selling glass out of the front room of my house. Carl had set-up seven

A 1980 advertisement for The Sea Witch Gift Shoppe, featuring the work of Carl Silva, "a retired Pairpoint craftsman." *Courtesy of Myldred Costa, North Dartmouth, Massachusetts.*

Carl Silva's "Hessler" pattern sketch, named after Myldred Costa's family name. *Courtesy of Myldred Costa, North Dartmouth, Massachusetts.*

Carl Silva's "Myldred" pattern sketch. *Courtesy of Myldred Costa, North Dartmouth, Massachusetts.*

tables and covered them with black cloth (you know it was unheard of to display glass on anything but black). I put mirrors down; it looked beautiful! He had customers from Boston, and Marlboro. That's when I decided to display at Sunshine Plaza every Sunday…some days he would make up to $400, plus get orders for next week. I'd then go out and buy more crystal to keep him busy for the next week. He used to say "Myldred, old Buddy, old Pal, you're working me harder than I ever worked at Pairpoint!" Although he would never show it to anyone but me, he was very guarded and reserved, he thrived on the work.

Mentioning Sunshine Plaza reminds me of a funny story about Carl. I told you how quiet and reserved he was; his nickname at Morse Twist Drill was "Old Stone Face." He could insult you, and you wouldn't realize you had been insulted for two weeks. I always stayed with him at the Plaza, because he wouldn't mingle or talk to the people coming by our display. One Sunday I went to get him something to eat, and when I returned he was giggling like a fool. As he told it, he was leaning back in his chair in the back corner of the booth…he had those dark tinted glasses on, that he always wore, when a little colored boy about six years old kept going back and forth in front of the display. Carl never moved or said a word. Finally this little boy got as close to the table as he could, stared at Carl for a few moments, and said "Hey, Mister! You dead?" I can't remember Carl laughing so hard. Those were good times.

QUESTION: You have mentioned that your mother worked at Pairpoint during the 1920s, and you worked there in the early 1950s. Is there any reminiscing you can share from your own experiences or stories you remember from your mother?

ANSWER: My mother and Carl grew up together; she was older than he. My mother was employed as an inspector while Carl was learning to engrave. That would have been in the late 20s. Her job paid good, and her pay went to help support my grandmother, who had three other children in addition to my mother. Two were married but she and her older sister were home to support the house. I don't have much bad to say about Pairpoint, but they had one fault, not only while my mother worked there, but when I worked there in the 1950s. The plant was loaded with black soot! Everytime someone opened the factory door into the office, the soot just blew in all over us. I looked like I worked in a coal mine by the end of the day. My mother became very ill from this while she worked at the factory. She had a lung that collapsed, but nevertheless, after recovering, she went back to work and kept a handkerchief over her face so she wouldn't have to breathe the soot. In 1929, my mother met and married a handsome sailor, and quit working when she became a mother. That's when Carl became my Godfather.

As a young girl, I spent time at Pairpoint carrying messages from department to department, walking through this huge factory. The men were a great bunch of guys. They'd jump out and scare me when they heard my heels tapping the floor as I went about on my merry way. But they were always respectful, no course or dirty comments. It was a dirty place, and the heat was unbearable, but these men worked hard and were dedicated to making Pairpoint glass the best in the world.

I have some pieces of Pairpoint from my grandmother and one vase my mother gave to me. I wish today that I had known how valuable Pairpoint glass would become. Fresh out of school, I didn't appreciate all the beautiful glass at my fingertips that I could have bought for practically nothing. And the Pairpoint lamps as well. In 1956, Pairpoint opened a store on William Street and sold seconds...perfume bottles, paperweights, vases, etc., not perfectly blown but beautiful just the same, and inexpensive. I did buy a few things. When I think back of what I could have bought and had today, it would be a small fortune in glass.

"Myldred's Garden," a delightful bouquet of hand-made glass flowers, a cherished gift to us from Myldred Costa.

I made one significant purchase that will always stand out for me. Back when Carl and I were going to yard sales and auctions, we went to a Tag Sale at someone's home. I spotted a long box under an old bed, so I dragged it out. Inside was a Pairpoint cut crystal chandelier! I bought it for $80, and donated it to the New Bedford Whaling Museum, in memory of my late husband, Rodney Costa. You can see it there today.

QUESTION: I know Carl lived with you and you provided his care during the final years of his life. Did he ever reflect on his years at Pairpoint and talk about the importance of his work there. Did he ever recognize the lasting significance of the products made there and how his contribution, along with many others, ensured Pairpoint's place in history?

ANSWER: Carl came to North Dartmouth to live with me in 1981, three or four years after his wife Blanche passed away. He hated city life and enjoyed the privacy and freedom that living in the country could provide. The first thing he did when he moved into his apartment was to set-up his engraving equipment. Carl was very upset when he had heard that the Pairpoint factory had burned down. He spoke often about how crazy the guys at Pairpoint were and how he missed them. As for his work there, he was just another employee, but always grateful that he had Ollie Cayton as his mentor and closest friend. Like me, Carl took Pairpoint for granted while he worked there, but when the fire destroyed the old plant, reality and memories set in. What he did there, to him, was a job he got paid to do to the best of his ability, not a contribution. I have the most important piece I think he ever engraved, a perfume bottle he engraved for his wife. Someday that will be placed in the Whaling Museum so that Carl will be remembered always, along with some of the other fine craftsmen, friends of his, who are recognized there through the display of their work.

A gift to Blanche Silva from her husband, Pairpoint engraver Carl Silva. The base of the perfume bottle is standard Gundersen-Pairpoint from the 1950s, but the 1/2" thick stopper was custom cut, engraved, and polished by Carl from a 1" thick block of glass. The work took approximately thirteen hours. *From the collection of Myldred Costa.*

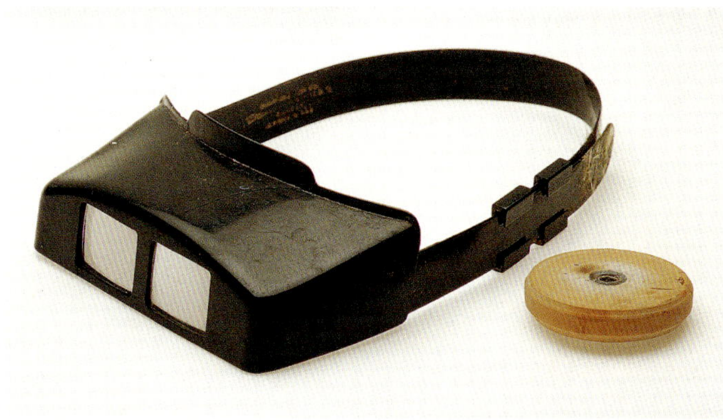

Two tangible reminders of the end of an era...Carl Silva's magnifying glasses and one of his engraving wheels. *Courtesy of Myldred Costa, North Dartmouth, Massachusetts.*

Chapter 2

Pairpoint Shapes

As you explore the various sections within this chapter, you will undoubtedly notice the difference in the way the shapes are shown in the photographs. Some will be photographs of items from within our personal collection, some will be photographs of finished catalog items having engraving or cutting patterns, and some will be frosted-looking images of shapes with rough edges and contours. This is due to the variety of source material we used to make this information available to you. The rough-looking frosted shapes came from original factory catalog pages displaying rough blanks for sale to other glass houses as well as for internal use. The shapes which appear to be finished with engraving or cutting patterns came from catalog pages that would have been used by jobbers and retailers.

Additionally, we have always been curious about the names that people give the different shapes. Vases and candlesticks are rather obvious, but when it comes to bowls and serving pieces, the variety of names given by dealers and collectors to the same type of item is fairly broad. To be very candid, we have always envied those that could look at a certain glass dish and call it a "lemon dish." Well, we've discovered the little secret, and we're going to let you in on it. Things can be named whatever you want them to be; Pairpoint certainly did! There are any number of identical blank shapes that have different names. Most likely it depended upon the type of marketing that was going on at the time, and changing trends of what items were popular with the public. I would imagine it was easier to sell any overstock of relish dishes when mayonnaise dishes became more popular by renaming your "relish" as a "mayonnaise." We have chosen in many cases to omit a "name" if we had any question about its factory description. The only discretion we used was to place the item into a general category. In other words we may have categorized a small bowl as a serving piece if we believed it to be so instead of grouping the bowl with the decorative bowls. So, if you can't find your bowl in the decorative bowls section, be sure to look in the section for serving pieces.

With regard to the factory identification numbers shown, we have taken a little liberty to make those numbers easier to read. Pairpoint did not use the symbol "#" as a prefix, nor did they use the "-" between the letter prefix and the actual number. In other words, our designation #A-294, would have actually been A294 on a Pairpoint catalog page.

We have provided sizes whenever possible and blank spaces for sizes if we knew that another size existed. Do not presume that our size information is complete; it merely represents that which we know at this point in time. As you discover new sizes, or any other new information for that matter, we recommend that you enter the information into the relevant section of this book.

The time period we have selected to cover is the same as that which we used for *The Essence of Pairpoint*, approximately 1918-1938. The rough-looking frosted shapes will pre-date 1918 by a modest margin, but most transitioned into the post-1918 period and will regularly be found decorated with the earlier "Brilliant-era" heavy cutting as well as the later light engraving patterns. The inclusion of these shapes, while spanning two different style periods, is crucial to providing a full picture of what could have been produced in the 1920s and 1930s. Additionally, many of the shapes we have identified were carried forward into the Gundersen and later years.

Near the end of each section, you will find items identified as Unk-???. This is our own numbering system for items known, or strongly believed, to be from Pairpoint, but have not yet been officially identified through factory documentation. We have assigned our own number to provide a conversational reference point.

Finally, if you have not found your particular shape within this chapter, we encourage you to go to Chapter 5, where you will find sketches reproduced from a notebook used by Pairpoint's engraving department during the 1920s. Included within these pages are several sketches of shapes not shown in this chapter. We have been able to successfully identify numerous shapes by using this unique and valuable resource.

Bowls-Decorative

BOWL #A-106, 13"d x 2.50"h. Bowls that are virtually identical to this shape will be found with color differences and engraving patterns strongly believed to be from Union Glass Company, Somerset, Massachusetts.

BOWL #A-109, 13"d. This bowl is an identical match to the Comport also identified by the factory as #A-109. *Illustration from a Pairpoint catalog.*

BOWL #123, 12"d x 8.50"h. *Illustration from a Pairpoint catalog.*

BOWL #111, 8"d x 3.25"h, 9"d x __"h, 10"d x __"h.

BOWL #124, 8"d, 9"d. *Illustration from a Pairpoint catalog.*

FLOWER HOLDER #131, 7.50"d, 8.50"d. *Illustration from a Pairpoint catalog.*

FLOWER BOWL #A-142, 8.375"d (rim) x 6.50"h. *Illustration from a Pairpoint catalog.*

FOOTED BOWL #A-145, 10.50"d x 5.25"h, 12.50"d x 5.25"h, 14.50"d x 6.25"h. An engraving department cost book references sizes: 8", 9", 10", 12", 14", and 15".

BOWL #145, 6"d x 3.50"h, 9"d x __"h. *Illustration from a Pairpoint catalog.*

CENTERPIECE BOWL ON PLATE #A-192, 10"d. *Illustration from a Pairpoint catalog.*

BOWL #A-193, 13"d. *Illustration from a Pairpoint catalog.*

BOWL #A-194, 8"d x __"h, 9"d x 3"h, 10"d x __"h, 12"d x 3.75"h, 14"d x 4"h, 16"d x __"h.

BOWL #197, 8"d. *Illustration from a Pairpoint catalog.*

NAPPY #210, 7"d. This is the identical shape as the #210.5 Bowl. (Pairpoint chose to call the smallest size a nappy instead of a bowl.) *Illustration from a Pairpoint catalog.*
BOWL #210.5, 8"d, 9"d, 10"d. (There is a 7"d size called a nappy and listed separately as #210.) *Illustration from a Pairpoint catalog.*

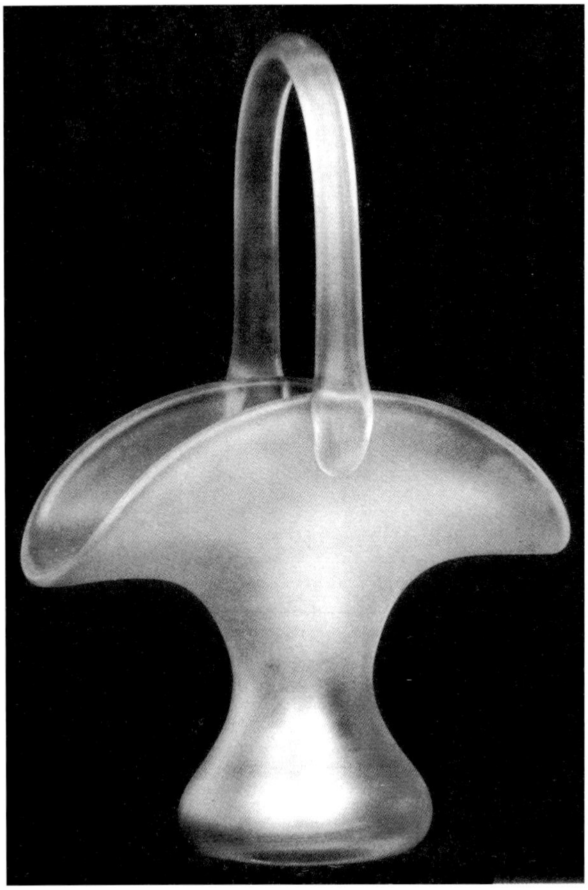

BASKET #A-235, 7"h, 8.25" body height x 14" overall height. *Illustration from a Pairpoint catalog.*

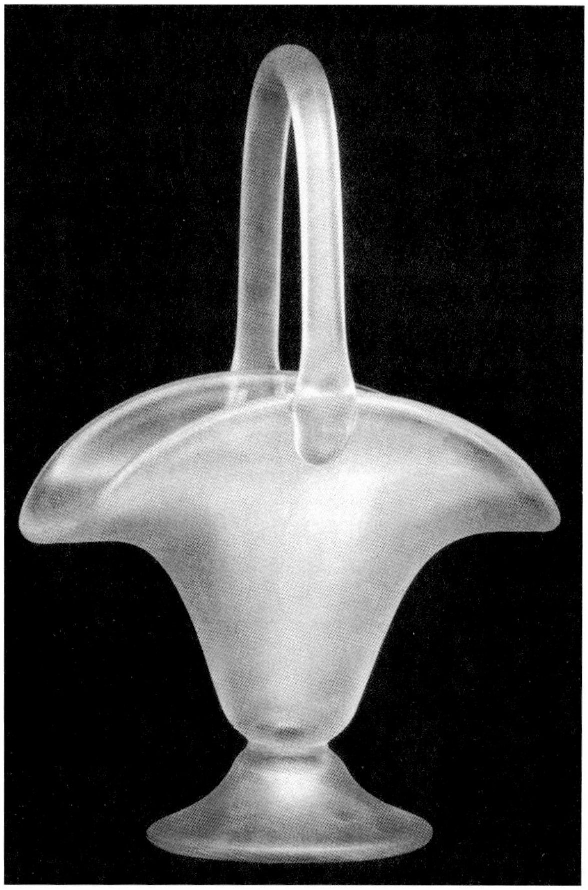

BASKET #A-237, 11"d x 15" overall height. *Illustration from a Pairpoint catalog.*

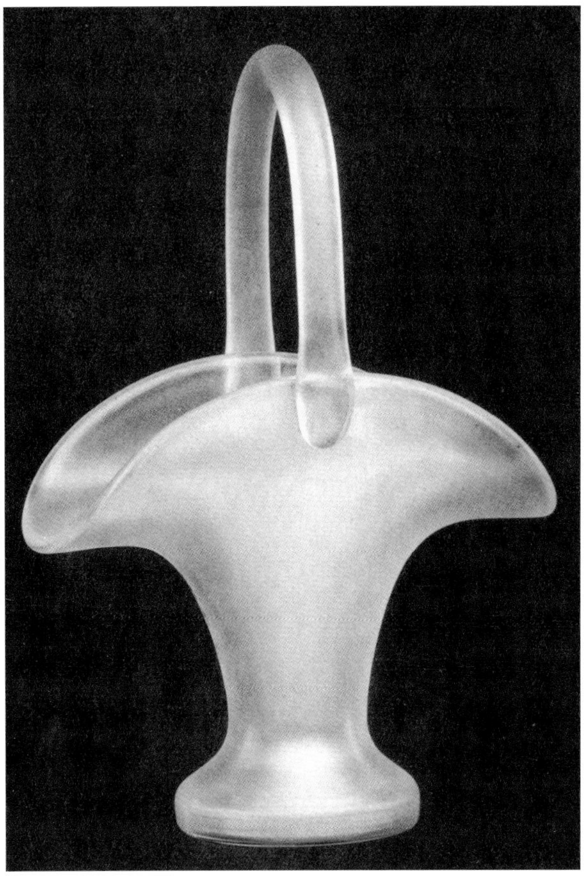

BASKET # A-236, 10.50"d x 14.50" overall height. *Illustration from a Pairpoint catalog.*

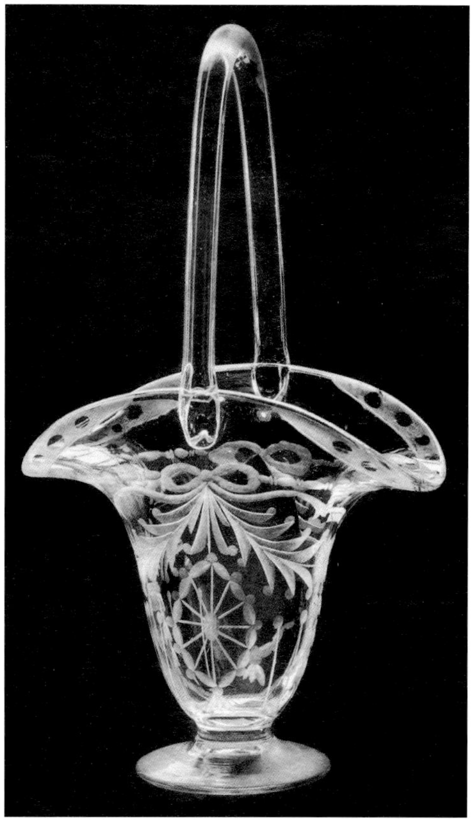

BASKET #A-237.5, 4"d x 7.25" overall height, 5.50"d x 9.25" overall height, 6.50"d x 10.75" overall height. *Illustration from a Pairpoint catalog.*

BASKET #A-242, 3.50"h. *Illustration from a Pairpoint catalog.*

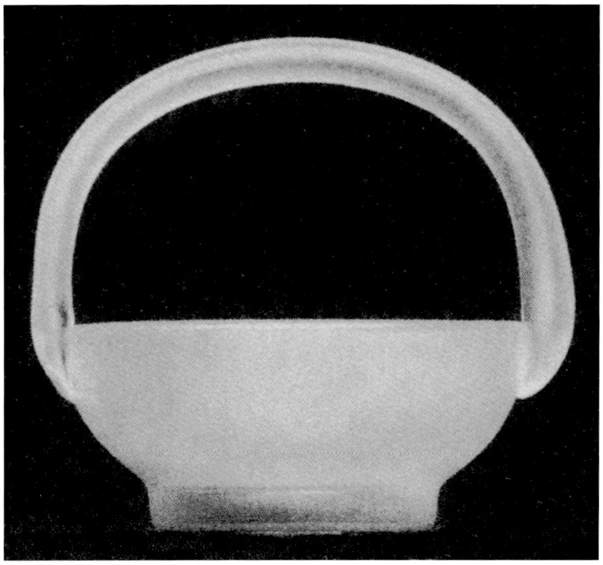

BASKET #A-243, 3.50"h. *Illustration from a Pairpoint catalog.*

VIOLET HOLDER A-244, 5"d x 3.875"h. *Illustration from a Pairpoint catalog.*

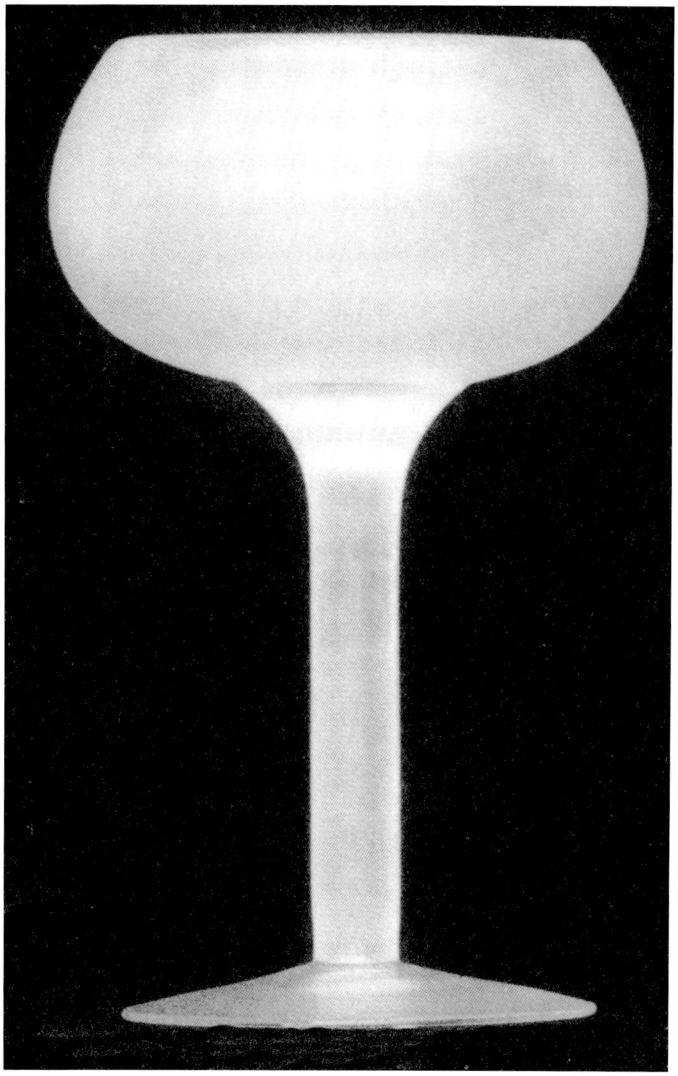

VIOLET HOLDER #A-245, 5"d x 8"h. *Illustration from a Pairpoint catalog.*

________ #303, 8"d, 9"d. *Illustration from a Pairpoint catalog.*

BOWL #304, 9"d. *Illustration from a Pairpoint catalog.*

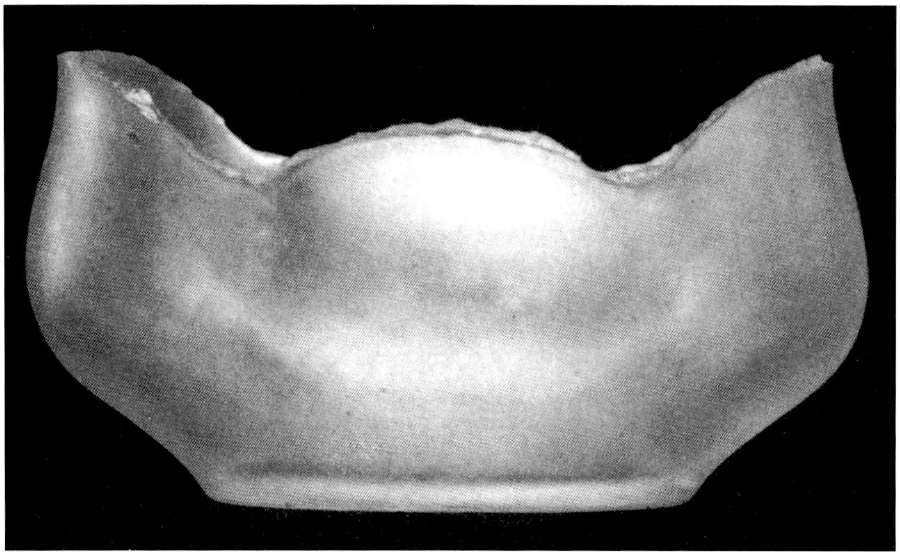

________ #311, 10.50" long x 7" wide x 5.75" high. *Illustration from a Pairpoint catalog.*

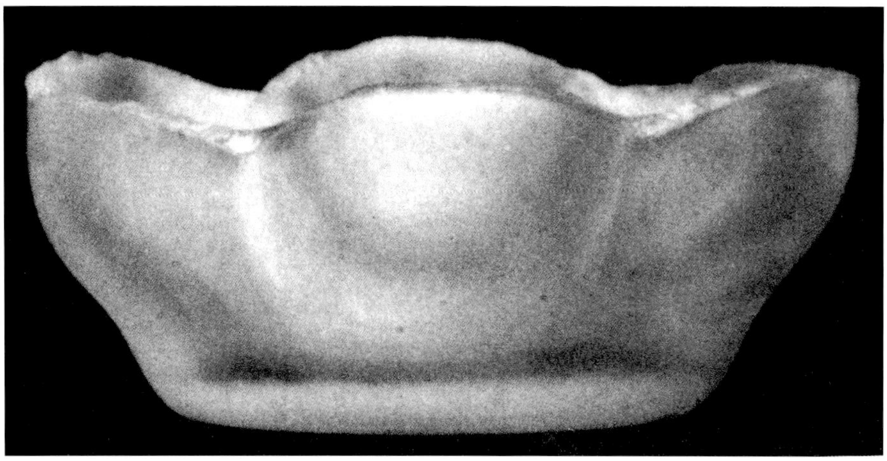

________ #312, 8"d, 9"d. *Illustration from a Pairpoint catalog.*

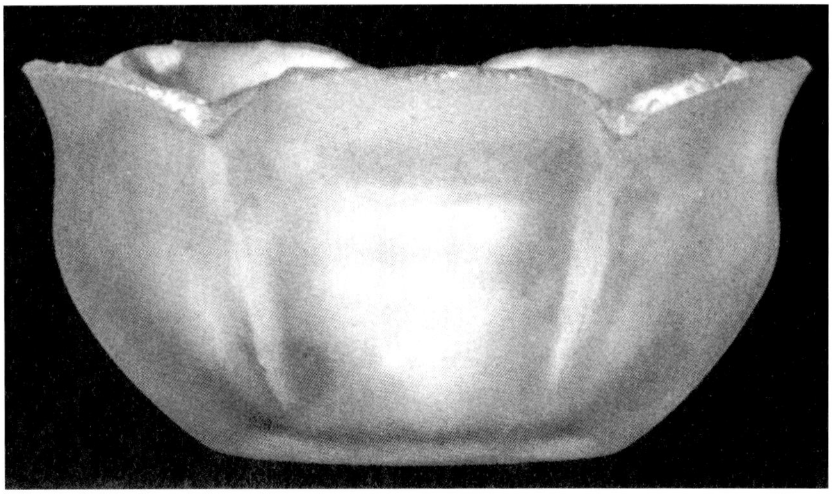

BOWL #313, 8"d, 9"d. *Illustration from a Pairpoint catalog.*

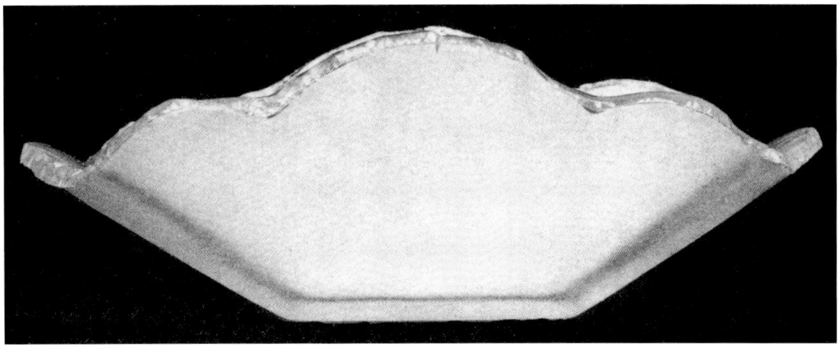

________ #315, 11" long x 6.75" wide. *Illustration from a Pairpoint catalog.*

________ #316, 10"d. *Illustration from a Pairpoint catalog.*

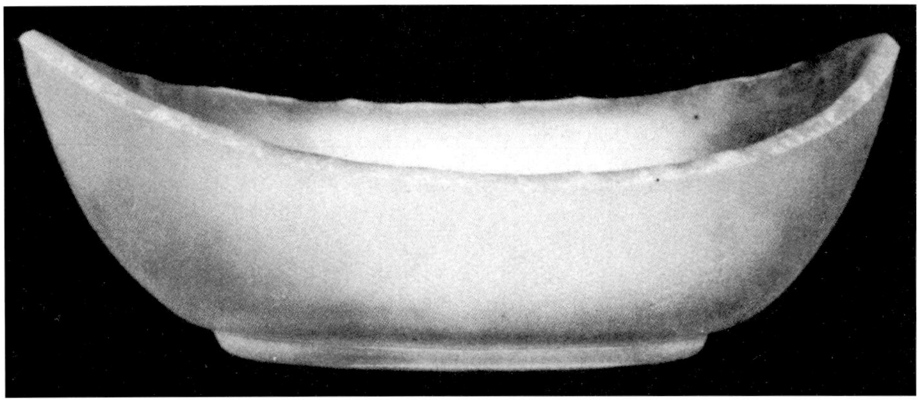

Oval Bowl #317, 11" long x 7" wide. *Illustration from a Pairpoint catalog.*

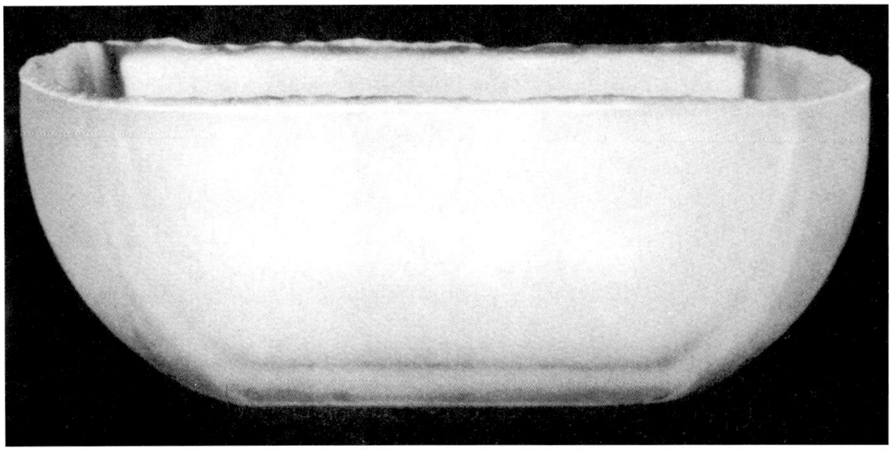

________ #318, 10" long x 6" wide. *Illustration from a Pairpoint catalog.*

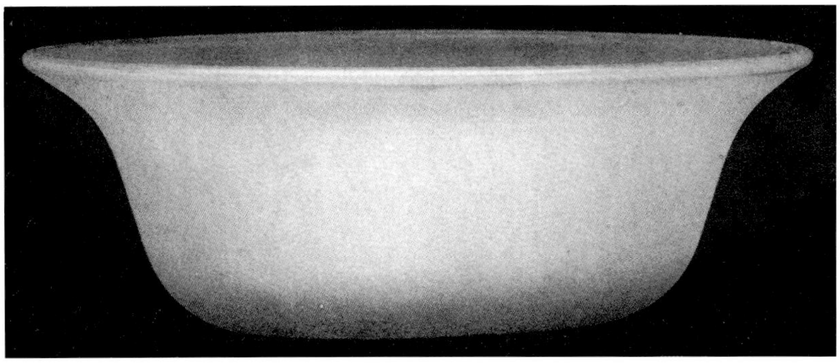

BOWL #323, 6.50"d, 7.50"d, 8.50"d, 9.50"d, 10.50"d. *Illustration from a Pairpoint catalog.*

FLOWER HOLDER #324, 9"d x 2.50"h, 10"d, 11"d, 12"d x 2.50"h, 13"d, 13.50"d x __"h, 15"d x 3"h. *Illustration from a Pairpoint catalog.*

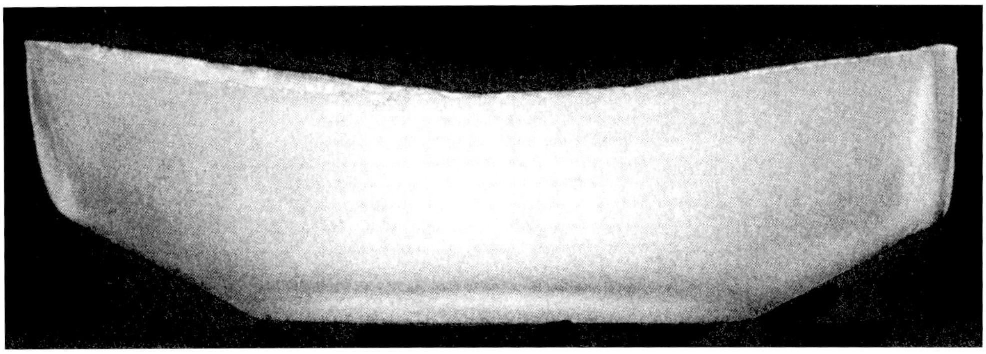

BOWL #328, 8" long, 9" long. *Illustration from a Pairpoint catalog.*

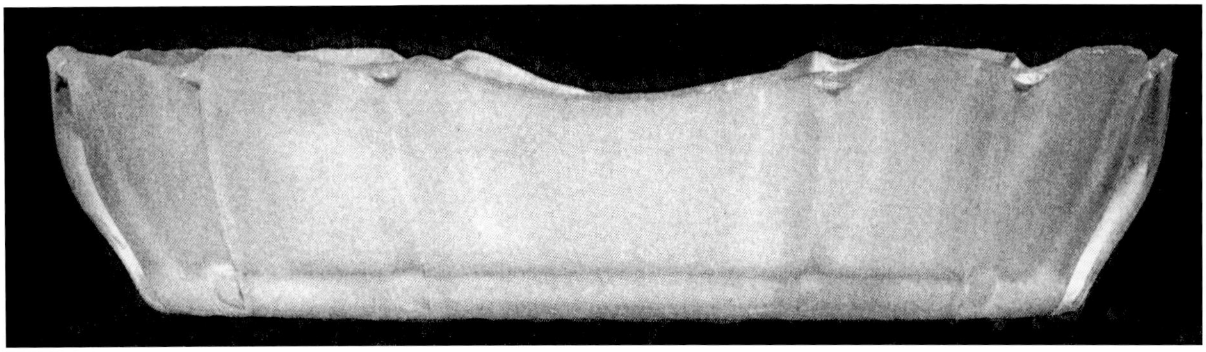

BOWL #331, 12" long x 6.875" wide. *Illustration from a Pairpoint catalog.*

LILY DISH #348, 12"d x 2"h. *Illustration from a Pairpoint catalog.*

BOWL #F-349, 8"d, 9"d. Form has three feet. *Illustration from a Pairpoint catalog.*

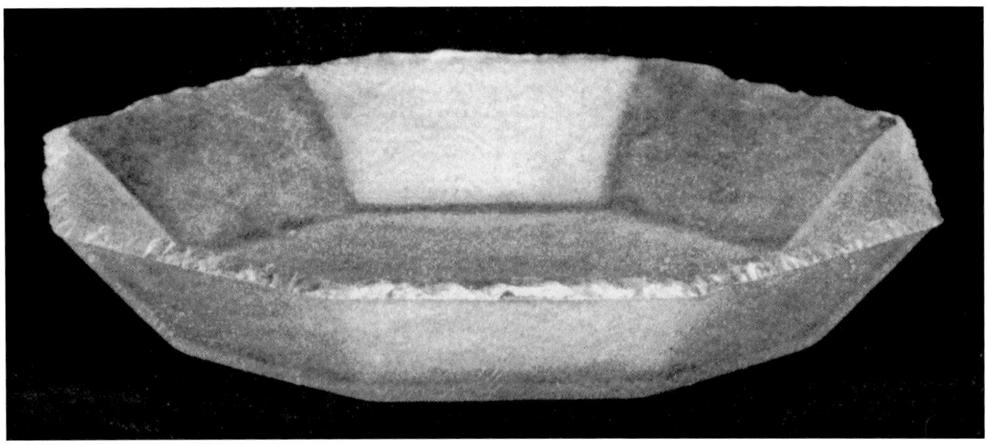

_______ #350, 8.50"d. *Illustration from a Pairpoint catalog.*

________ #351, Octagonal shape, 5"d, 6"d, 7"d, 9"d. *Illustration from a Pairpoint catalog.*

BOWL #F-356, 10"d. *Illustration from a Pairpoint catalog.*

BOWL #F-357, 10"d. This bowl has a lower profile than F-356. *Illustration from a Pairpoint catalog.*

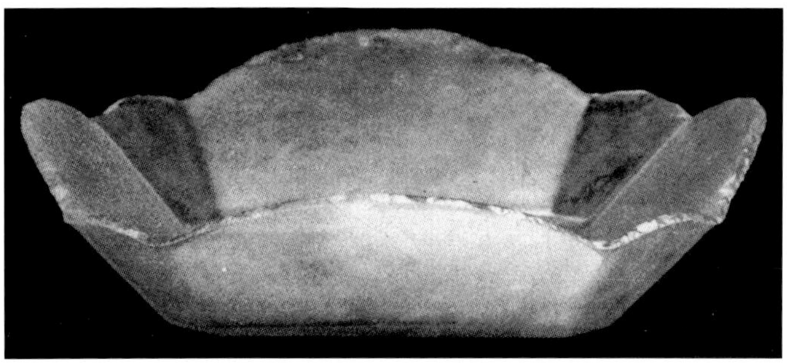

________ #365, 8"d, 10"d. *Illustration from a Pairpoint catalog.*

BOWL #B-368. *Illustration from a Pairpoint catalog.*

BOWL #B-369, 10"d x 6"h, 12"d x 6.75"h, 14" d x 7.625" h.

FISH BOWL #B-371, 10.50"d x 12"h. *Illustration from a Pairpoint catalog.*

OVAL BOWL #387, 15.50" long x 10.50" wide x 4" high. *Illustration from a Pairpoint catalog.*

BOWL #1010, 10"d x 3.50"h, 12"d x 4"h. *Illustration from a Pairpoint catalog.*

BOWL #A-1065, 10"d x 4.50"h, 12"d x 5.25"h, 14"d x __"h, 16"d x __"h.

BOWL #B-1065, 12"d x 6.75"h.

FLOWER HOLDER #A-1091. *Illustration from a Pairpoint catalog.*

_______ #1700, 6"d x 4"h. *Illustration from a Pairpoint catalog.*

BOWL #A-1106, 12"d, 13"d. *Illustration from a Pairpoint catalog.*

_______ #1701, 8"d, 3 Footed. *Illustration from a Pairpoint catalog.*

BOWL #1174, 5.75"d x 5.50"h.

_____ #1702, 6.50"d x 5.75"h. *Illustration from a Pairpoint catalog.*

_______ #1703, 8"d. *Illustration from a Pairpoint catalog.*

_______ #1705, 5"d x 2.375" deep. *Illustration from a Pairpoint catalog.*

FERN #1704, 4"d x 6.25"h.

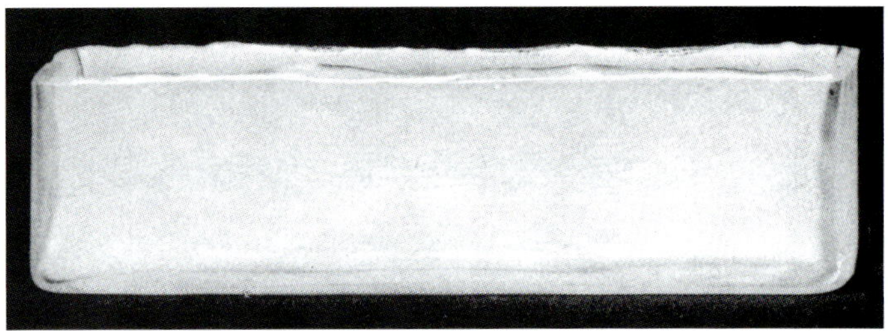

_______ #1706, 9" long x 2.375" wide x 2.375" high. *Illustration from a Pairpoint catalog.*

_______ #1707, 9" long x 3.50" wide x 3.50" deep. *Illustration from a Pairpoint catalog.*

________ #1708, 6" square at bottom x 6" high. *Illustration from a Pairpoint catalog.*

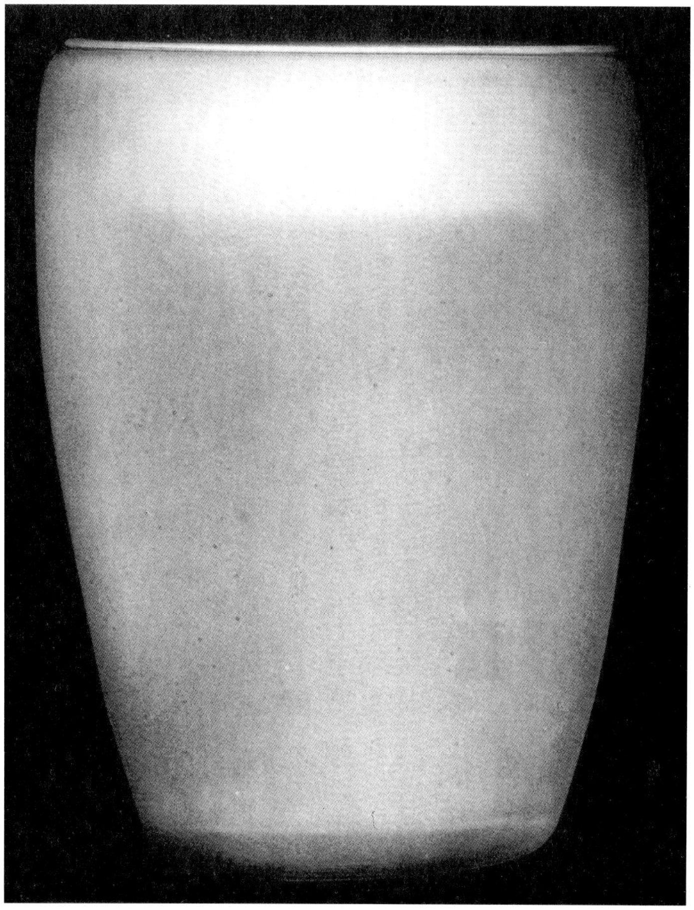

FERN #1710, 8"d x 11"h. *Illustration from a Pairpoint catalog.*

FERN #1709, 8.50"d. *Illustration from a Pairpoint catalog.*

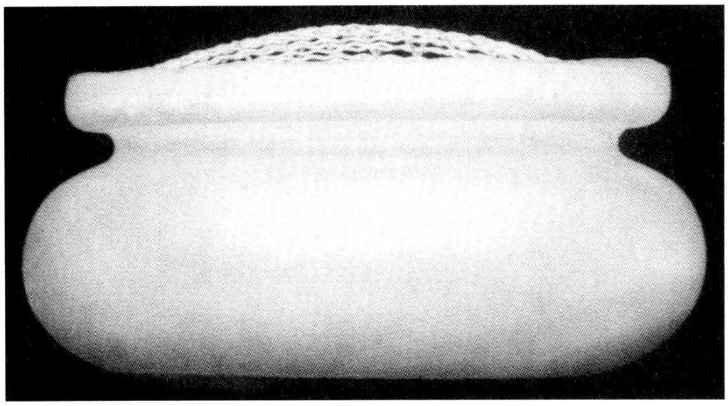

FLOWER HOLDER #1711, 7.50"d, 8.50"d, 9.50"d. *Illustration from a Pairpoint catalog.*

FLOWER HOLDER #1714, 10" long x 4.50" wide. *Illustration from a Pairpoint catalog.*

FLOWER POT #1712, 5.50"d, 6.50"d, 7.50"d. *Illustration from a Pairpoint catalog.*

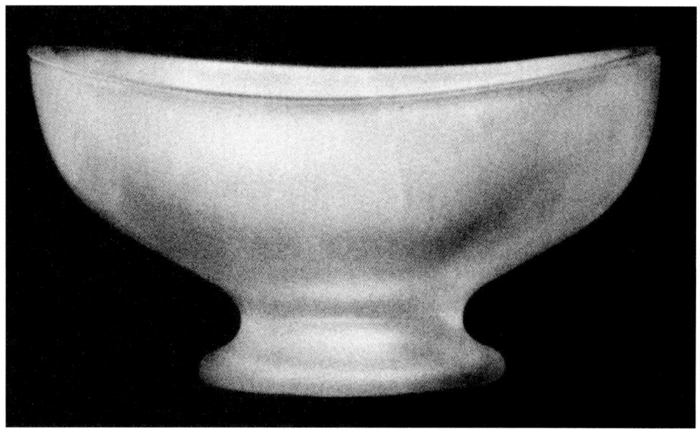

FERN DISH #1715, 9.50" long x 5.50" wide. *Illustration from a Pairpoint catalog.*

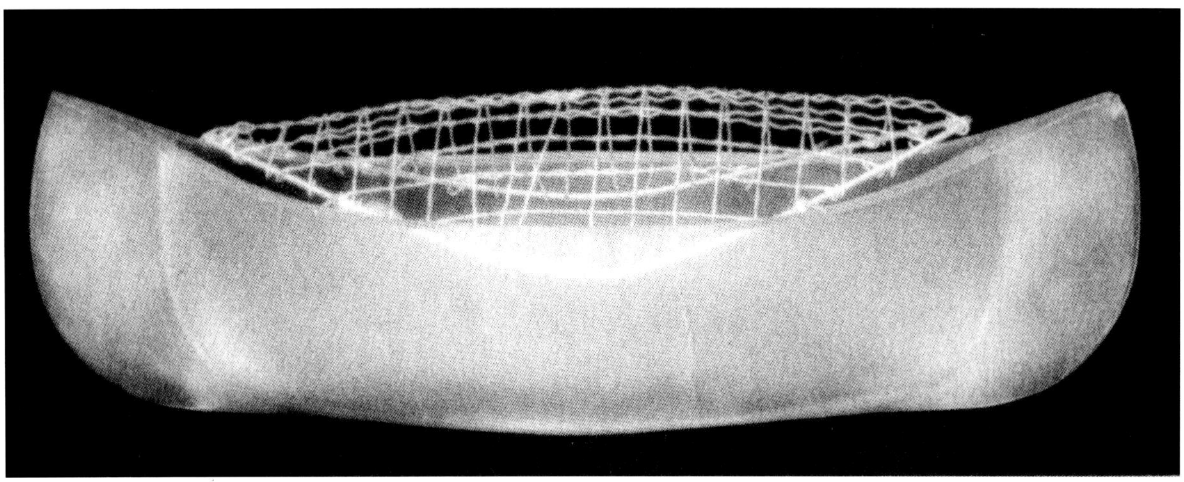

FLOWER HOLDER #1713, 12" long x 5" wide. *Illustration from a Pairpoint catalog.*

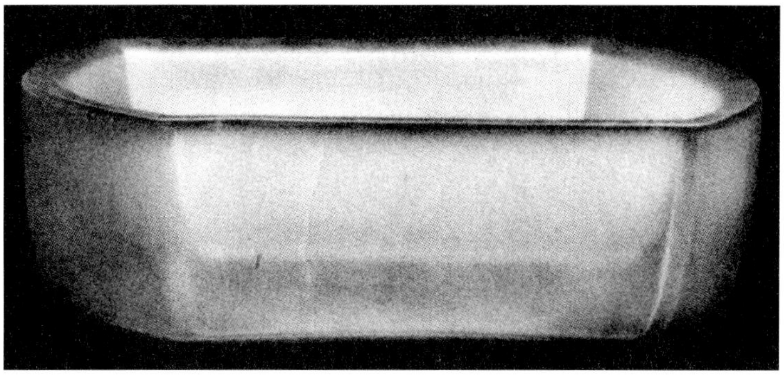

FERN #1716, 8.25" long x 7.25" wide. *Illustration from a Pairpoint catalog.*

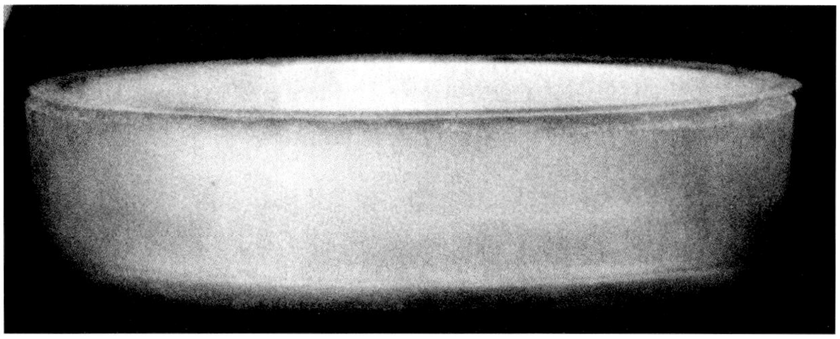

FERN #1717, 9.75" long x 6.75" wide. *Illustration from a Pairpoint catalog.*

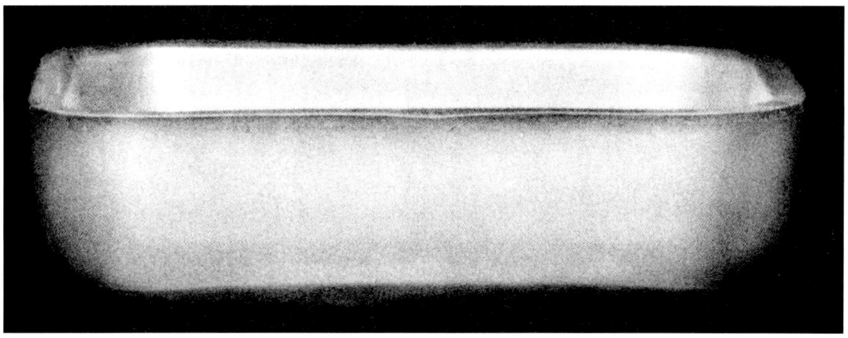

FERN #1718, 10.25" long x 7.75" wide, *Illustration from a Pairpoint catalog.*

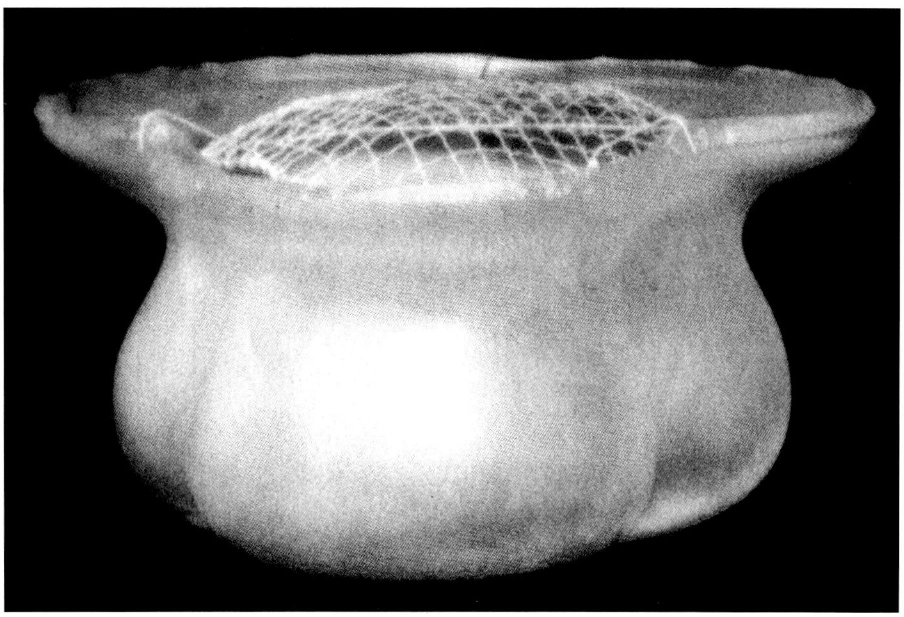

FLOWER HOLDER #1719, 11"d x 5"h. *Illustration from a Pairpoint catalog.*

BOWL #2227, Square Foot, 14"d x 4"h. *Illustration from a Pairpoint catalog.*

BOWL #2228, 10"d x 7"h. *Illustration from a Pairpoint catalog.*

BOWL #2229, 10"d x 6.25"h. *Illustration from a Pairpoint catalog.*

BOWL #2230, 10"d x 3.25"h. *Illustration from a Pairpoint catalog.*

FLOWER GLOBE #Unknown 01, 3"d, 3.50"d, 4"d, 5"d x 4"h, 6"d, 7"d, 8"d, 9"d.

BOWL #Unknown 02, 13"d, 15"d x 3"h. This shape has been referred to as the "Merry Widow" bowl.

BOWL #Unknown 03, 13"d x __"h, 14"d x 3.25"h, 15"d x __"h, 16"d x __"h, 16.50"d x 3.50"h.

BOWL #Unknown 05, 10.50"d x 6.75"h, 12"d x 6.75"h.

BOWL #Unknown 06, 13"d x 4"h.

BOWL #Unknown 08, 7.50"d x 2.50"h, 9"d x 2.75"h

FLOWER HOLDER (?) #Unknown 87, 5"d x __"h, 5.50"d x __"h, 7.125"d x 5.125"h x 4.50" base diameter, 7.50"d x 5.50"h. *Previously in the collection of Scott Grant.*

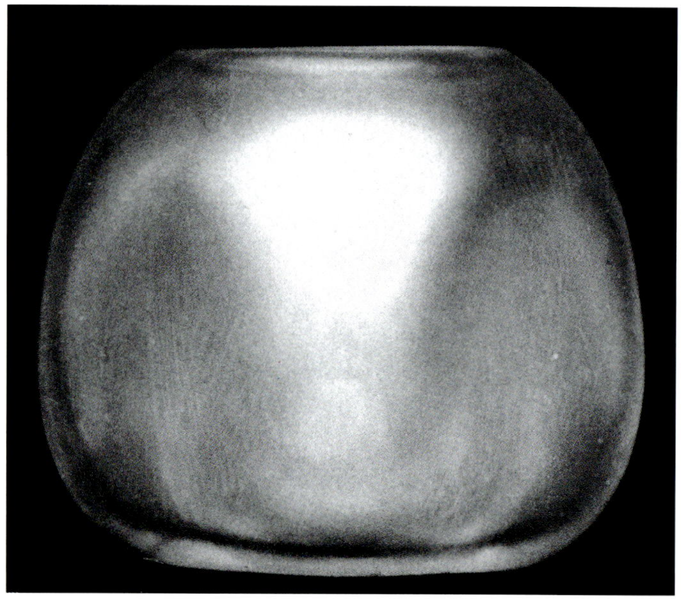

MOULDED FLOWER GLOBE #_____, 6"d. *Illustration from a Pairpoint catalog.*

BOWL #Unknown 91, 9.75"d x 4.75"h.

Pedestal Bowl #Unknown 113, 9"d x 7"h.

Candlesticks

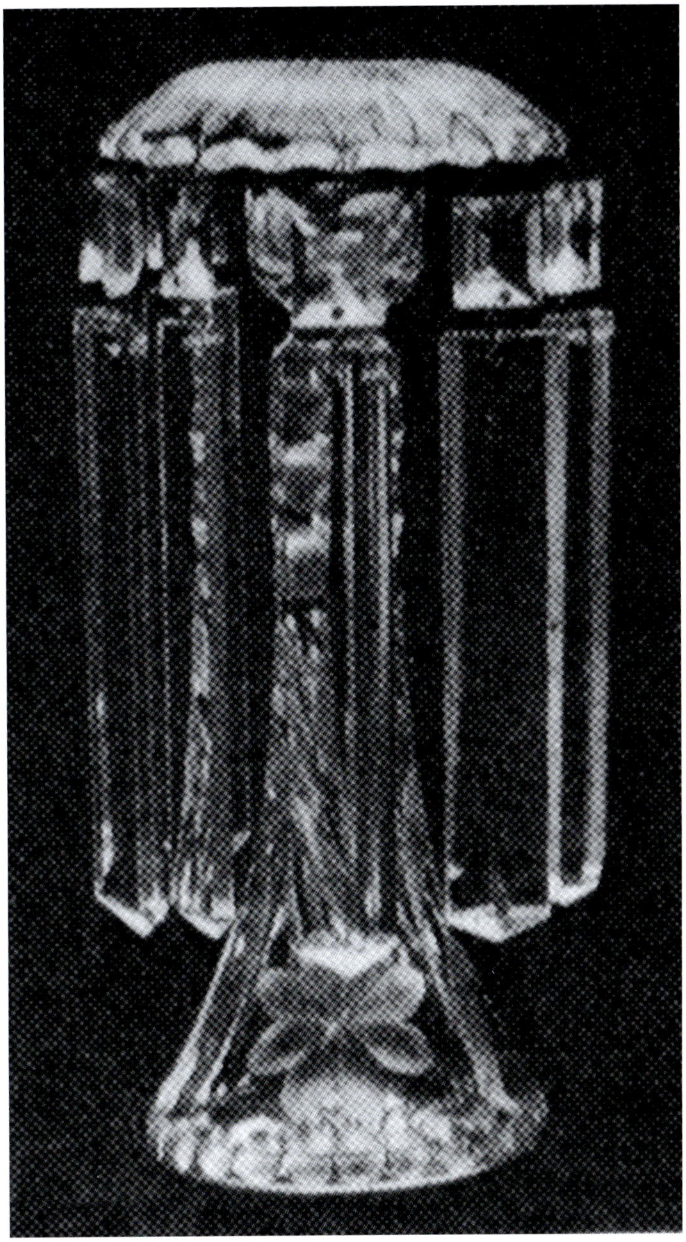

CANDLE #642, 9"h with (10) 5" Blunt Prisms. *Illustration from a Pairpoint catalog.*

CANDLE #1600, 8"h, 9"h, 10.75"h, 12"h, 14"h, 16"h.

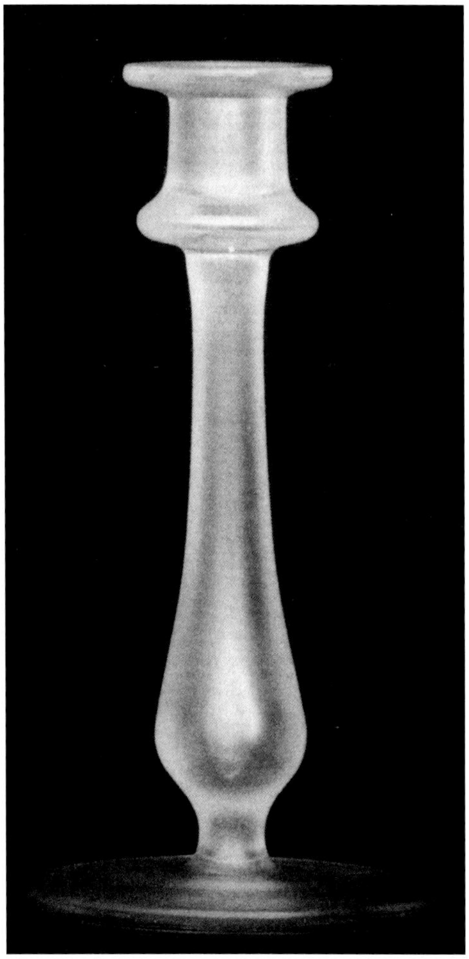

CANDLE #1604, 11.25"h. *Illustration from a Pairpoint catalog.*

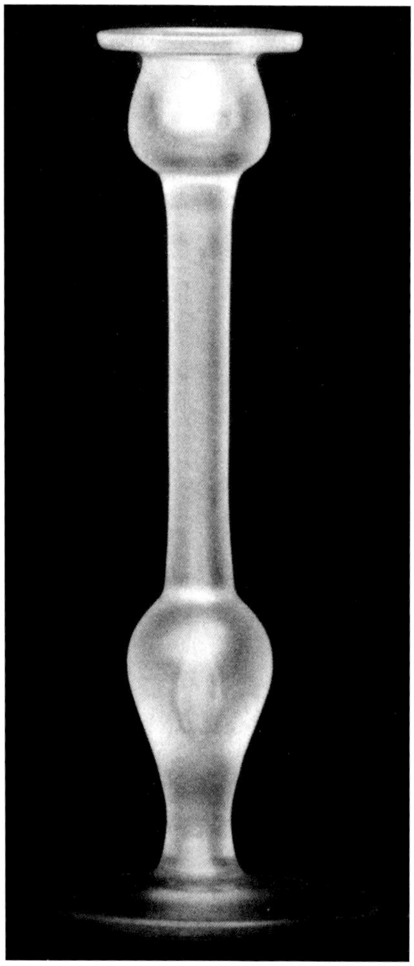

CANDLE #1605, 13.50"h. *Illustration from a Pairpoint catalog.*

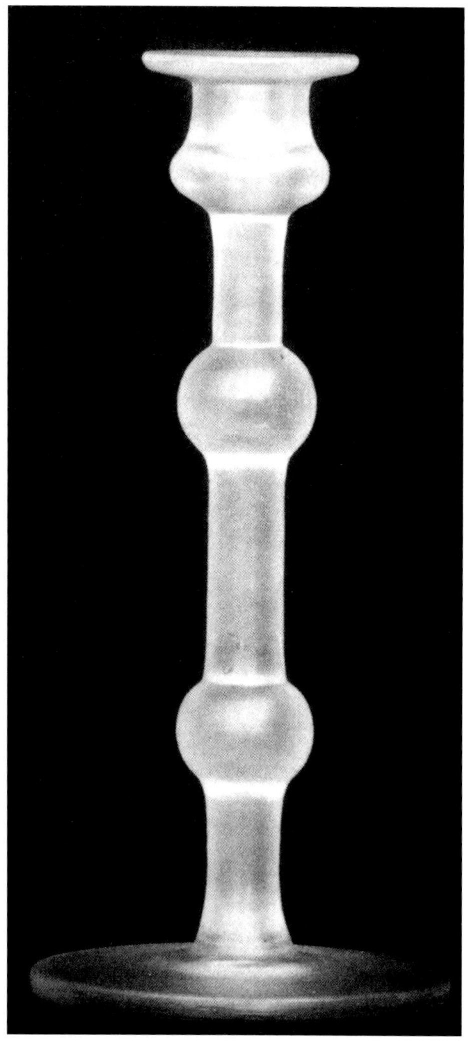

CANDLE #1606, 12.50"h. *Illustration from a Pairpoint catalog.*

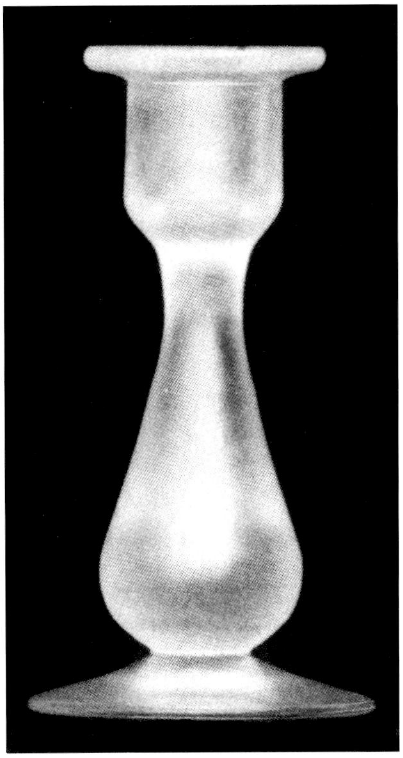

CANDLE #1607, 6.25"h. *Illustration from a Pairpoint catalog.*

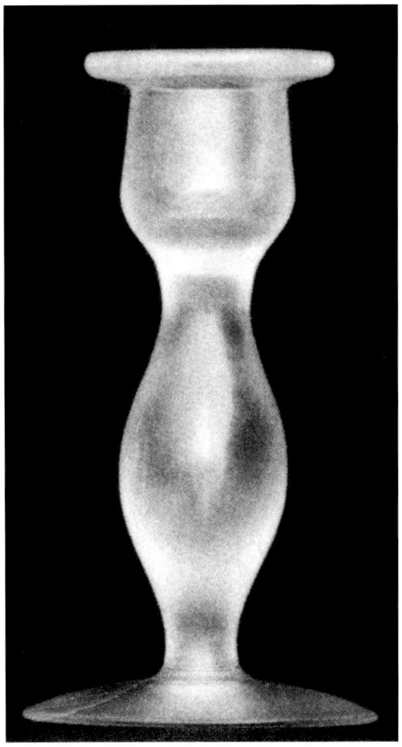

CANDLE #1608, 6"h, 8"h, 10"h. *Illustration from a Pairpoint catalog.*

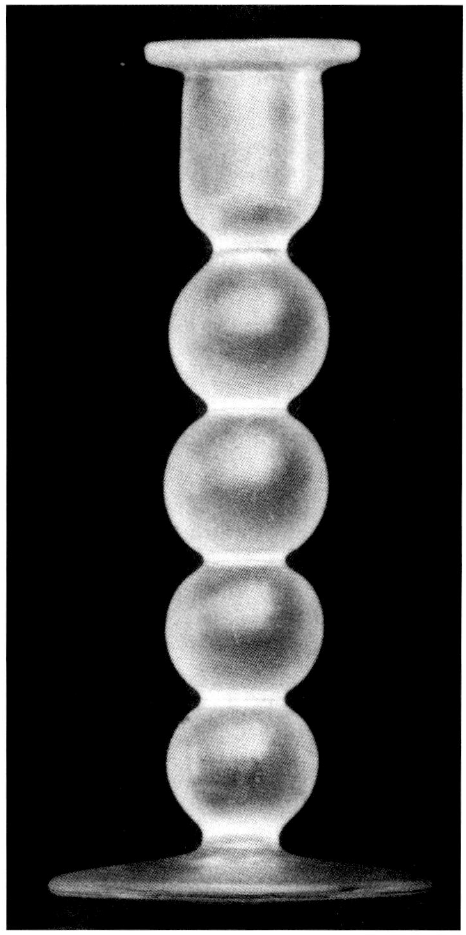

CANDLE #1609, 9.25"h. *Illustration from a Pairpoint catalog.*

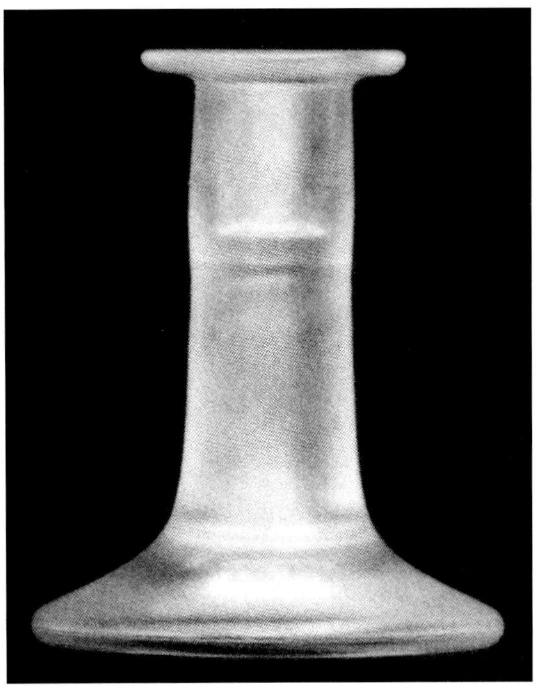

CANDLE #1610, 5.50"h. *Illustration from a Pairpoint catalog.*

CANDLE #1616, 10.50"h with (8) 3" Spear Prisms.

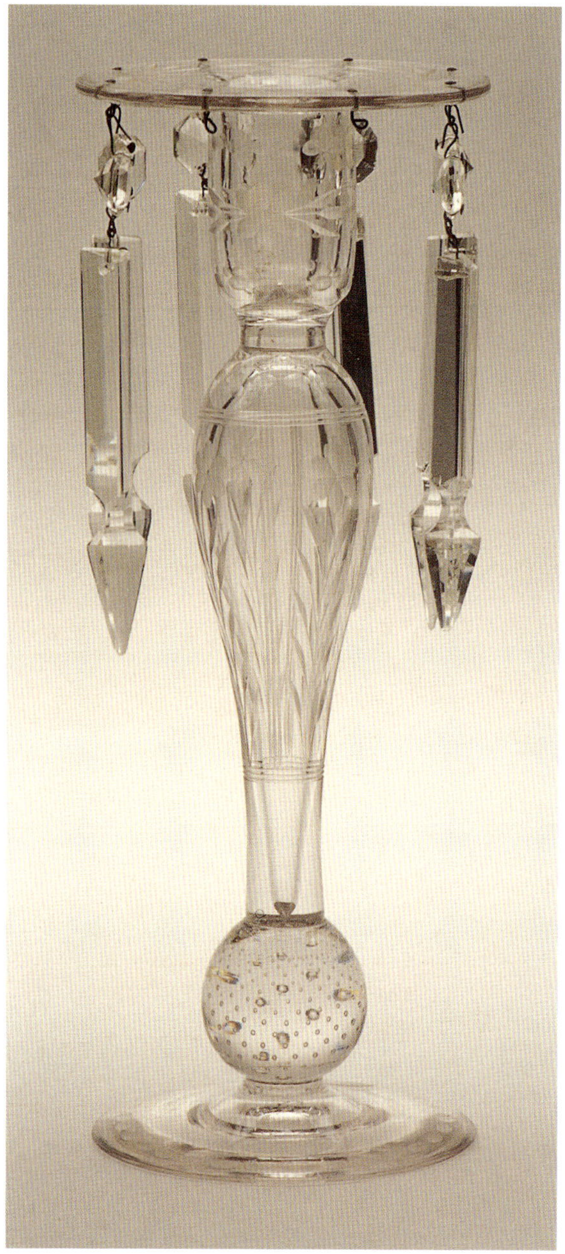

CANDLE #B-1617, 10"h with (8) 5" Spear Prisms.

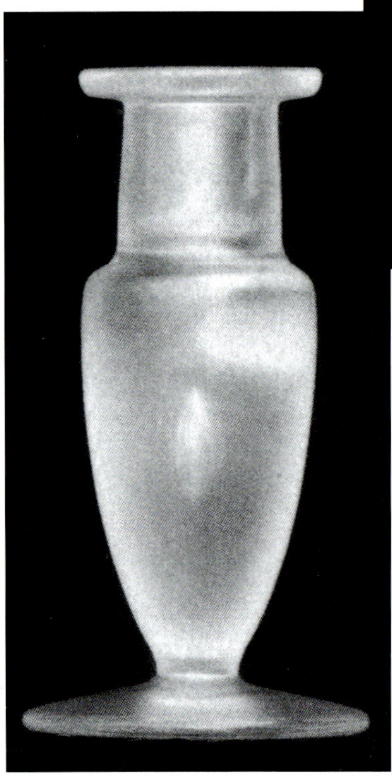

CANDLE #1611, 6"h. *Illustration from a Pairpoint catalog.*

CANDLE #F-1622, 10"h. *Illustration from a Pairpoint catalog.*

CANDLE #F-1624, 10.50"h. (This shape was previously identified in *The Essence of Pairpoint* as Unknown 11.)

CANDLE #F-1623, 10"h (This shape was previously identified in *The Essence of Pairpoint* as Unknown 12.)

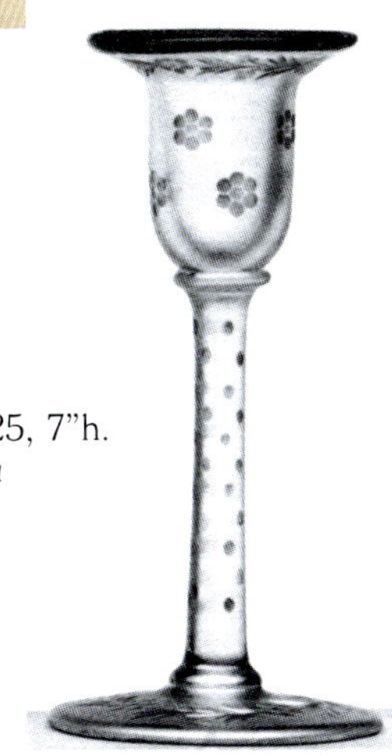

CANDLE #F-1625, 7"h. *Illustration from a Pairpoint catalog.*

CANDLE #B-1626, 8.50"h, 10"h, 12"h. *Illustration from a Pairpoint catalog.*

CANDLE #B-1627, 9"h, 10.50"h, 12.50"h.

CANDLE #1629, 9.50"h, 10"h, 10.75"h, 12"h, 14"h, 16"h.

CANDLE #B-1628, 12"h (usually found with (8) 5" Spear Prisms). *Illustration from a Pairpoint catalog.*

CANDLE #B-1634, 9.25"h with (8) 4" Blunt Prisms.

CANDLE #1635, 7.50"h.

CANDLE #1640, 5"h. A 1926 Pairpoint engraving department cost book references a "Large" and "Small" size.

CANDLE #1641, 9.50"h, 12"h, 14"h. *Illustration from a Pairpoint catalog.*

CANDLE #1642, 4"h.

CANDLE #B-1811, 12"h (may be found with (8) 5" Spear Prisms), 16"h.

CANDLE #B-3024, 5"h.

CANDLE #1811, 12"h, 16"h.

CANDLE #Unknown 10, 4"h. A 1926 Pairpoint engraving department cost book references a "Large" and "Small" size.

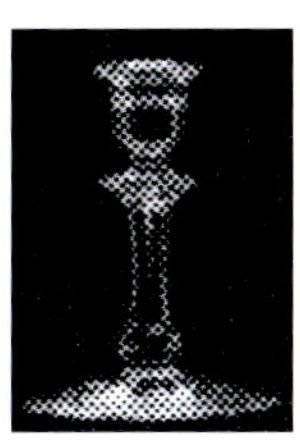

CANDLE #Unknown 09, 6"h. *Illustration from a Pairpoint catalog.*

CANDLE #Unknown 13, 9"h, 10.50"h with (8) 5" Spear Prisms.

CANDLE #Unknown 15, 3.50"h.

CANDLE #Unknown 100. 8"h. This blank has a heavy optic swirl intended to be used with the Ardsley pattern. *From the collection of Chris Vizvarie.*

CANDLE #Unknown 101.
Sketch from a 1926 Pairpoint engraving department cost book.

THREE LIGHT CANDELABRA #______, 16.25" wide x 15.25" high. This candelabra has a heavy optic spiral and is engraved with the Ardsley pattern. This is an extremely rare and desirable item. *Illustration from a Pairpoint catalog.*

Comports or Compotes

COMPORT #A-104, 6"d x 3.25"h, 8"d x 4.25"h, 10"d x 5"h, 12.50"d x 5.50"h.

COMPORT #A-198, 7"d x 8"h. *Illustration from a Pairpoint catalog.*

COMPORT #A-109, 8.50"d. This is identical to Bowl #A-109, but in the smaller size it is referred to as a comport. *Illustration from a Pairpoint catalog.*

COMPORT #A-199. *Illustration from a Pairpoint catalog.*

COMPORT #A-210, 6.50"d x __"h, 7.50"d x __"h, 8.50"d x __"h. *Illustration from a Pairpoint catalog.*

COMPORT #A(F)-215, 5"d x 6.50"h, 6"d x 7.50"h, 8"d x 6.75"h. *Illustration from a Pairpoint catalog.*

COMPORT #A-213, 5"d x 3.25"h, 6"d x 3.50"h.

COMPORT #A-214, 5"d x 3.25"h, 6"d x 3.25"h. *Illustration from a Pairpoint catalog.*

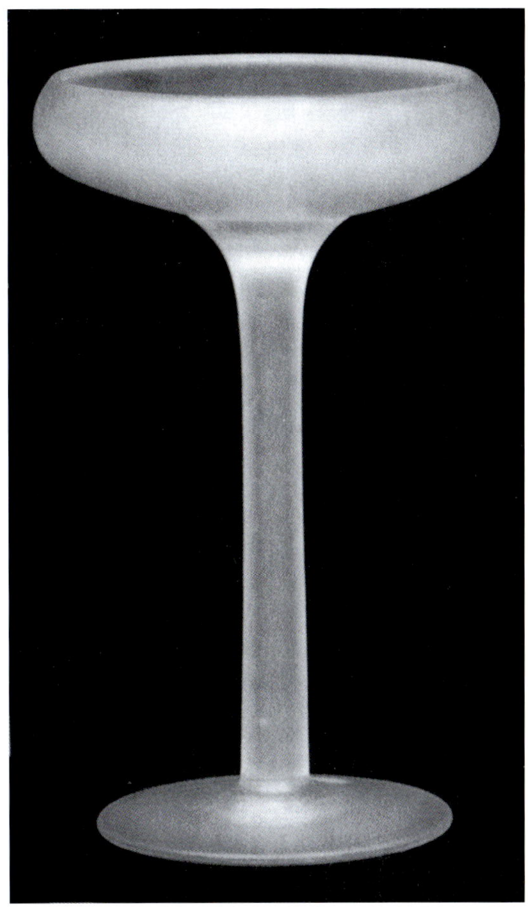

COMPORT #A-223, 6"d x 9"h. *Illustration from a Pairpoint catalog.*

COMPORT #A-228, 6"d x 3.75"h, 7"d x 4"h, 8"d x 4.50"h, 8.75"d x 4.50"h, 10"d x 4.75"h, 12"d x 5"h.

________ #A-238, 8"d x 8"h, 9"d x 9"h. *Illustration from a Pairpoint catalog.*

COMPORT #B-228, 6"d x 4.375"h, 7"d x __"h, 8"d x 4.75"h, 9"d x __"h.

OVAL COMPORT #A-239, 3.50" long, 4.25" long, 5.25" long, 6.75" long.

COMPORT #A-246, 6"d x 6"h. *Illustration from a Pairpoint catalog.*

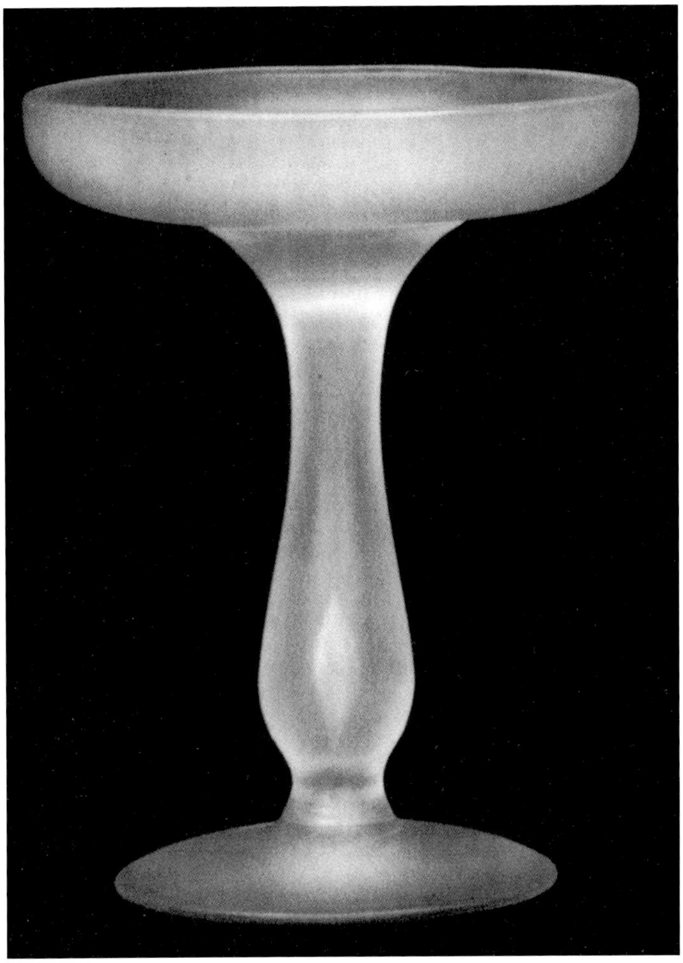

COMPORT #A-240, 5.50"d x 6.50"h, 6"d x 8.25"h. *Illustration from a Pairpoint catalog.*

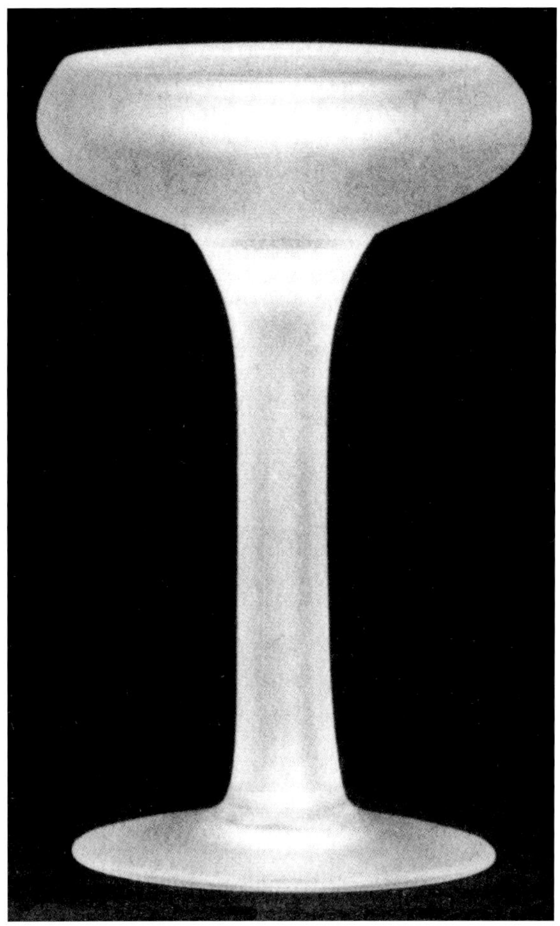

_______ #248.5, 6"d x 9"h. *Illustration from a Pairpoint catalog.*

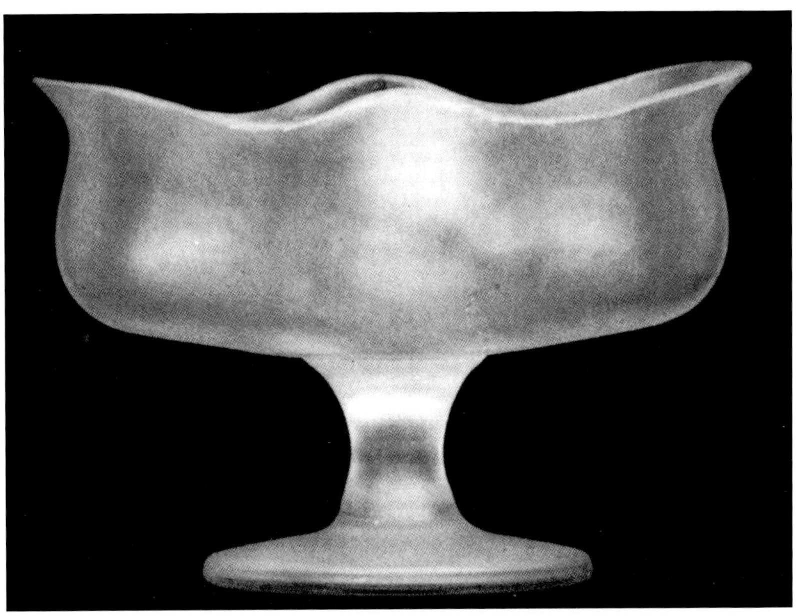

_______ #A-241, 9" long x 7" wide x 6.50" high. *Illustration from a Pairpoint catalog.*

________ #A-255, 7" long x 7.25" high. *Illustration from a Pairpoint catalog.*

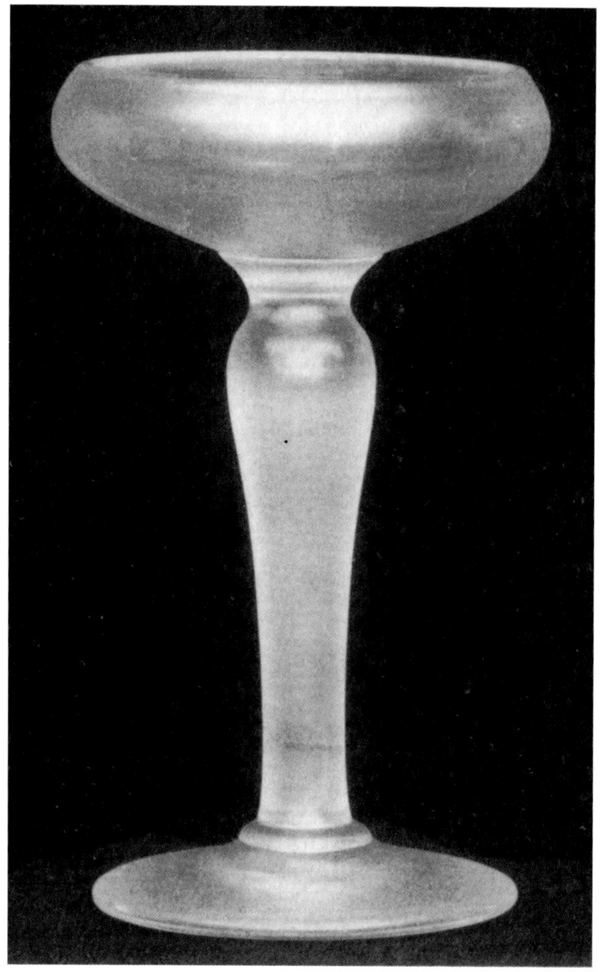

________ #256, 7"h, 10"h. *Illustration from a Pairpoint catalog.*

COMPORT #A-256, 4.25"d x 5.25"h

COMPORT #A-258, 9"d x 8"h, 10"d x 9"h. *Illustration from a Pairpoint catalog.*

COMPORT #A-278, 5"d x 4.25"h, 6"d x 5.375"h, 7"d x 6"h, __"d x __"h.

COMPORT #A-259, 5.50"d x 7.50"h. *Illustration from a Pairpoint catalog.*

COMPORT #A-262, 6.50"d x 5.50"h, 7.50"d x __"h, 8.50"d x __"h, 9.50"d x __"h. (This shape was previously identified in *The Essence of Pairpoint* as Unknown 22.)

COMPORT #A-294, 5.50"d x 5"h, 6.50"d x 6"h, 7"d x 6.50"h, 7.50"d x __"h, 8"d x __"h, 8.50"d x 7.25"h, 9.50"d x __"h, 10"d x 10.50"h, 10.50"d x __"h.

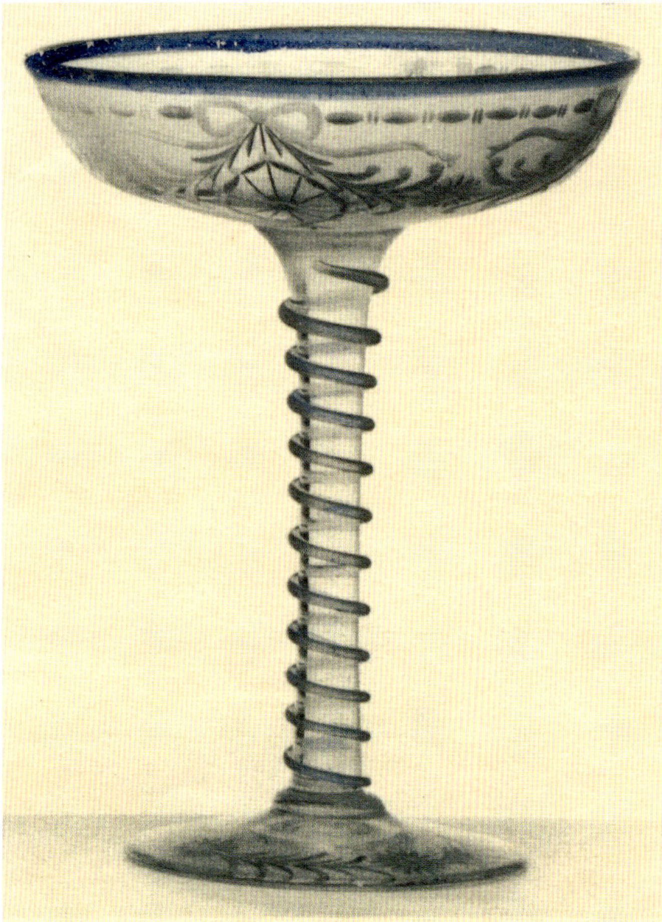

COMPORT #F-290, 5"d x __"h, 6"d x __"h, 8"d x 7"h. (This shape was previously identified in *The Essence of Pairpoint* as Unknown 21.) *Illustration from a Pairpoint catalog.*

COMPORT #F-291, 9"d x 6.75"h. *Illustration from a Pairpoint catalog.*

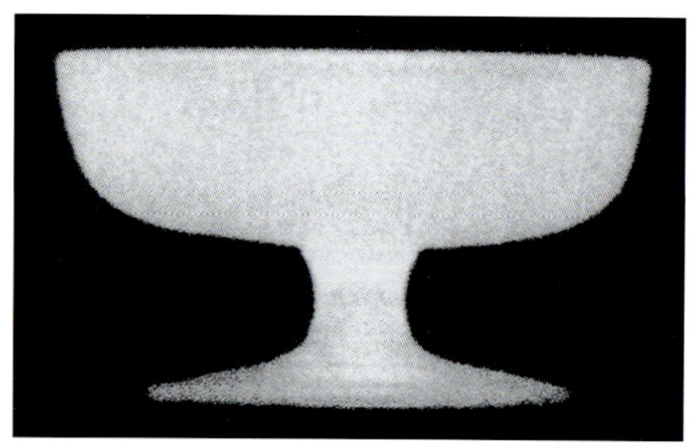

COMPORT #298, 3"d x __"h, 4"d x __"h, 5"d x 2.25"h. *Illustration from a Pairpoint catalog.*

COMPORT #A-299, 4.50"d x 3.625"h, 8"d x 7"h, 9"d x __"h, 11.50"d x 7.25"h.

_______ #309, 12" long x 9" wide x 8.50" high. *Illustration from a Pairpoint* catalog.

COMPORT #364, 6"d x 5.50"h, 7.50"d x 6"h. (This shape was previously identified in *The Essence of Pairpoint* as Unknown 17.)

COMPORT #B-366, 6.50"d x 6"h, 7.50"d x __"h, 8"d x 7"h, 8.50"d x __"h.

COMPORT #B-367, 8"d x 5"h.

COMPORT #B-372, 7"d x 8.25"h, 7.50"d x __"h, 8.50"d x __"h. (Same as #372, but having a bubble ball connector)

COVERED COMPORT #B-382, 9" high overall.

COMPORT #372, 7"d x __"h, 7.50"d x __"h, 8.50"d x __"h. (Same as B-372, but without the bubble ball connector) *Illustration from a Pairpoint catalog.*

COMPORT #Unknown 19, 8.50"d x 8"h.

OBLONG COMPORT #Unknown 16, 9.50" long x 5.25" wide x 5.50" high. *Illustration from a Pairpoint catalog.*

COMPORT #Unknown 20, 8"d x 8"h.

COMPORT #Unknown 85, 9"d x 8.75"h.

TALL COVERED COMPORT #Unknown 23, 12" high overall.

COMPORT #Unknown 86, 6.375"d x 6"h. This form is the same as #B-366, but it has a "hollow" foot.

COVERED COMPORT #Unknown 92, 7"d x 6.75"h (overall), 7.75"d x 6.50"h (overall). This form has been seen with two differently styled lids, hence the inconsistency of the two height dimensions relative to the diameters.

OVAL COMPORT #Unknown 96, 5.25" long x 3.50" wide x 4.50" high. *Courtesy of Charles and Barbara Coulter, Easton, Massachusetts.*

COMPORT #Unknown 97, 7.50"d x 7.25h.

COMPORT #Unknown 98, 6"d x 2.75"h, 9"d x 3.75"h. It is highly probable that this blank is NOT of Pairpoint origin. When tapped lightly the bell-tone "ring" you would expect from a Pairpoint clear blank is noticeably missing. Instead you will hear a very dull, non-resonating "clunk." Additionally, you will find the foot has a welt edge with the fold turning down and under; this characteristic just isn't found on Pairpoint shapes. Each of the two sizes of this shape have been seen with true Pairpoint engraving patterns, the 9" comport having "Clarina' and the 6" comport having "Waterford." The pontils are ground and polished.

COMPORT #Unknown 102, 6"d x 6.75"h. This blank has a heavy optic swirl intended for use with the Ardsley pattern. *From the collection of Chris Vizvarie.*

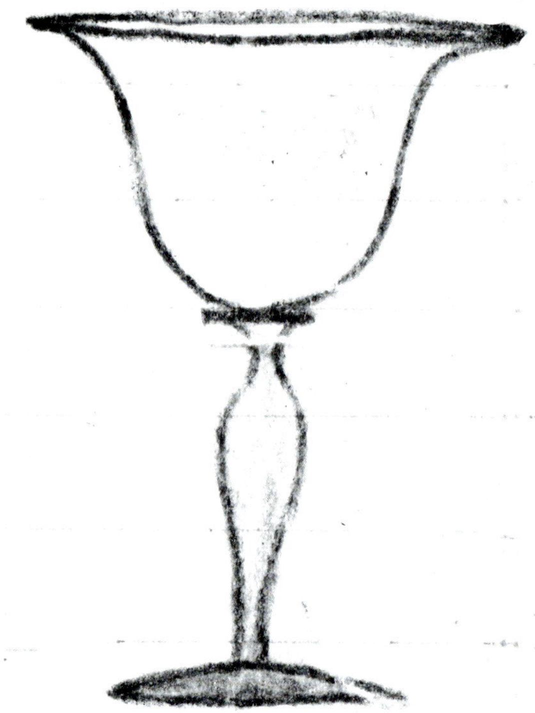

COMPORT #Unknown 103. *Sketch from a 1926 Pairpoint engraving department cost book.*

Vases

VASE #A-292, 6.50"h, 7"h, 8"h. (All measurements are to the top of the lower body.)

VASE #A-295, 6"h, 5.50"h, 8"h. (All measurements are to the top of the lower body.)

VASE #A-297, 8.25"h, 10.50"h. (All measurements are to the top of the lower body.) *Illustration from a Pairpoint catalog.*

VASE #A-298, 8" (measured to top of lower body) x __" overall height, 11" (measured to top of lower body.) x 14.75" overall height.

VASE #B-373, 6.75"d x 11"h with (10) 6" Spear Prisms, __"d x 12"h.

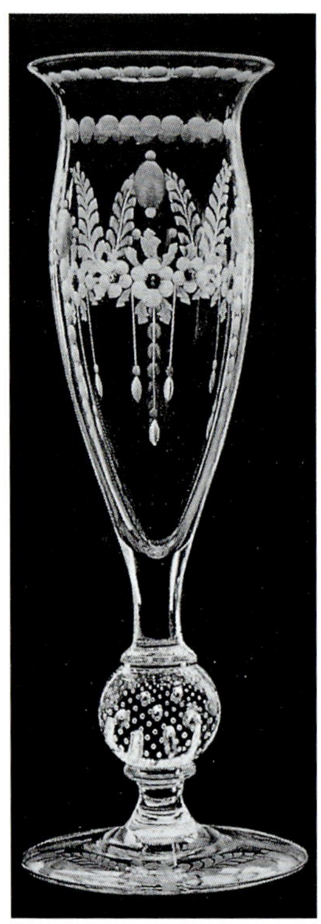

VASE #B-958. *Illustration from a Pairpoint catalog.*

VASE #B-959, 10"h, 12"h, 14"h.

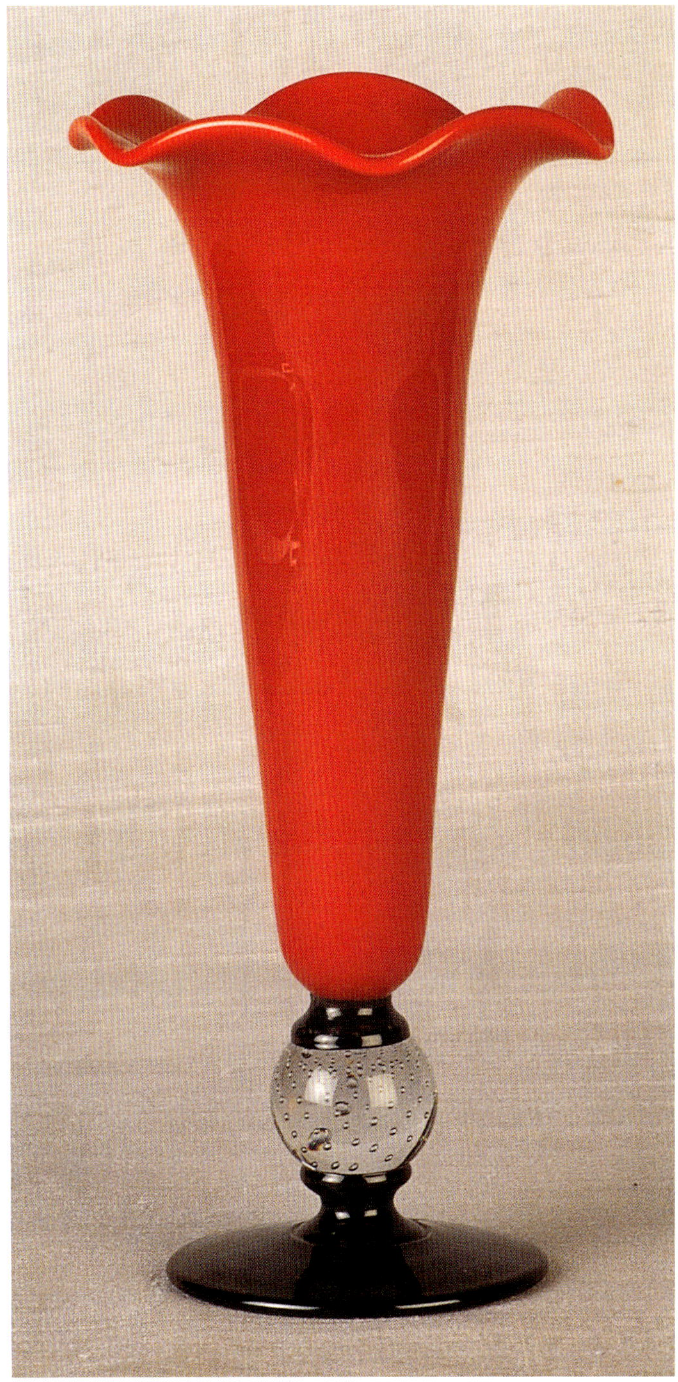

VASE #B-960, 9"h, 12"h. (Same as A-960, but with the bubble ball connector) A 1926 Pairpoint engraving department cost book references the following sizes, but does not differentiate between A-960 or B-960: 8"h, 9"h, 10"h, 10.50"h, 12"h.

VASE #A-960. (Same as B-960, but without the bubble ball connector) A 1926 Pairpoint engraving department cost book references the following sizes, but does not differentiate between A-960 or B-960: 8"h, 9"h, 10"h, 10.50"h, 12"h.
Illustration from a Pairpoint catalog.

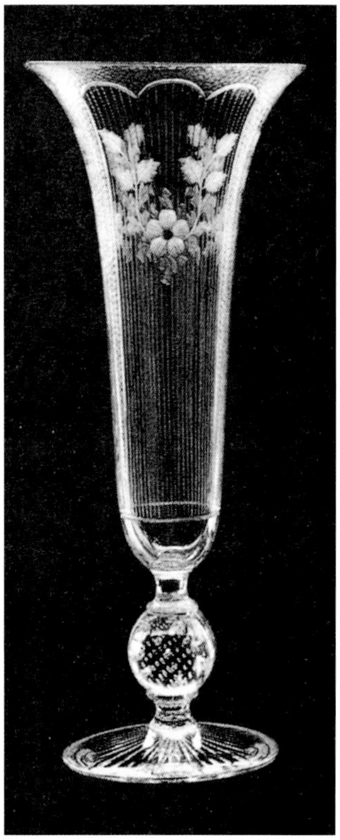

VASE #B-961, 10"h, 12"h. *Illustration from a Pairpoint catalog.*

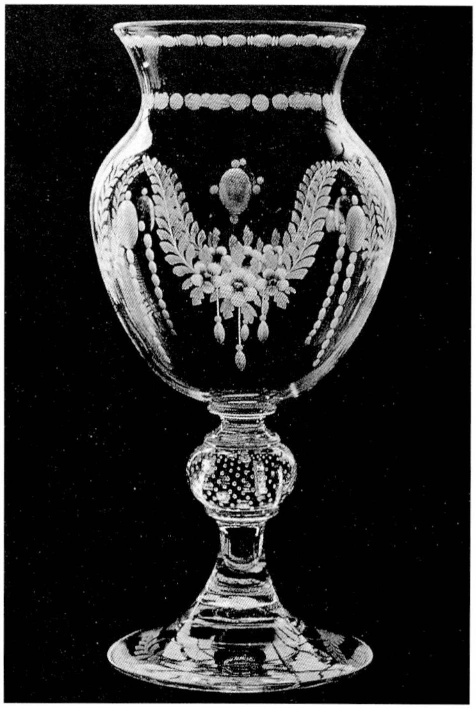

VASE #B-962, 10"h x 4.50"d. *Illustration from a Pairpoint catalog.*

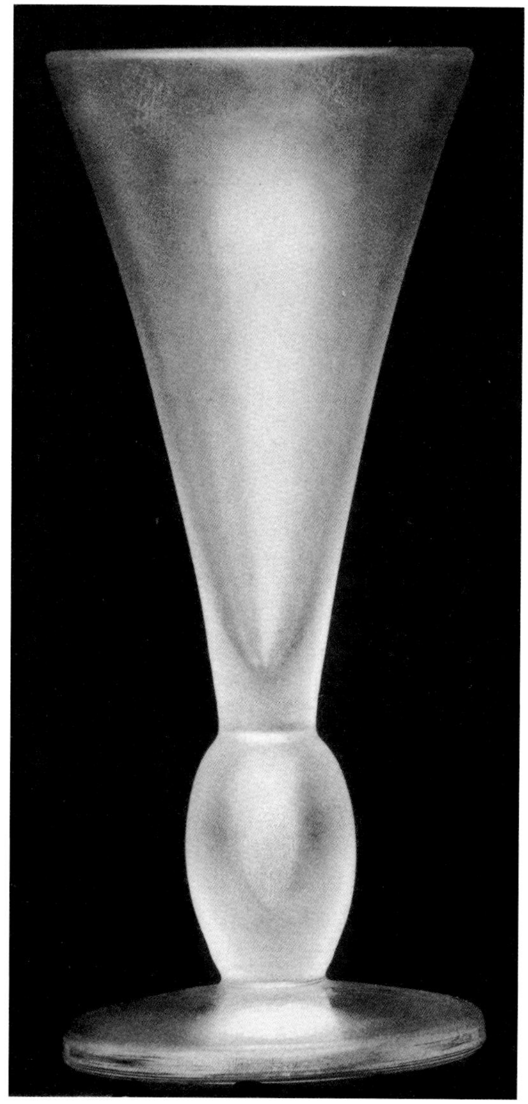

_______ #A-1002, 14"h. *Illustration from a Pairpoint catalog.*

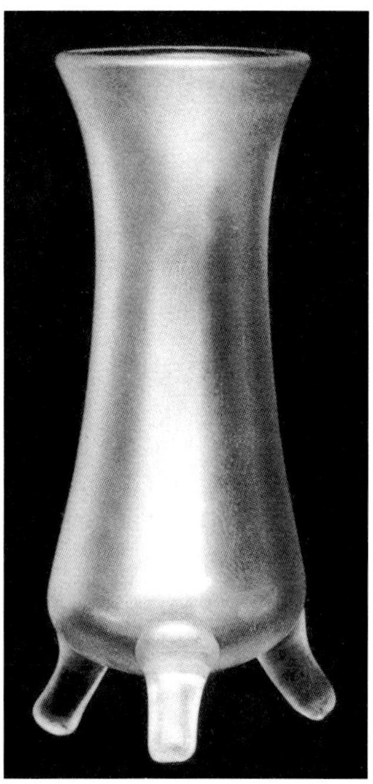

_______ #A-1000, 12"h, 14"h, 16"h, three feet. *Illustration from a Pairpoint* catalog.

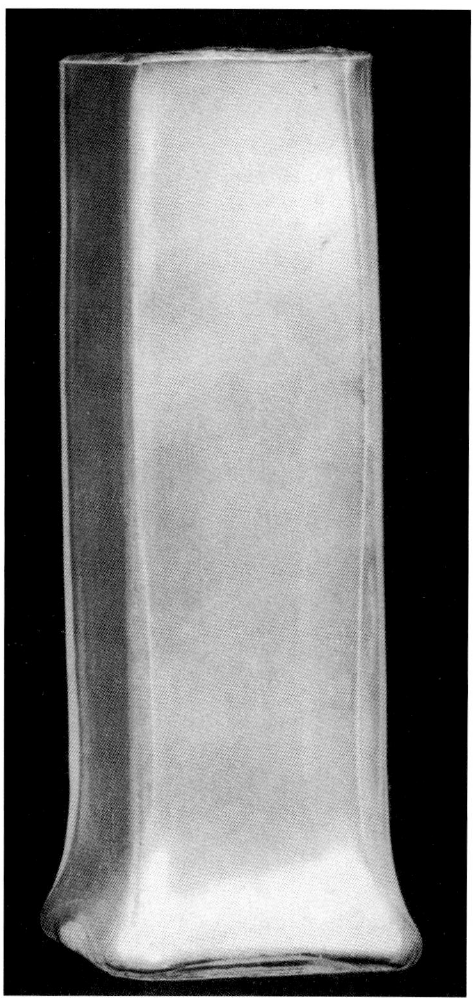

_______ #A-1001, 14"h x 4.50" square. *Illustration from a Pairpoint catalog.*

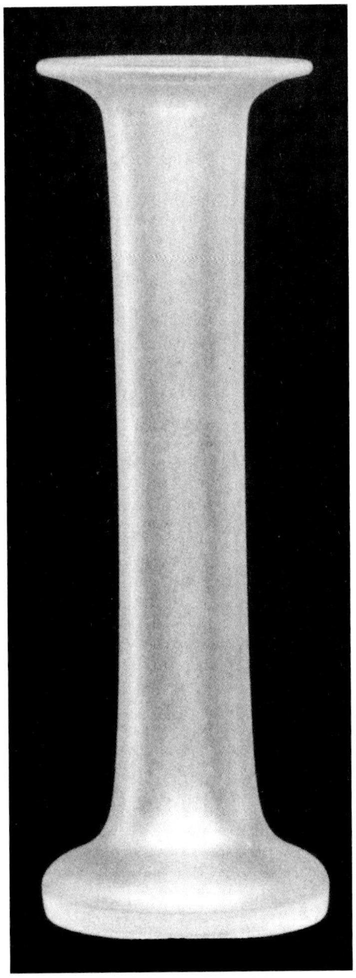

#1002, 15.50"h. *Illustration from a Pairpoint catalog.*

________ #1003, 14"h. *Illustration from a Pairpoint catalog.*

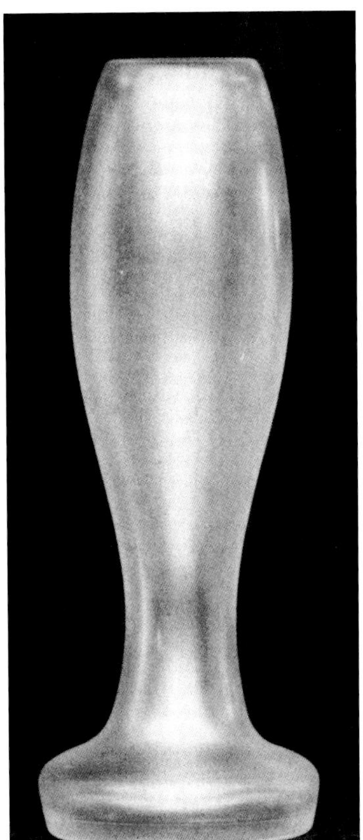

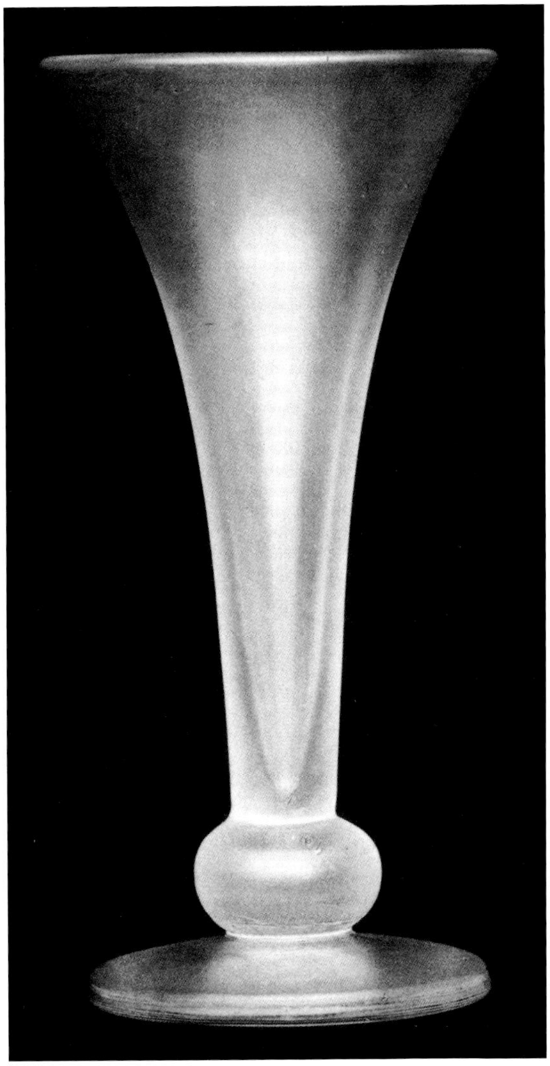

________ #A-1003, 14"h. *Illustration from a Pairpoint catalog.*

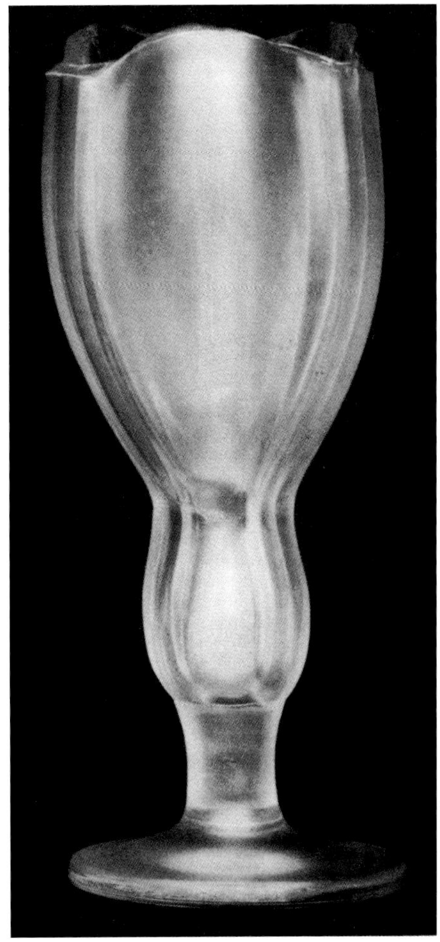

________ #A-1004, 15"h. *Illustration from a Pairpoint catalog.*

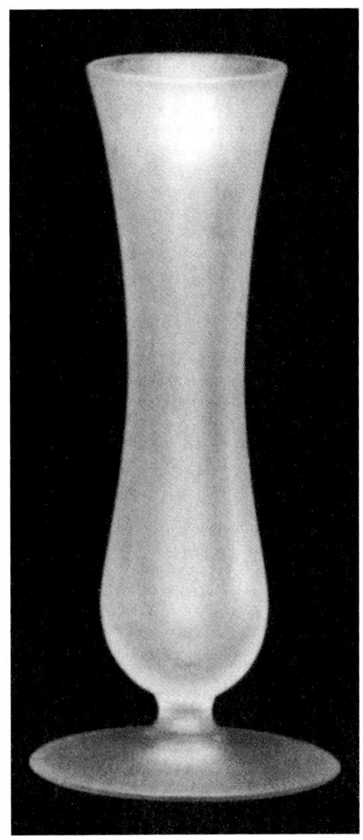

VASE #A-1005, 6.50"h, 8.50"h, 10"h. *Illustration from a Pairpoint catalog.*

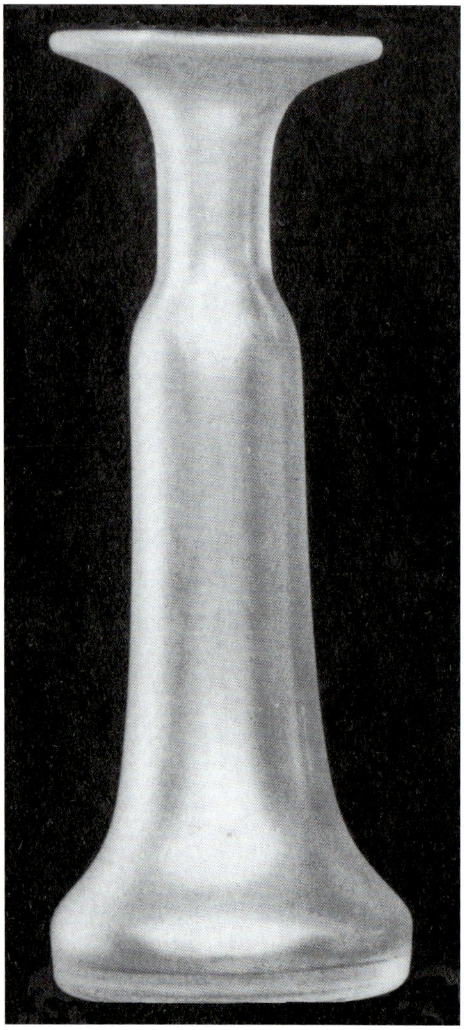

_______ #1005, 16.50"h. *Illustration from a Pairpoint catalog.*

VASE #A-1007, 6"d x 6.75"h, 7.75"d x 7.25"h, 10"d x __"h. (Same as B-1007, but without the bubble ball connector) A 1926 Pairpoint engraving department cost book references the following sizes, but does not differentiate between A-1007 or B-1007, or whether the sizes are diameters or heights: 6", 8", 10". *Illustration from a Pairpoint catalog.*

VASE #B-1007, 8.50"d x 8"h, 10.25"d x 9.25"h. (Same as A-1007, but with the bubble ball connector) A 1926 Pairpoint engraving department cost book references the following sizes, but does not differentiate between A-1007 or B-1007, or whether the sizes are diameters or heights: 6", 8", 10".

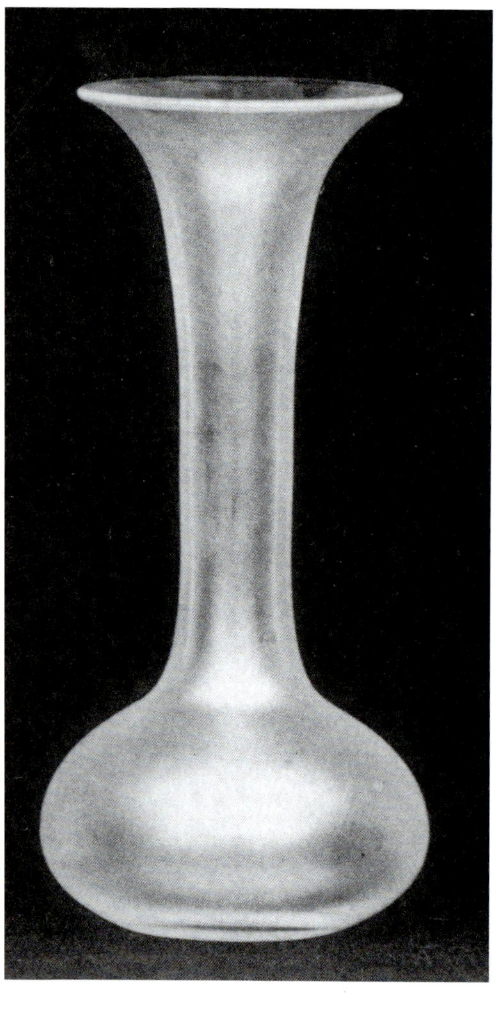

_______ #1013, 7"h. *Illustration from a Pairpoint catalog.*

VASE #A-1018, 5.50"h, 9"h (2.50" top dia and 3" foot dia). *Illustration from a Pairpoint catalog.*

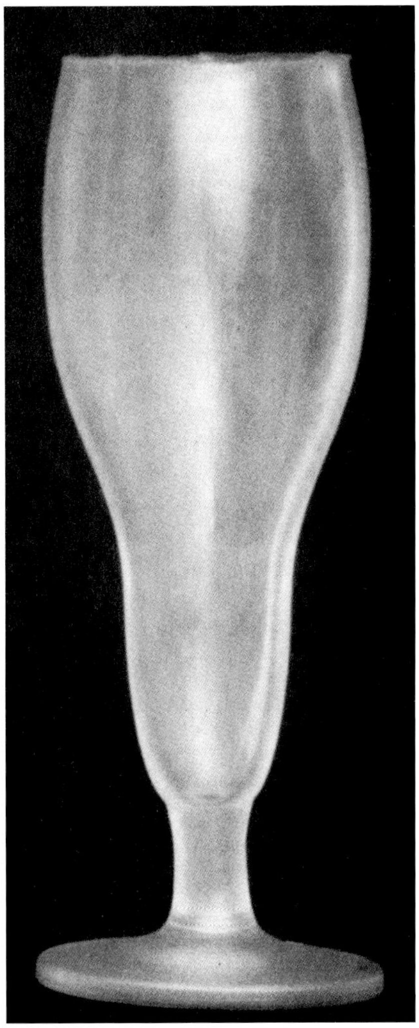

________ #1018, 12"h. *Illustration from a Pairpoint catalog.*

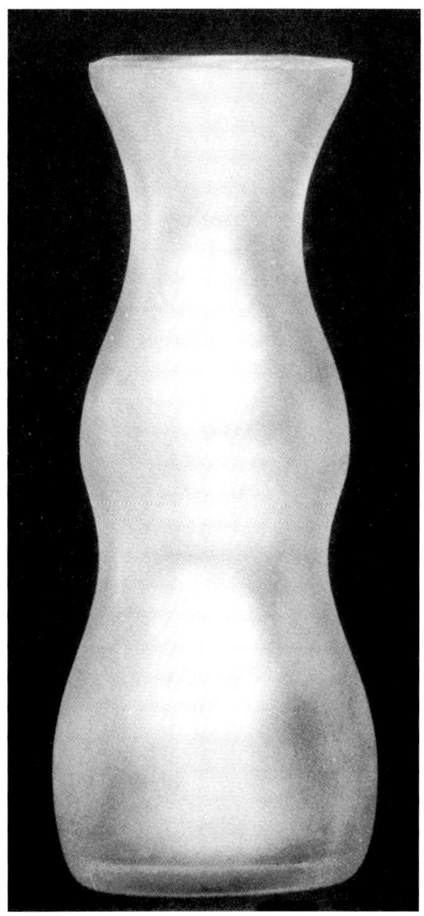

VASE #1020, 10"h, 12"h, 14"h. *Illustration from a Pairpoint catalog.*

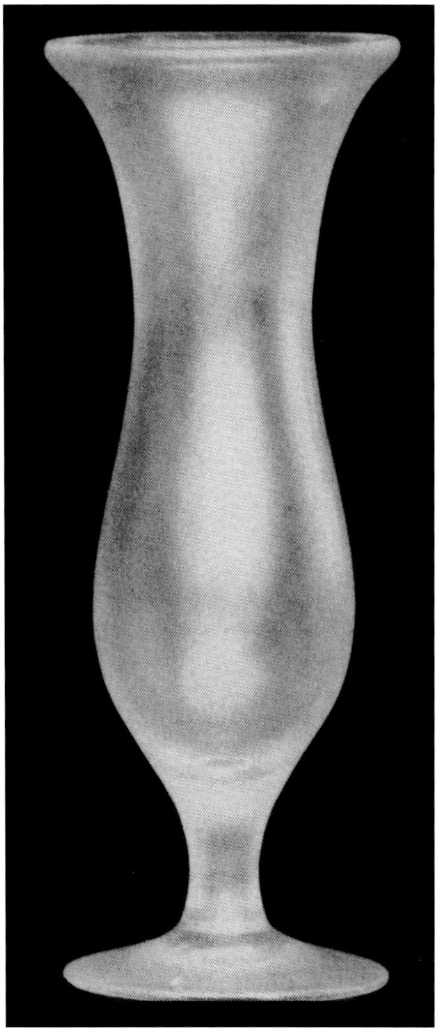

________ #1026, 8"h, 10"h, 12"h. *Illustration from a Pairpoint catalog.*

VASE #A-1027, 4.50"h. *Illustration from a Pairpoint catalog.*

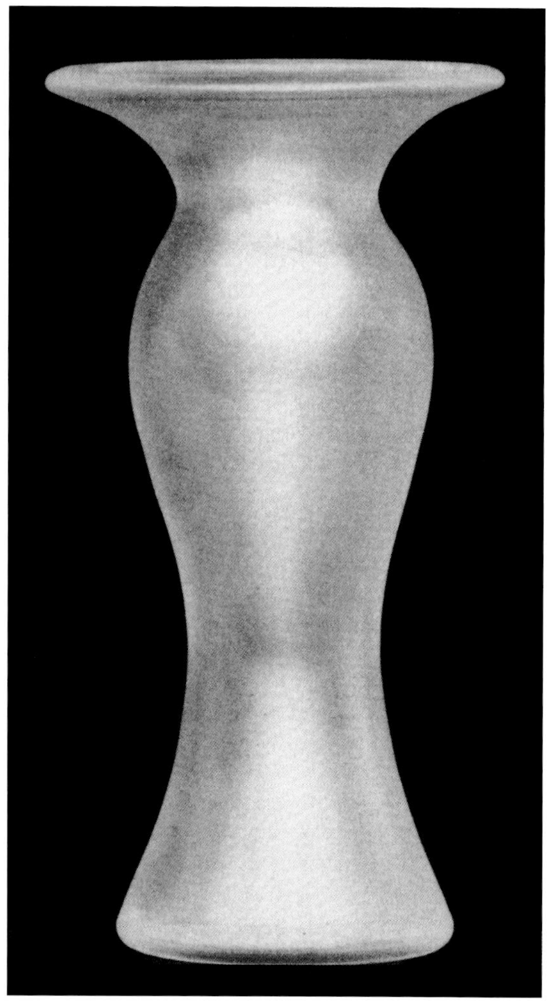

________ #1031, 11"h, 13"h. *Illustration from a Pairpoint catalog.*

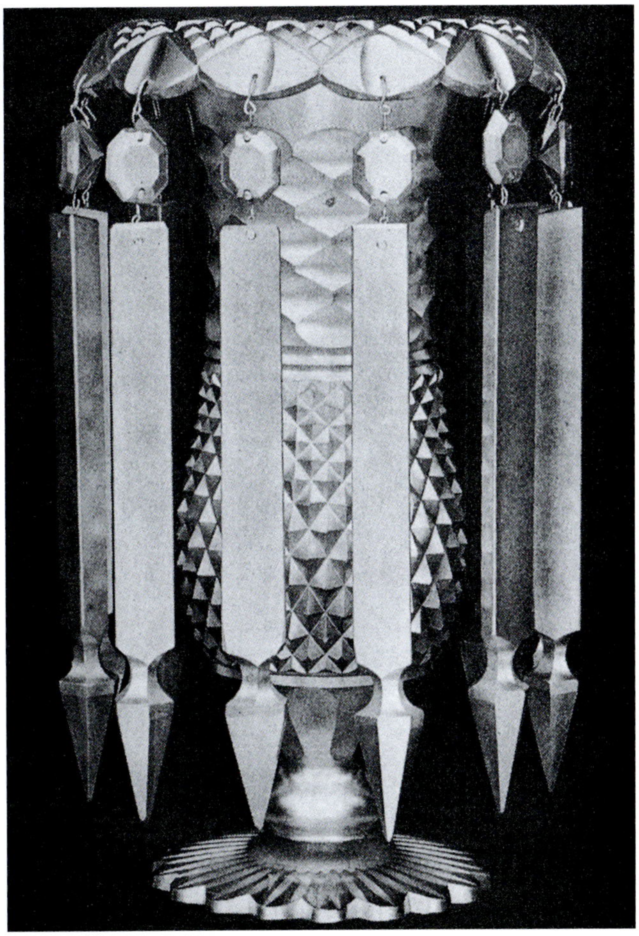

VASE #A-1032, 11.25"h. Made with or without prisms. (This shape was previously identified in *The Essence of Pairpoint* as Unknown 32.) *Illustration from a Pairpoint catalog.*

VASE #1032, 6"h, 8"h, 10"h, 12"h, 14"h. (This shape was previously identified in *The Essence of Pairpoint* as A-1032.)

VASE #A-1034, 6"h, 9"h. *Illustration from a Pairpoint catalog.*

VASE #A-1035. *Illustration from a Pairpoint catalog.*

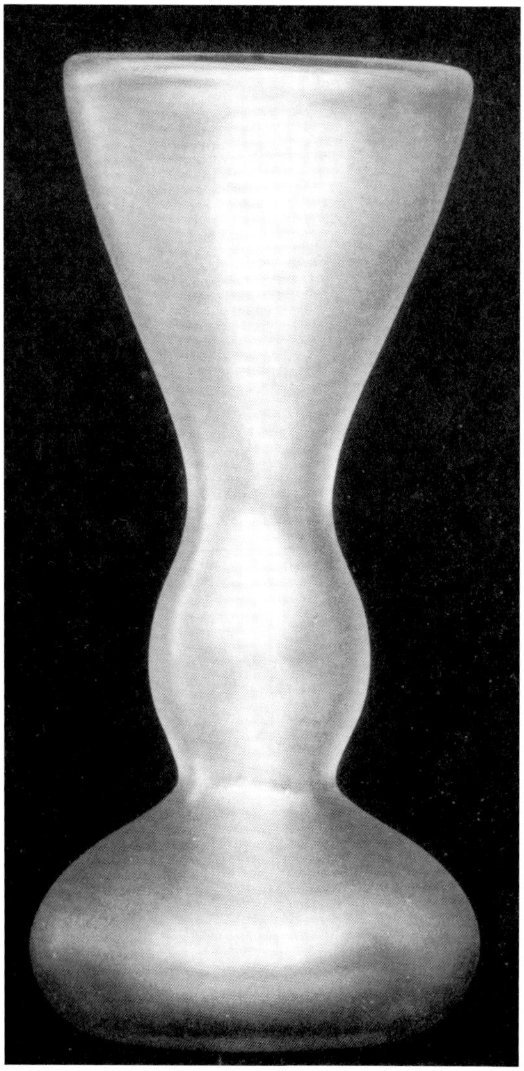

VASE #1035, 14"h. *Illustration from a Pairpoint catalog.*

VASE #A-1036, 8"h x 6.25"d. *Illustration from a Pairpoint catalog.*

VASE #A-1037. *Illustration from a Pairpoint catalog.*

VASE #A-1038, 8"h. *Illustration from a Pairpoint catalog.*

VASE #A-1039. *Illustration from a Pairpoint catalog.*

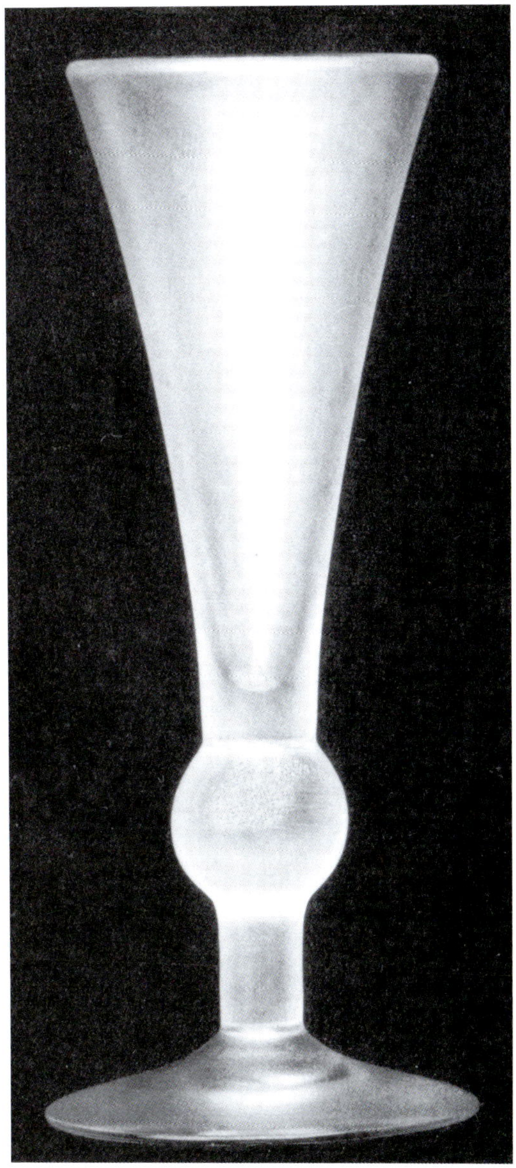

_______ #1047, 10"h, 12"h, 14"h. *Illustration from a Pairpoint catalog.*

VASE #A-1045, 6"h, 8"h, 10"h, 12"h, 14"h.

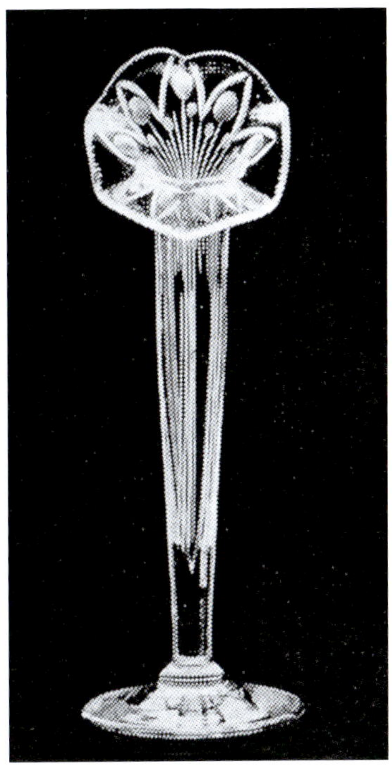

VASE #A-1046, __"h, __"h, __"h.
Illustration from a Pairpoint catalog.

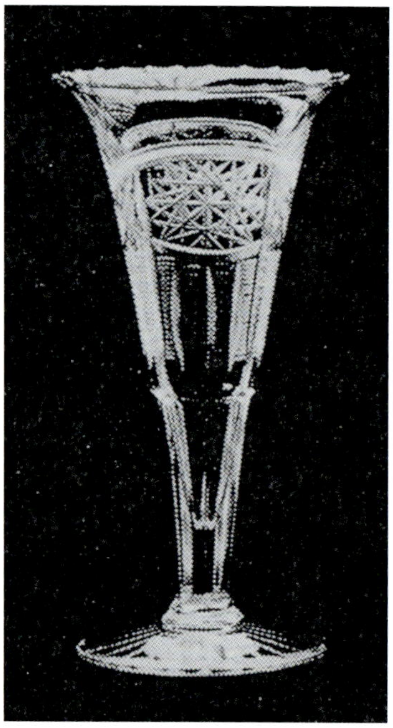

VASE #1050, 7"h. (This shape was previously identified in *The Essence of Pairpoint* as Unknown 80.) *Illustration from a Pairpoint catalog.*

VASE #A-1052, 8"h, 10"h, 12"h.

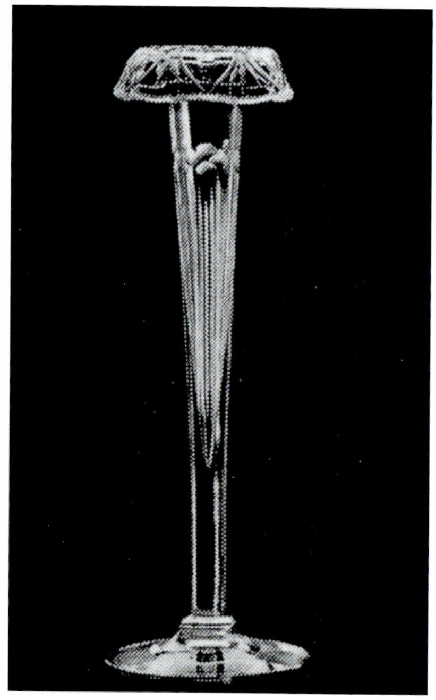

VASE #A-1053, __"h, __"h, __"h, __"h. *Illustration from a Pairpoint catalog.*

VASE #A(F)-1055, 6"h, 9"h, 11"h. *Illustration from a Pairpoint catalog.*

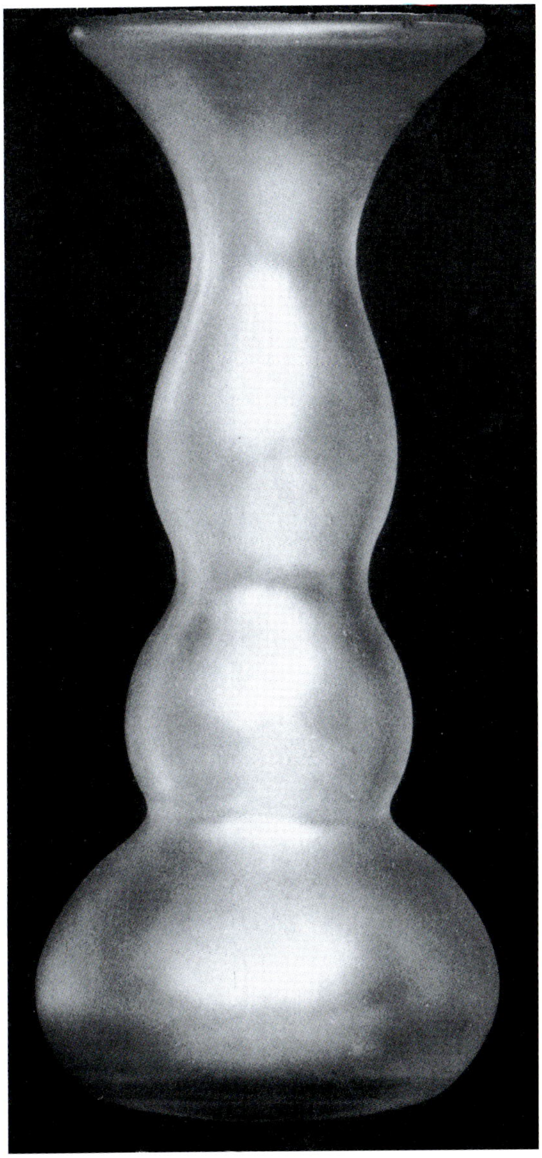

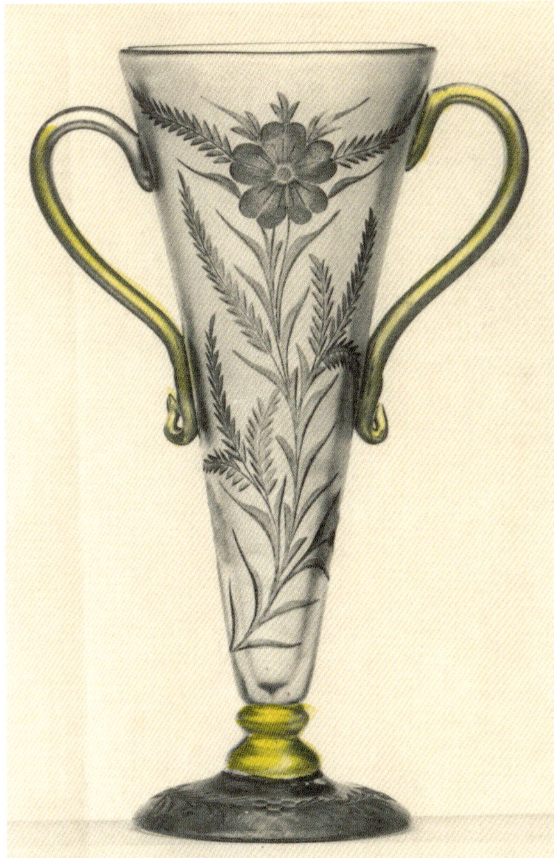

VASE #F-1056, 12"h. *Illustration from a Pairpoint catalog.*

VASE #1055, 16.50"h. *Illustration from a Pairpoint catalog.*

VASE #1056, 11"h, 12.50"h, 13"h. *Illustration from a Pairpoint catalog.*

VASE #F-1057, 8"h, 10"h, 12"h, 14"h.

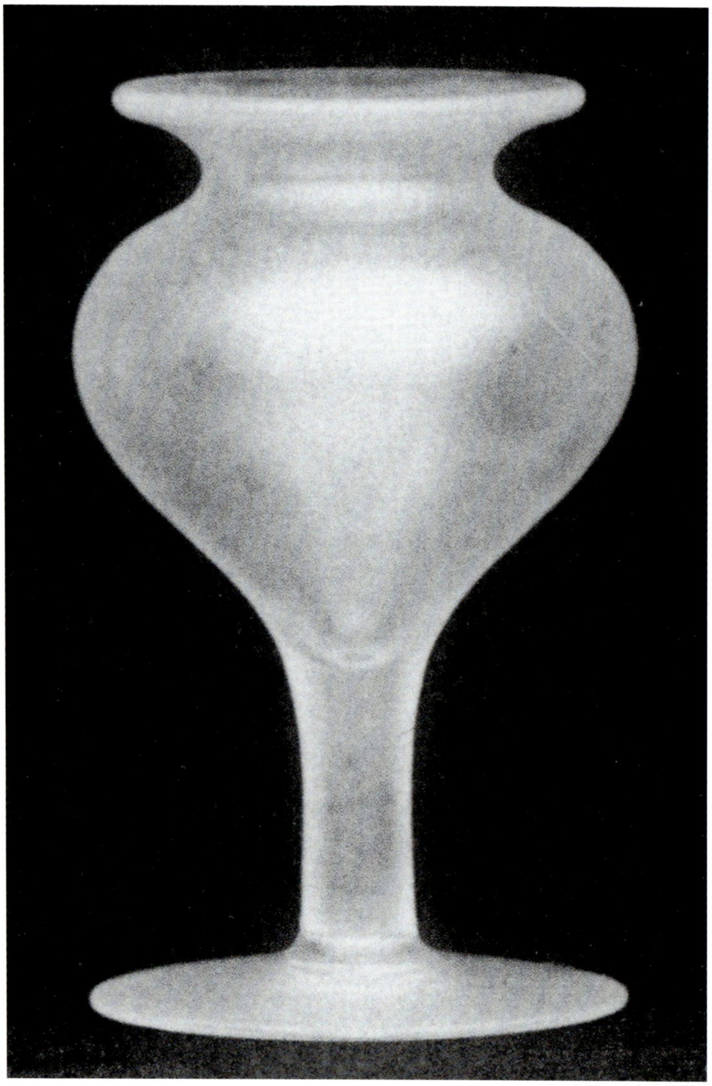

________ #1058, 5"h. *Illustration from a Pairpoint catalog.*

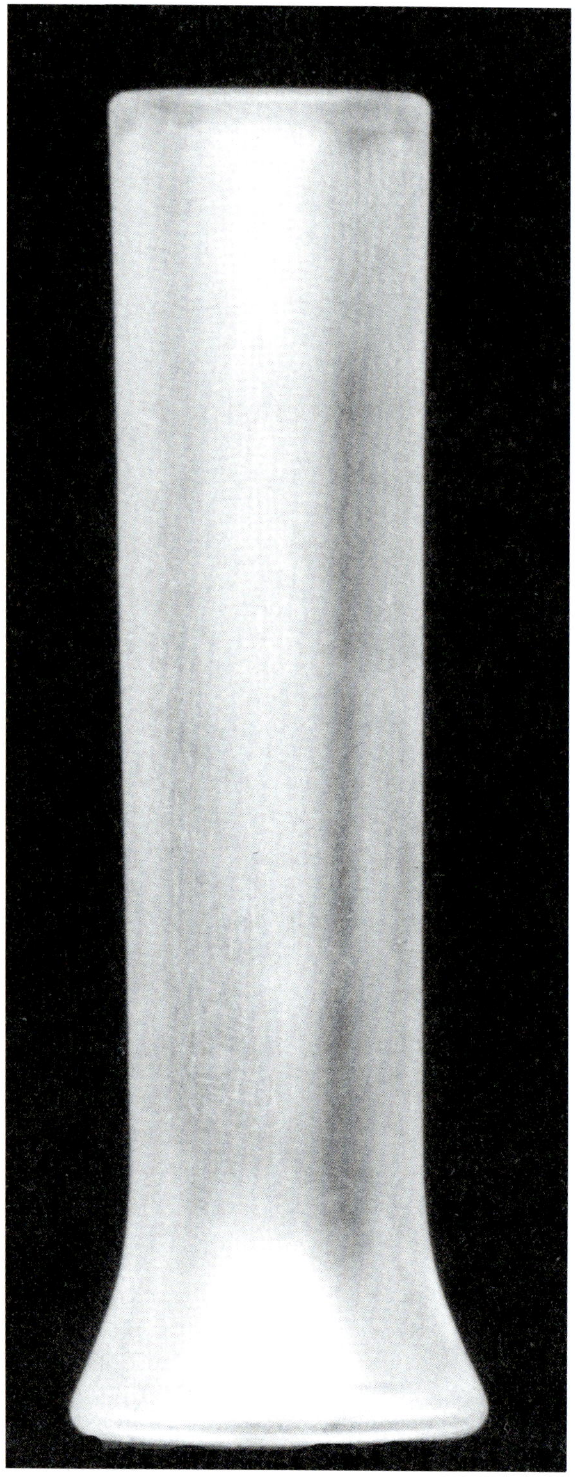

VASE #1060, 6"h, 8"h, 10"h, 12"h. *Illustration from a Pairpoint catalog.*

VASE #F-1058, 11"h. *Illustration from a Pairpoint catalog.*

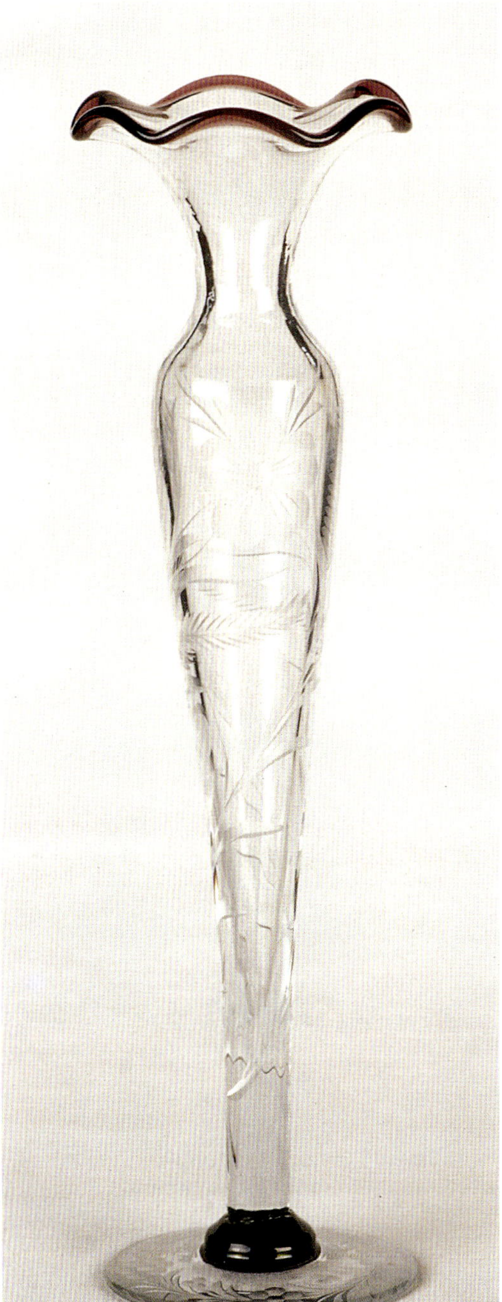

VASE #F-1061, 10"h, 12"h, 14"h.

VASE #A(F)-1062, 6"h, 8"h, 8.50"h, 10"h, 12"h, 14"h, 16"h.

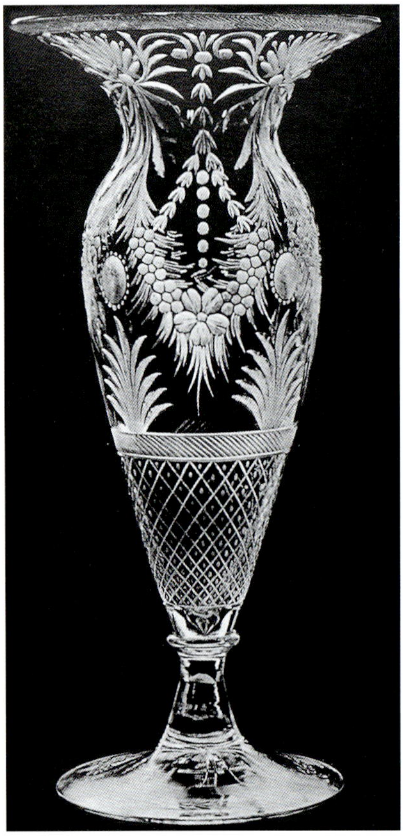

VASE #A-1063, 10"h x 5" flare diameter, 12"h, 14"h. *Illustration from a Pairpoint catalog.*

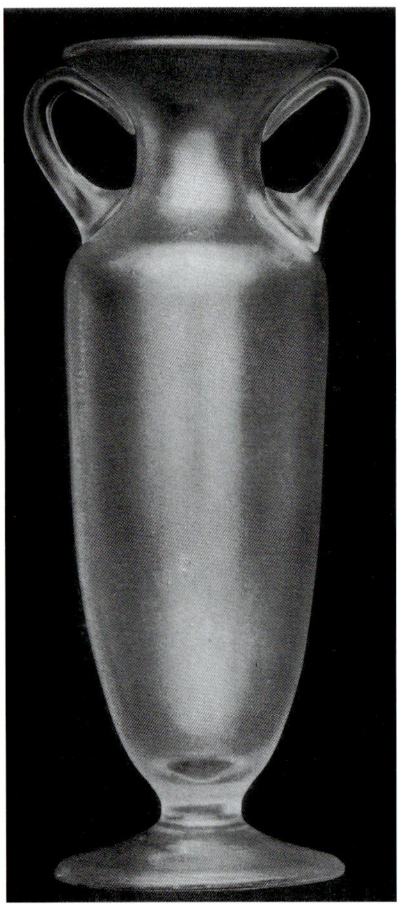

________ #1063, 17.50"h. *Illustration from a Pairpoint catalog.*

VASE #A-1064, 12"h.

VASE #A-1066. *Illustration from a Pairpoint catalog.*

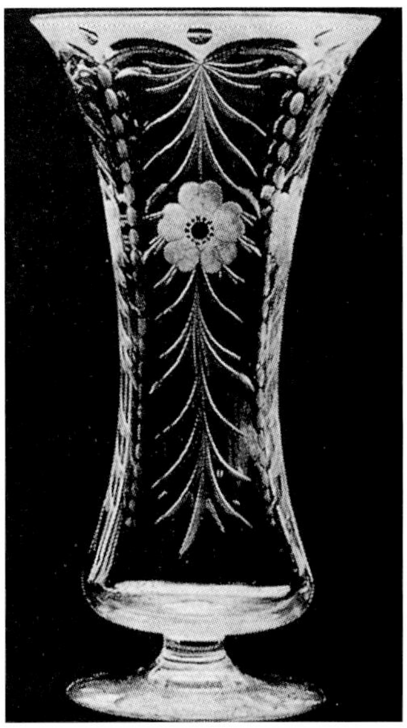

VASE #A-1067. *Illustration from a Pairpoint catalog.*

VASE #A-1068, 8"h, 10"h. These vases were made with or without the loop handles on the outer body near the top. *Illustration from a Pairpoint catalog.*

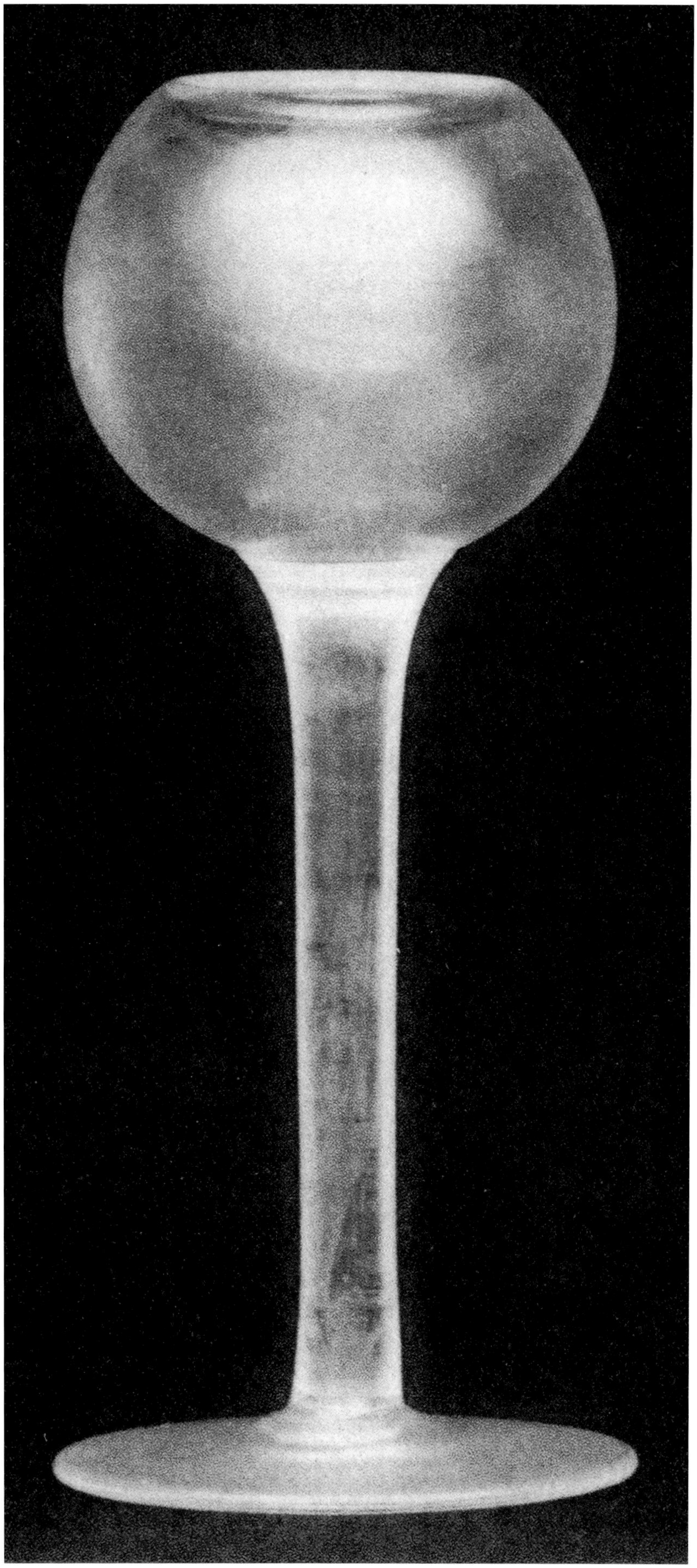

_______ #1068, 7"h. *Illustration from a Pairpoint catalog.*

VASE #A(F)-1069, 11.50"h.

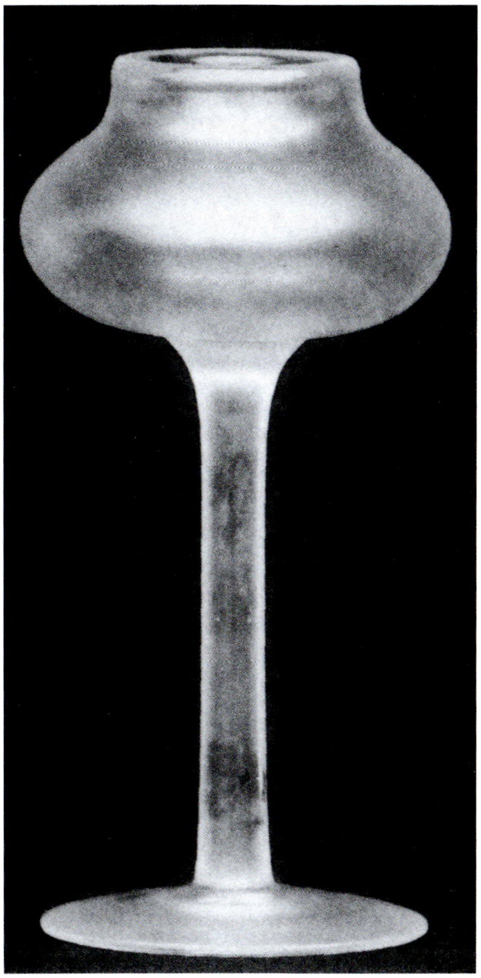

________ #1069, 7"h. *Illustration from a Pairpoint catalog.*

VASE #A(F)-1070, 7.50"h, 11"h. *Illustration from a Pairpoint catalog.*

VASE #1070, 6"h, 8"h, 10"h, 12"h x 3.75"d.

VASE #1071, 7.75"h. *Illustration from a Pairpoint catalog.*

VASE #F-1071, 12"h. *Illustration from a Pairpoint catalog.*

VASE #A-1072, 9"h, 9.50"h.

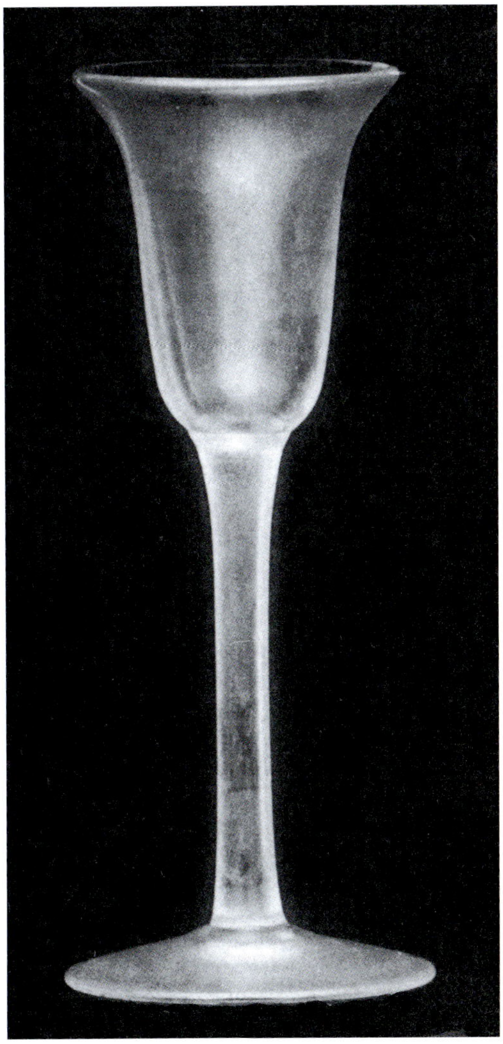

________ #1072, 7.75"h. *Illustration from a Pairpoint catalog.*

VASE #A-1073, 6"h, 9"h, 10"h.

VASE #A-1075, 12.50"h x 3.50" top diameter. *Illustration from a Pairpoint catalog.*

VASE #A(F)-1074, 10.75"h, 14"h. *Illustration from a Pairpoint catalog.*

VASE #A-1076, 12"h x 4.25" base diameter. *Illustration from a Pairpoint catalog.*

VASE #A-1077. *Illustration from a Pairpoint catalog.*

VASE #A-1078, 10.375"h. *Illustration from a Pairpoint catalog.*

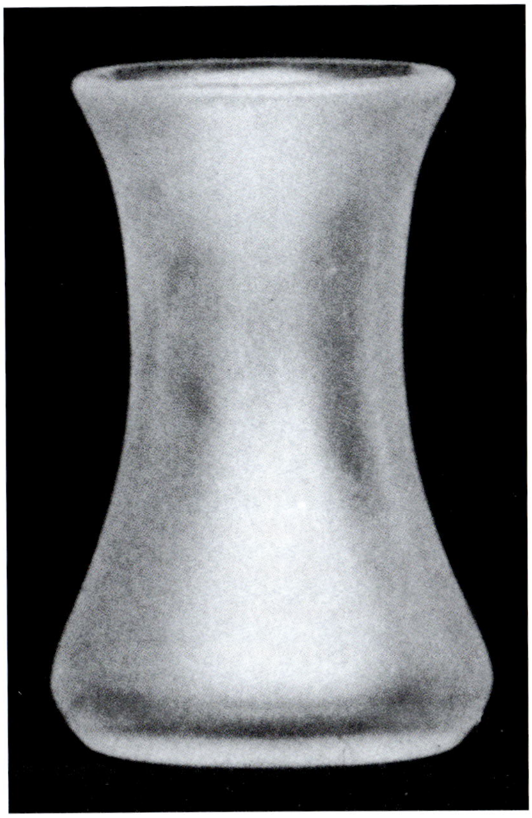

_______ #1078, 4.50"h. *Illustration from a Pairpoint catalog.*

VASE #A-1081, 10"h.

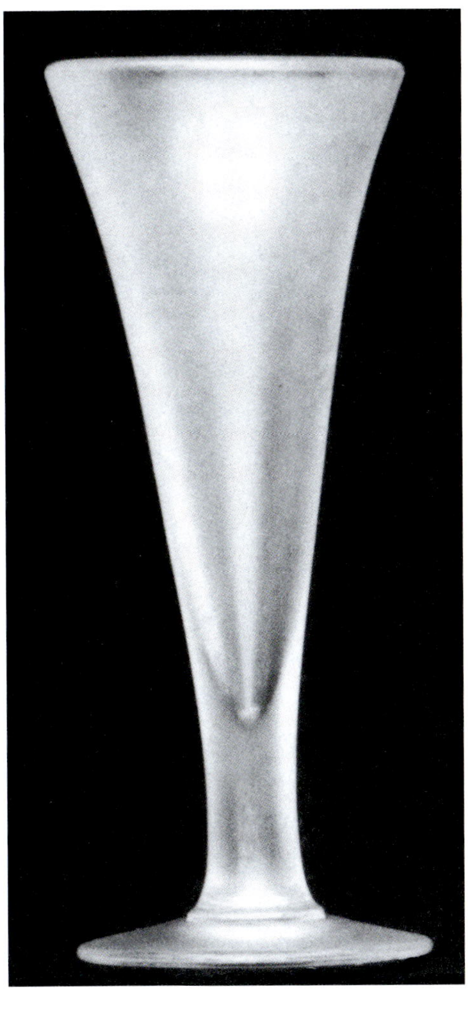

_______ #1080, 6"h, 8"h, 10"h, 12"h, 14"h, 16"h. (This shape was previously identified in *The Essence of Pairpoint* as A-1080.) *Illustration from a Pairpoint catalog.*

VASE #1082, Oval, 9"h, 11"h x 4.50"w x 6"l. (This shape was previously identified in *The Essence of Pairpoint* as A-1082.)

VASE #B-1083, 12"h. This vase was available with or without a cover. A 1926 Pairpoint engraving department cost book references this vase to have also been made 10" high, a size we have never seen.

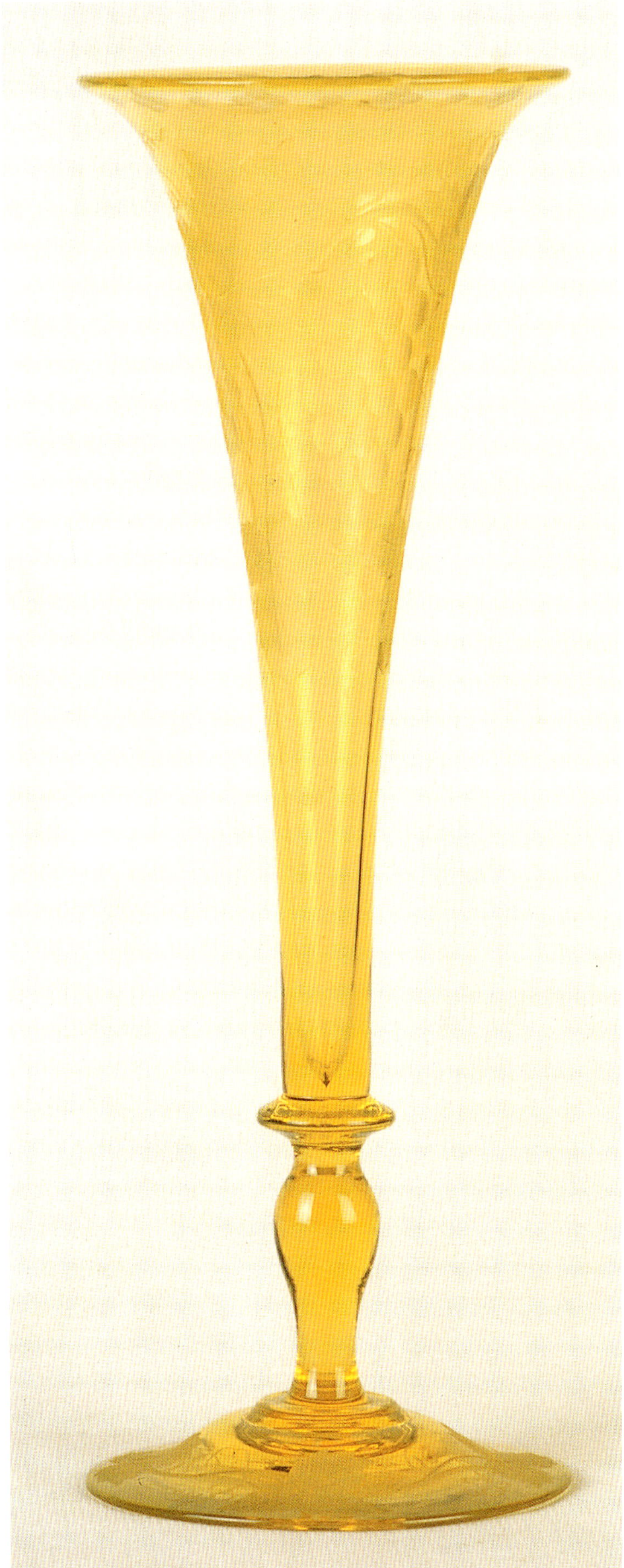

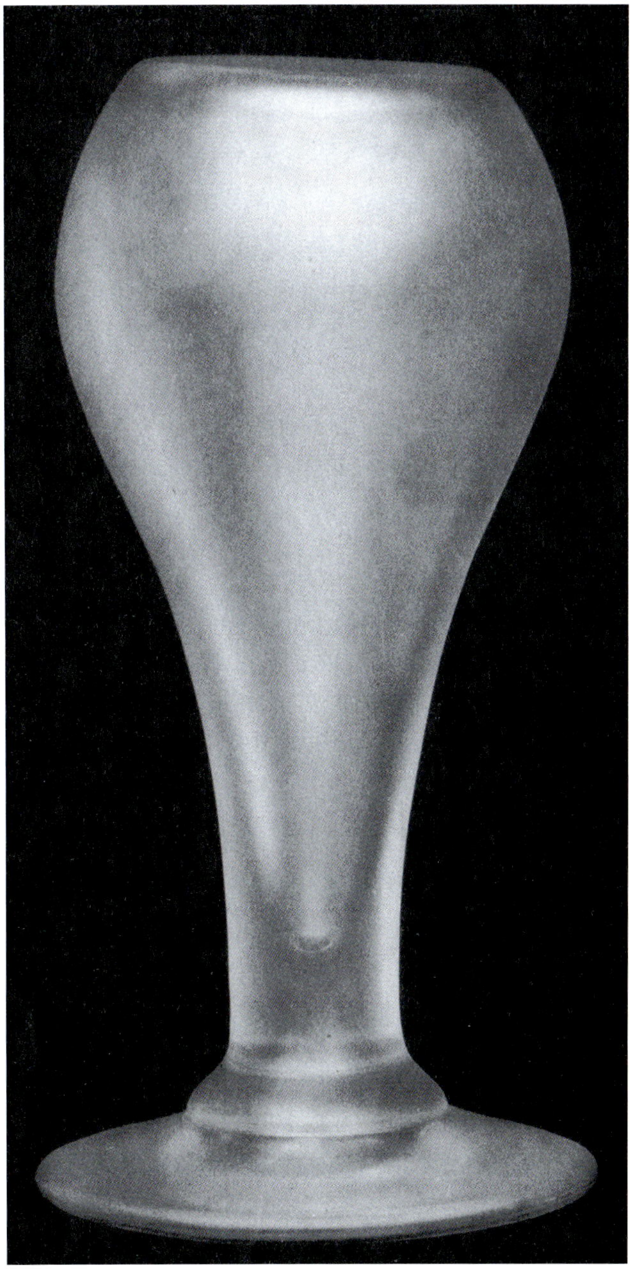

_______ #1084, 14"h. *Illustration from a Pairpoint catalog.*

VASE #A-1084, 12"h.

VASE #F-1087, 10"h. *Illustration from a Pairpoint catalog.*

VASE #F-1088, 12"h. *Illustration from a Pairpoint catalog.*

SWEET PEA VASE #1089, __"d x __"h, 6"d x 4.75"h, 7"d x __"h, 8"d x 5.50"h, 9"d x __"h, 10"d x 7.25"h, 10.50"d x __"h.

VASE #1095, 4.50"h. *Illustration from a Pairpoint catalog.*

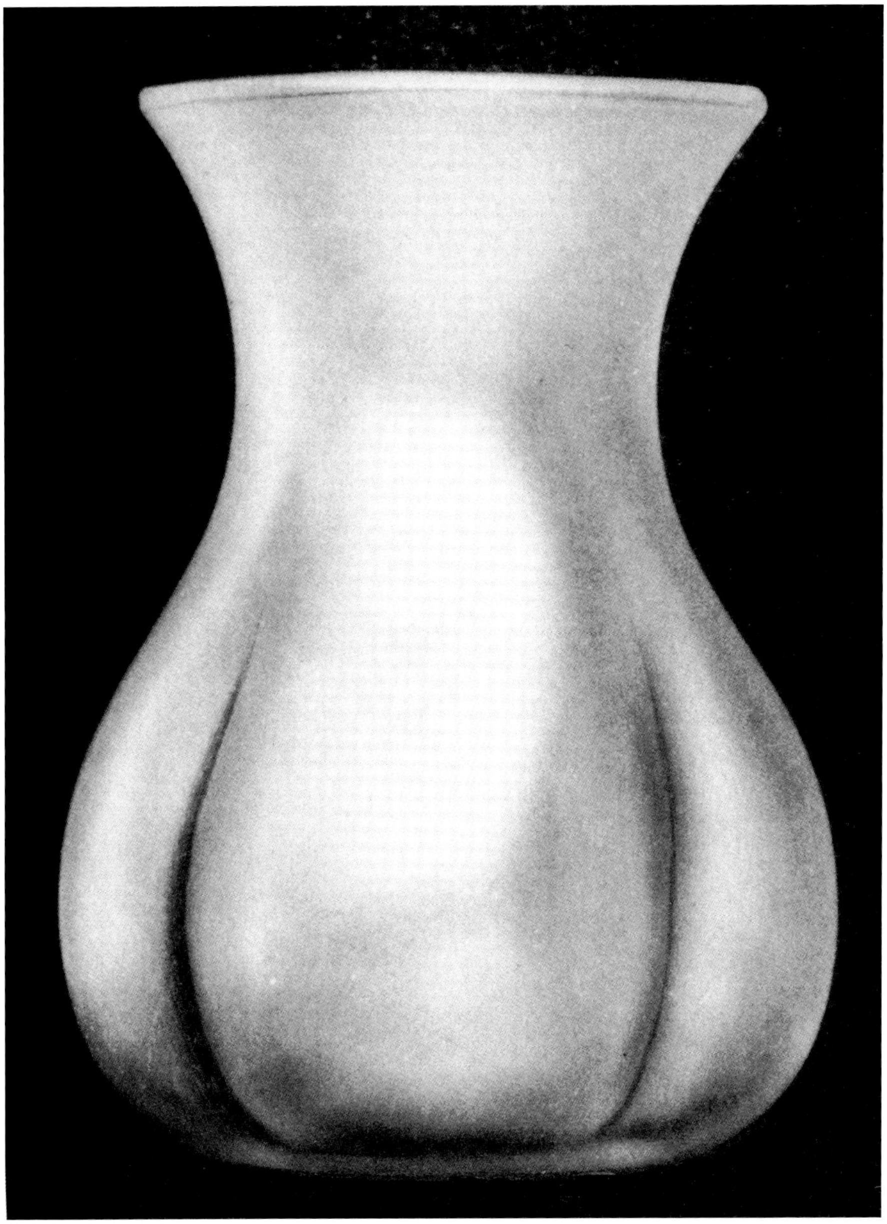

VASE #1094, 9"h. *Illustration from a Pairpoint catalog.*

VASE #A(F)-1099, 10"h. *Illustration from a Pairpoint catalog.*

_______ #1099, 6"d, 7"d, 8"d, 9"d. *Illustration from a Pairpoint catalog.*

VASE #A-1103, 7.50"d x 6.25"h. *Illustration from a Pairpoint catalog.*

VASE #A-1100. *Illustration from a Pairpoint catalog.*

VASE #A-1104. *Illustration from a Pairpoint catalog.*

VASE #A-1107.
Illustration from a Pairpoint catalog.

VASE #1158, 8"h, 8.50"h, 9.50"h, 12"h, 16"h. This vase was referred to at Pairpoint as a "Submarine Vase." (This shape was previously identified in *The Essence of Pairpoint* as A-1158.) *Illustration from a Pairpoint catalog.*

VASE #B-1107, 10"h, 11.50"h, 12"h, 13"h, 14"h.

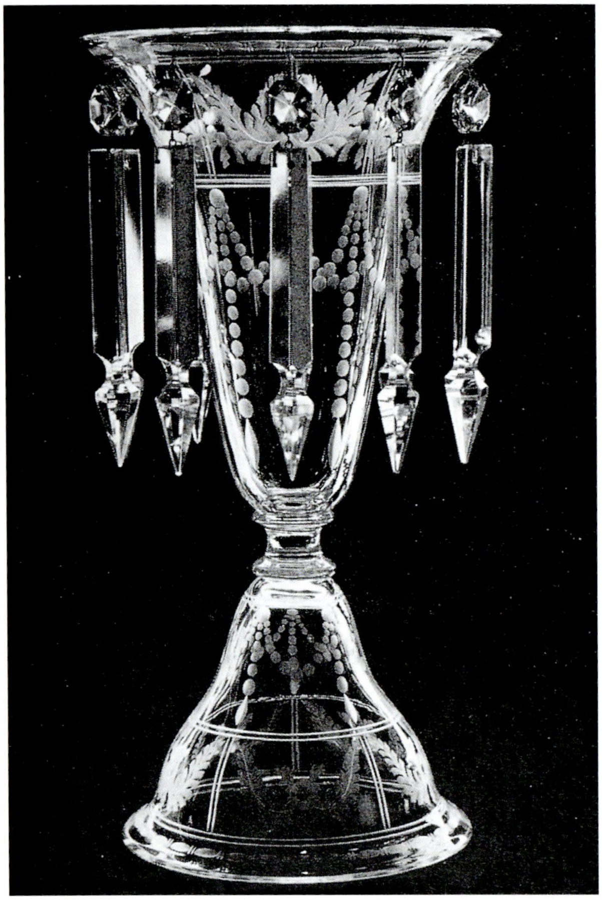

VASE #A-1164, 12"h. *Illustration from a Pairpoint catalog.*

VASE #1474, 8"h, 10"h. *Illustration from a Pairpoint catalog.*

VASE #B-1485, 13.25"h.

VASE #B-1488, 12"h. *Illustration from a Pairpoint catalog.*

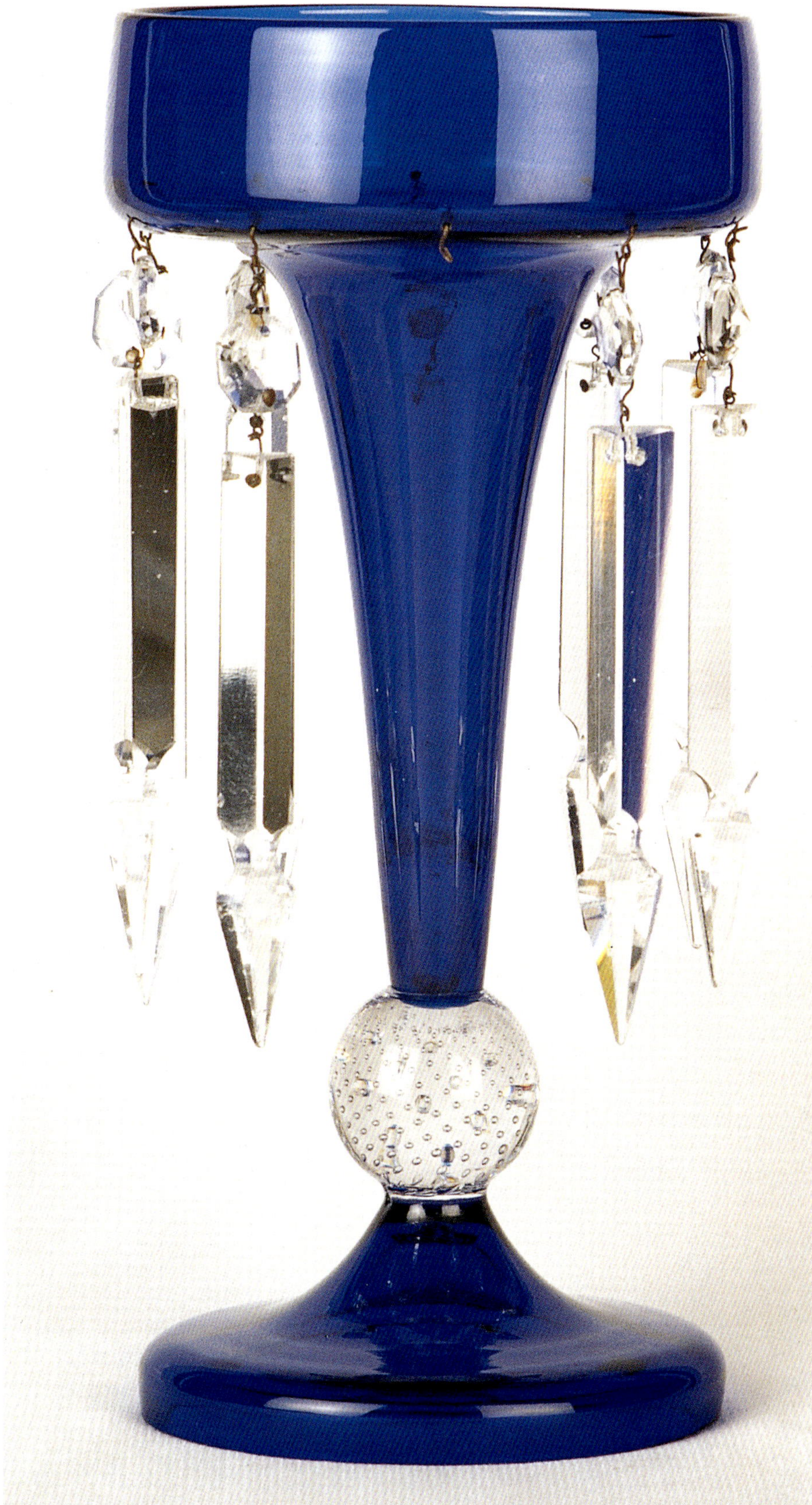

LUSTRE VASE #FB-1612, 11.50"h (12"h) with (10) 6" Spear Prisms and silver-plated candle cup insert. (This shape was previously identified in *The Essence of Pairpoint* as Unknown 27.)

HANDLED & FOOTED VASE #2231, 11.50"h. *Illustration from a Pairpoint catalog.*

HANDLED & FOOTED VASE #2232, 11.50"h. *Illustration from a Pairpoint catalog.*

VASE #Unknown 24, 10"h x 4"d, 12"h x 4.50"d, 13.75"h x 5"d. *Illustration from a Pairpoint catalog.*

LUSTRE VASE #Unknown 26. *Illustration from a Pairpoint catalog.*

Below: LUSTRE VASE #Unknown 28, 11.50"h with (9) 6" Spear Prisms (previously stated in *The Essence of Pairpoint* to be with ten prisms)

VASE #Unknown 25, 10"h. *Illustration from a Pairpoint catalog.*

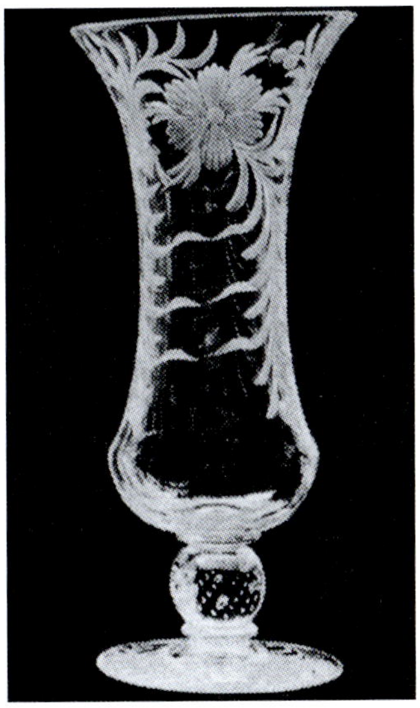

VASE #Unknown 30. *Illustration from a Pairpoint catalog.*

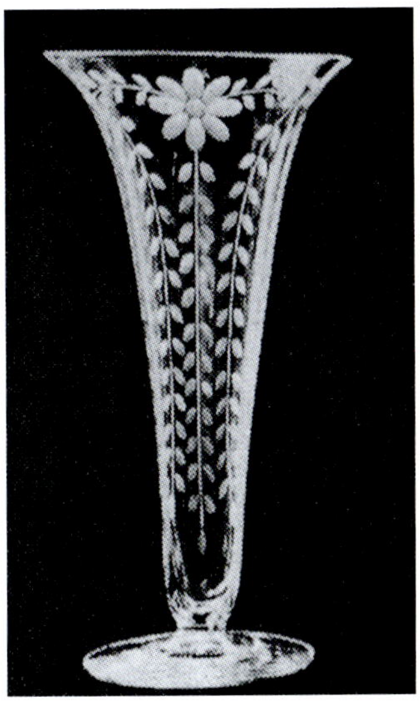

VASE #Unknown 31. *Illustration from a Pairpoint catalog.*

IVY VASE #Unknown 39, 12"h.

VASE #Unknown 42, 6" (estimated), 8"h, 10"h, 12"h.

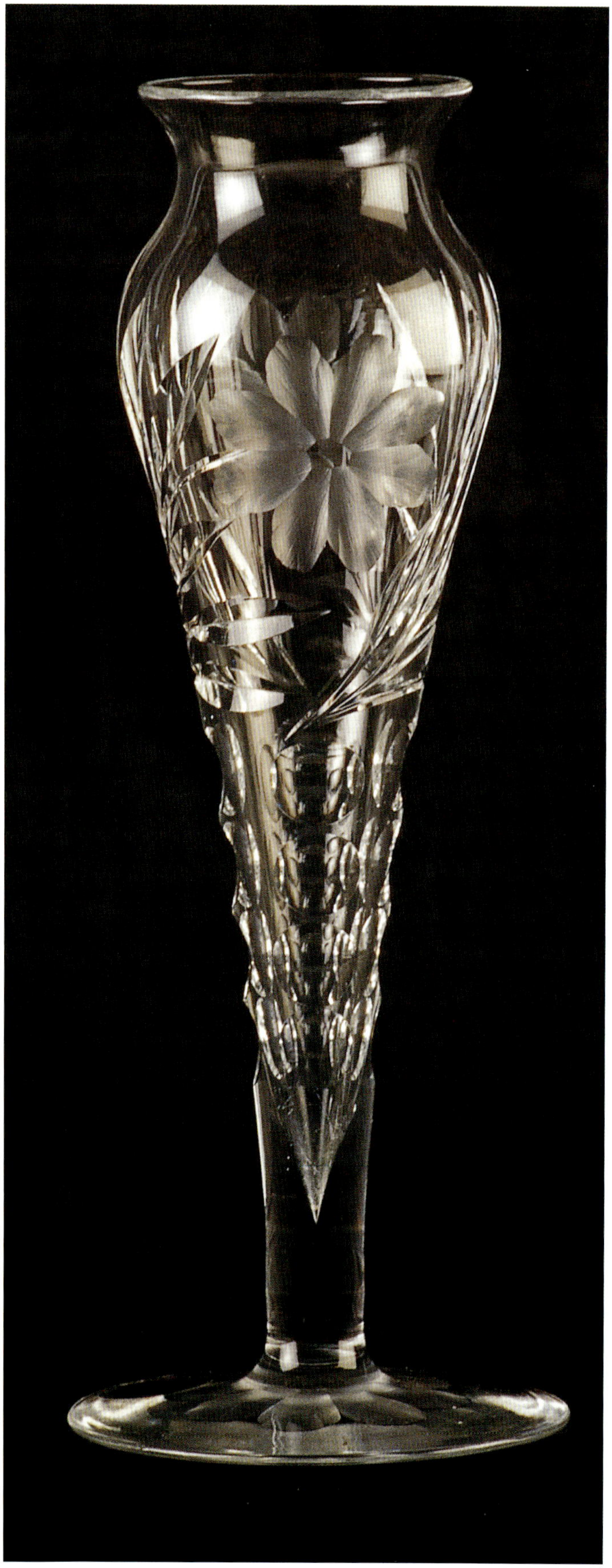

VASE #Unknown 43, 8.25"h.

VASE #Unknown 44, 8.50"d x 8.25"h, 9"d x 10.75"h.

VASE #Unknown 88, 8"h x 6.50"d, 10"h x __"d.

VASE #Unknown 89, 14"h.

VASE #Unknown 90, 10"h.

VASE #Unknown 95, 8"h.

VASE #Unknown 94, 6"h.

VASE #Unknown 104. *Sketch from a 1926 Pairpoint engraving department cost book.*

VASE #Unknown 105. *Sketch from a 1926 Pairpoint engraving department cost book.*

VASE #Unknown 106. *Sketch from a 1926 Pairpoint engraving department cost book.*

VASE #Unknown 107. *Sketch from a 1926 Pairpoint engraving department cost book.*

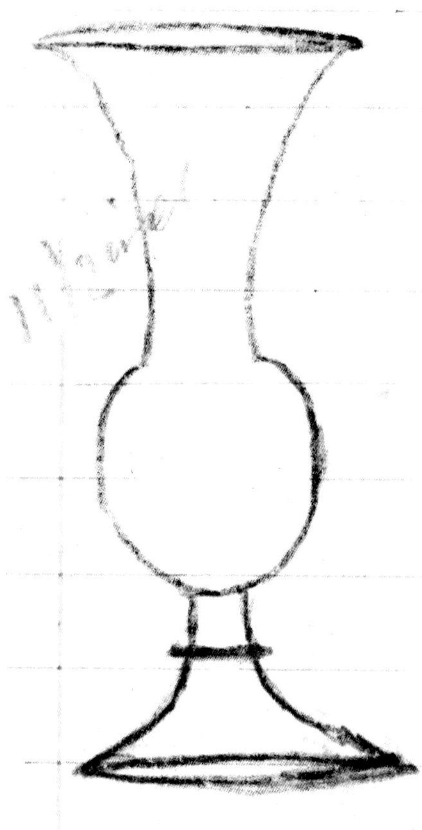

VASE #Unknown 108. *Sketch from a 1926 Pairpoint engraving department cost book.*

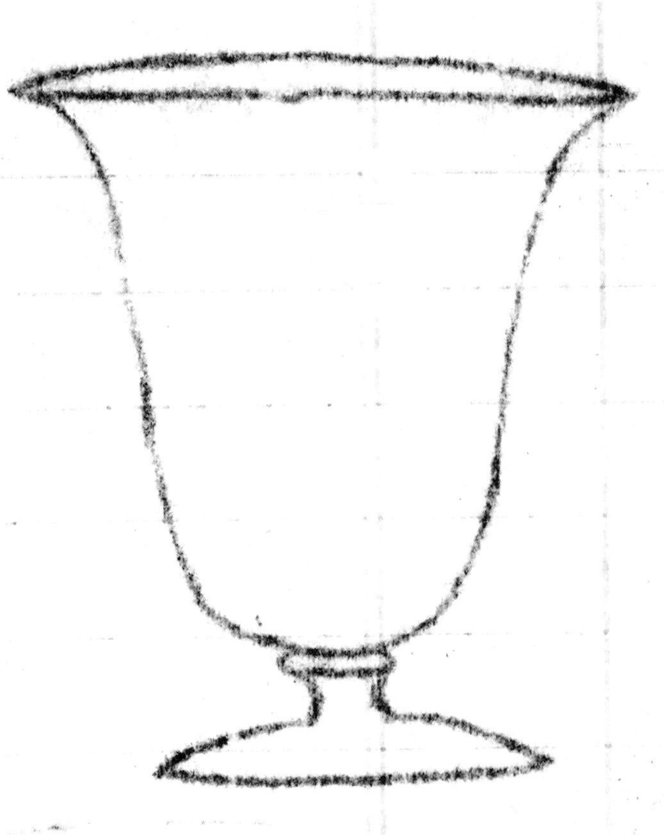

VASE #Unknown 109. *Sketch from a 1926 Pairpoint engraving department cost book.*

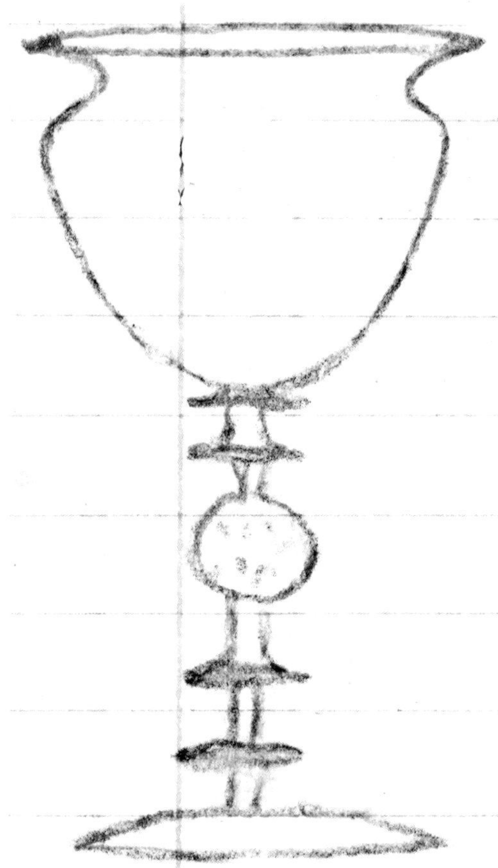

VASE #Unknown 111. *Sketch from a 1926 Pairpoint engraving department cost book.*

VASE #Unknown 110. *Sketch from a 1926 Pairpoint engraving department cost book.*

Personal Items

COLOGNE #6, 1-oz, 2-oz, 3-oz. *Illustration from a Pairpoint catalog.*

COLOGNE #7, 3-oz. *Illustration from a Pairpoint catalog.*

COLOGNE #8, 1-oz. *Illustration from a Pairpoint catalog.*

COLOGNE #9, 4-oz. *Illustration from a Pairpoint catalog.*

COLOGNE #10, 8-oz. *Illustration from a Pairpoint catalog.*

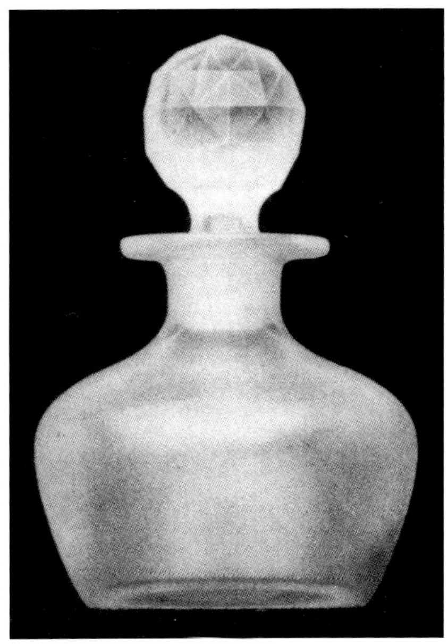

COLOGNE #14, 1-oz, 3-oz, 6-oz. *Illustration from a Pairpoint catalog.*

COLOGNE #19, 1-oz, 2-oz, 4-oz, 8-oz, 10-oz. *Illustration from a Pairpoint catalog.*

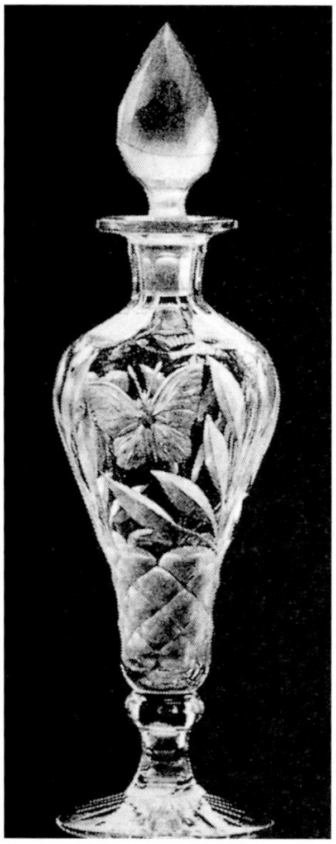

TOILET BOTTLE #21. *Illustration from a Pairpoint catalog.*

COLOGNE #26, 1-oz, 2-oz, 3-oz. *Illustration from a Pairpoint catalog.*

SMELLING SALTS JAR #546, Small (3.25"h), Medium (4"h), Large (4.75"h). *Illustration from a Pairpoint catalog.*

COLOGNE #22, 10.25" overall height. *Illustration from a Pairpoint catalog.*

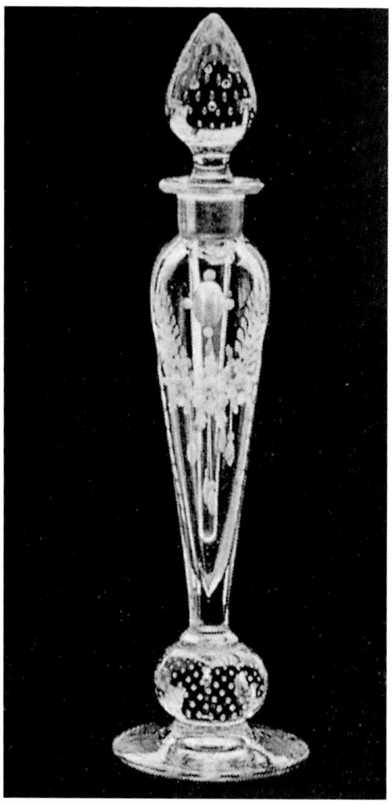

COLOGNE #B-31. *Illustration from a Pairpoint catalog.*

HAIR RECEIVER or PUFF #920, 5"d x 3"h. The Hair Receiver has a lid with an opening, while the lid on the Puff does not. *Illustration from a Pairpoint catalog.*

NIGHT CAP BOTTLE #637, 7.50" overall height. This is a very interesting and scarce item. The bottle stopper is a bottle unto itself and is precision fitted to the bottle.

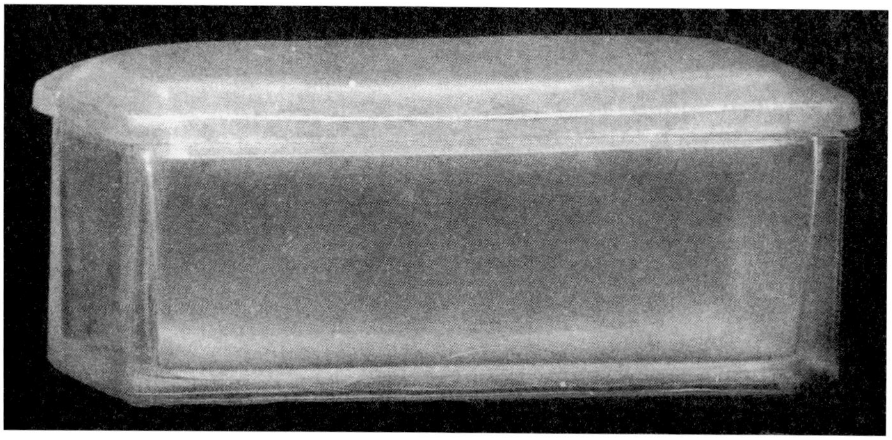

JEWEL and COVER #921, 6.50"l x 2.50"w. *Illustration from a Pairpoint catalog.*

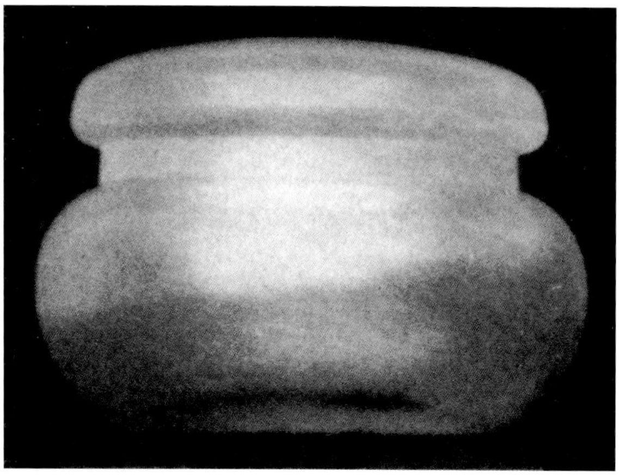

PUFF #923, 3.50"d. *Illustration from a Pairpoint catalog.*

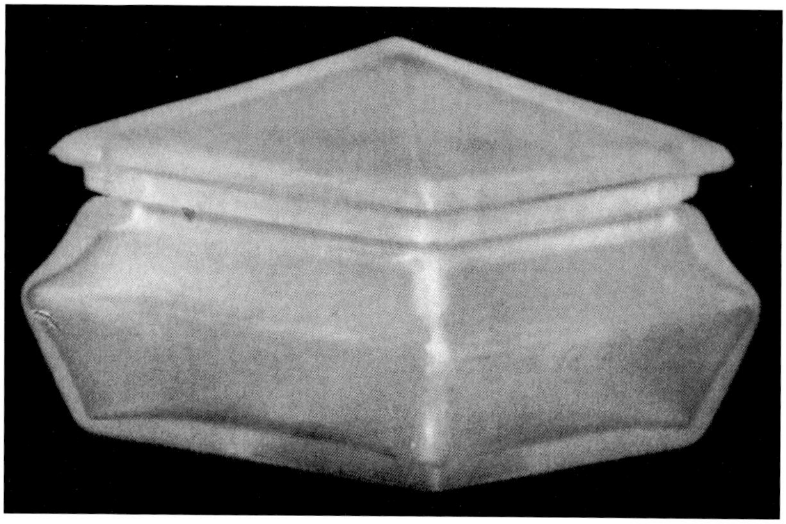

JEWEL #926, 6.50"long x 5.50"wide. *Illustration from a Pairpoint catalog.*

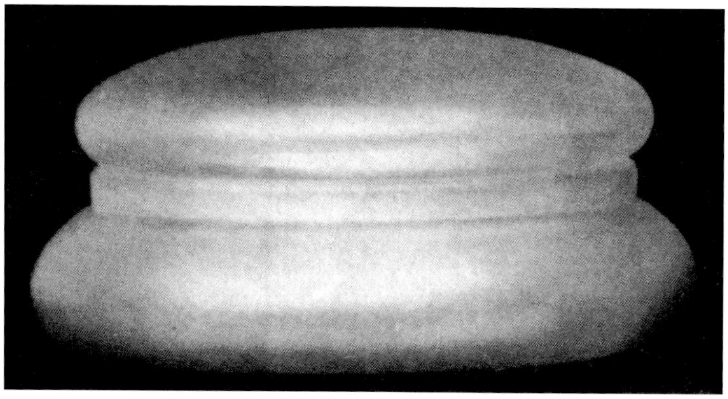

JEWEL #924, 5"d, 6"d, 7.50"d. *Illustration from a Pairpoint catalog.*

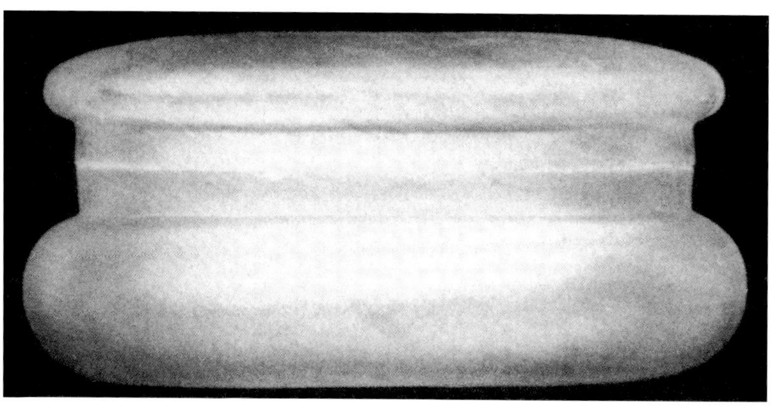

OVAL JEWEL #925, 5.50"long, 6.50"long. *Illustration from a Pairpoint catalog.*

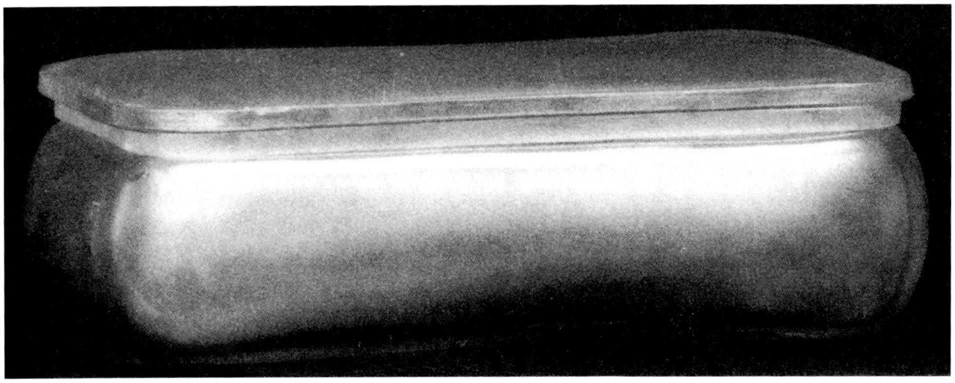

JEWEL and COVER #927, 9.25"long x 5"wide. *Illustration from a Pairpoint catalog.*

LEFT: HAIR RECEIVER #931, 4.25"d. (Cover has a round opening.) *Illustration from a Pairpoint catalog.*
RIGHT: PUFF #931, 4.25"d. (Cover has no opening.) *Illustration from a Pairpoint catalog.*

HANDKERCHIEF BOX #936, 6.75" square. *Illustration from a Pairpoint catalog.*

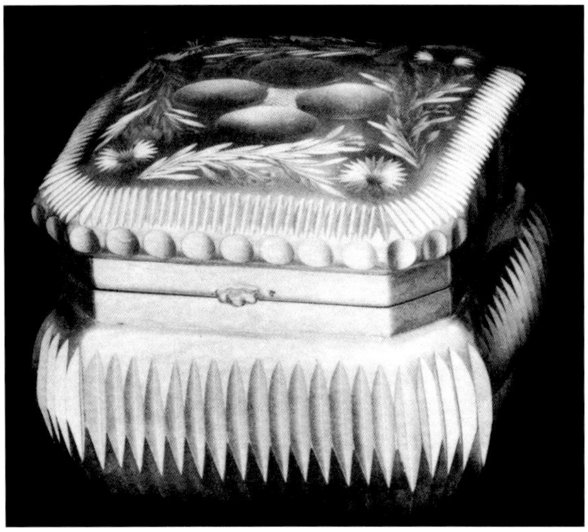

JEWEL BOX #938. *Illustration from a Pairpoint catalog.*

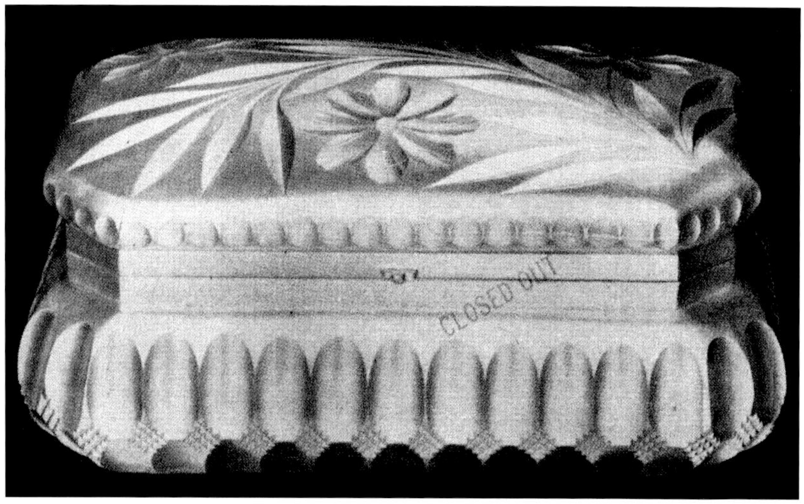

JEWEL #950, 9.50"long x 6.25"wide. *Illustration from a Pairpoint catalog.*

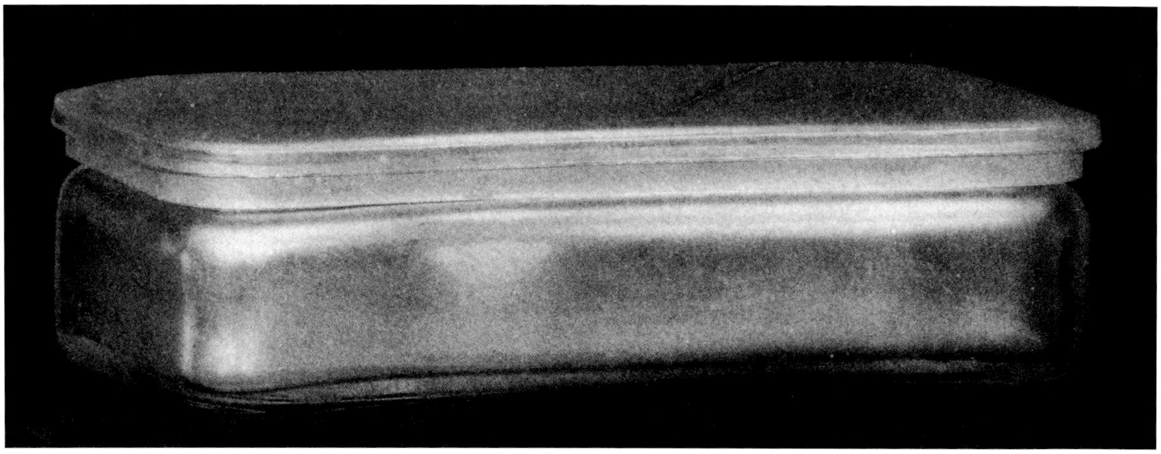

JEWEL and COVER #944, 8.625"long x 4.375"wide. *Illustration from a Pairpoint catalog.*

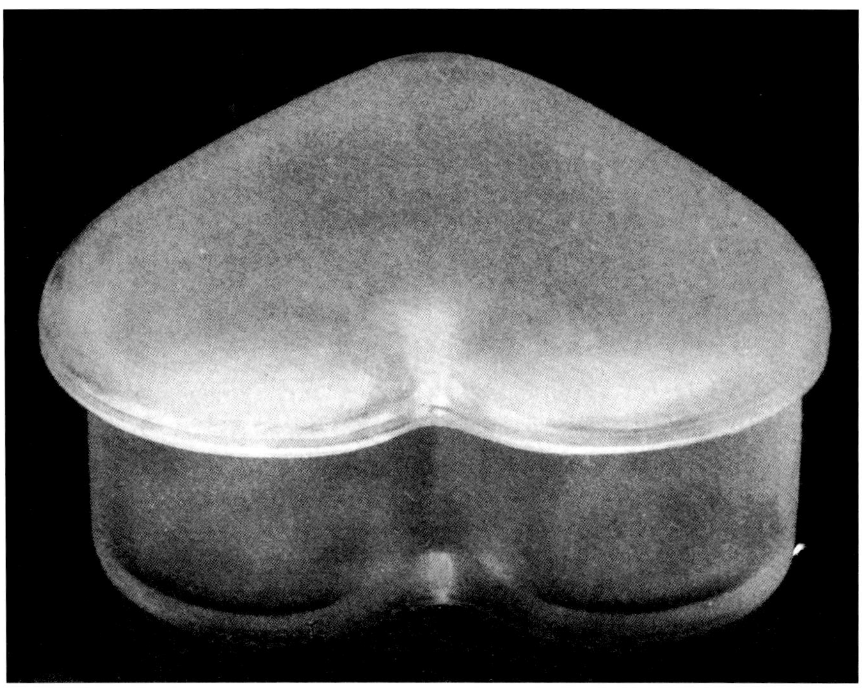

JEWEL and COVER #948, 5"wide. *Illustration from a Pairpoint catalog.*

TOOTH BRUSH HOLDER #1101. *Illustration from a Pairpoint catalog.*

JEWEL and COVER #4647, Small (5"d). Same as #4648 and #4649. *Illustration from a Pairpoint catalog.*
JEWEL and COVER #4648, Medium (6"d). Same as #4647 and #4649. *Illustration from a Pairpoint catalog.*
JEWEL and COVER #4649, Large (7.50"d). Same as #4647 and #4648. *Illustration from a Pairpoint catalog.*

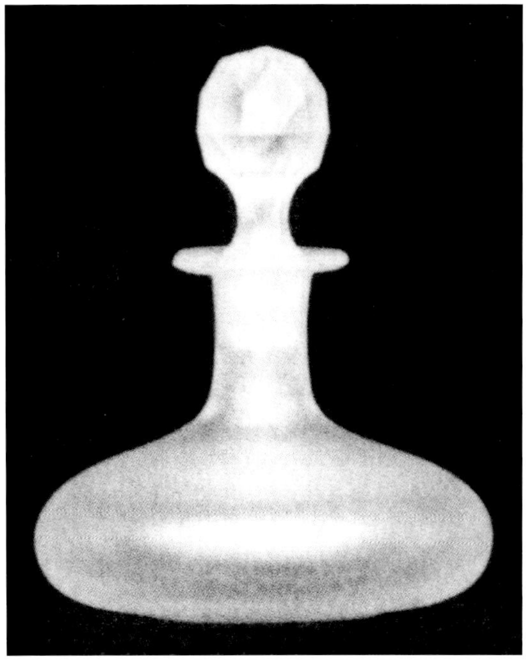

SQUAT COLOGNE, 2.75", 3.25", 4", 5", 6". *Illustration from a Pairpoint catalog.*

GLOVE BOX #Unknown 47, 10.75"long x 4.50"wide. *Illustration from a Pairpoint catalog.*

GLOBE COLOGNE, 4-oz, 6-oz, 8-oz. The stoppers were available with long daubers. *Illustration from a Pairpoint catalog.*

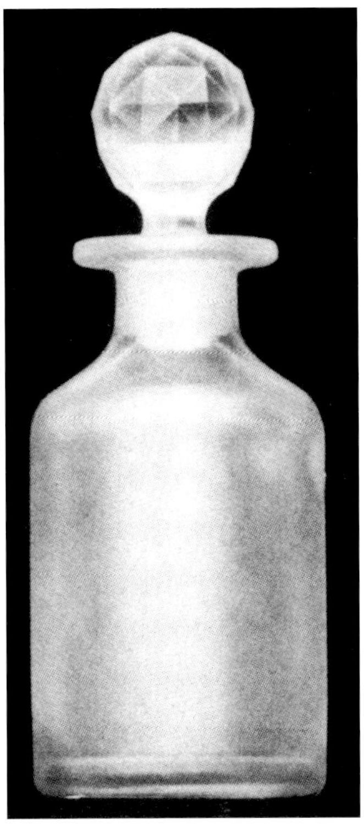

CYLINDER COLOGNE, 8-oz. *Illustration from a Pairpoint catalog.*

Serving Pieces and Bar Items

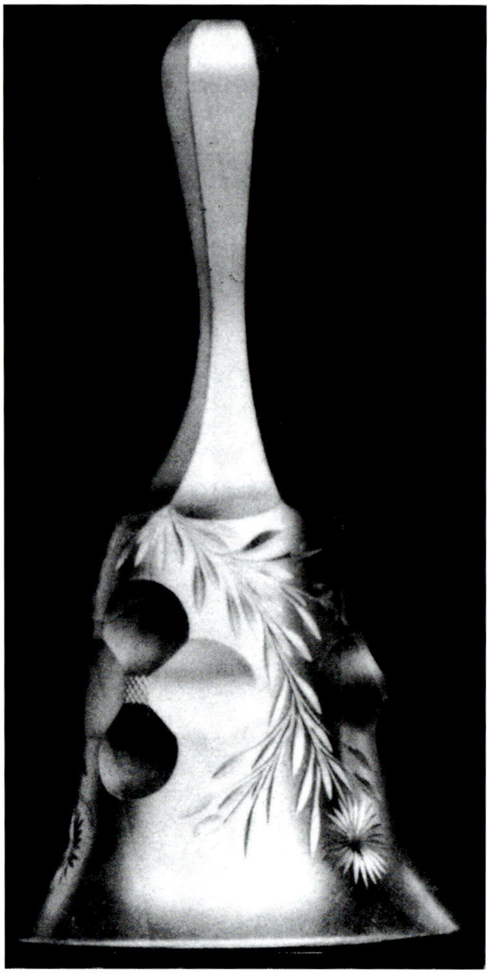

TEA BELL #1, 6"h x 3"d. *Illustration from a Pairpoint catalog.*

GRAPE JUICE BOWL #138, 9"h. This bowl is part of a set which includes the #928 juice glasses. *Illustration from a Pairpoint catalog.*

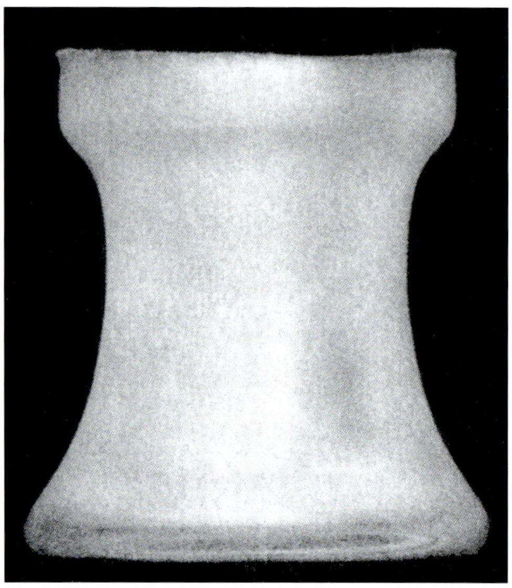

JAM JAR #18. *Illustration from a Pairpoint catalog.*

SPOON #203, 5.50". *Illustration from a Pairpoint catalog.*

NAPPY #205, 5"d, 6"d. (This shape was previously identified in *The Essence of Pairpoint* as Unknown 69.) *Illustration from a Pairpoint catalog.*

SAUCER #212, 5"d, 6"d. This is the same as the #205 Nappy but without a handle. *Illustration from a Pairpoint catalog.*

BON BON #216, 7.50" long. *Illustration from a Pairpoint catalog.*

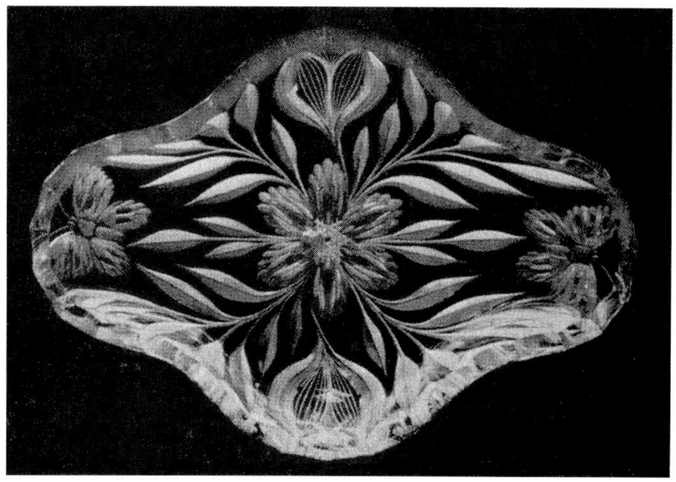

BON BON #217, 7.50" long. *Illustration from a Pairpoint ,catalog.*

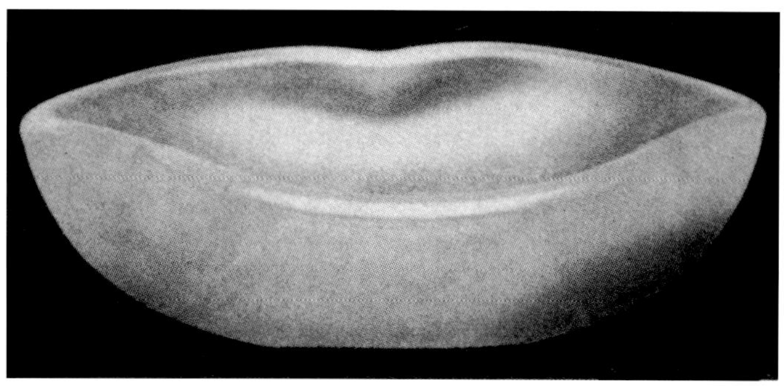

________ #220, 6"d. *Illustration from a Pairpoint catalog.*

NAPPY #222. *Illustration from a Pairpoint catalog.*

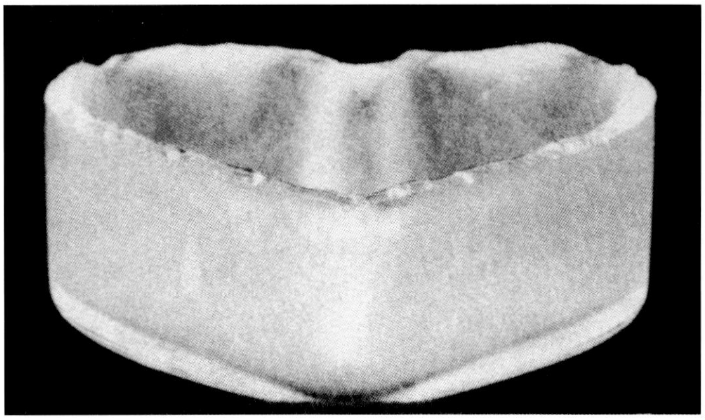

________ #A-227, 4"d, 5"d. *Illustration from a Pairpoint catalog.*

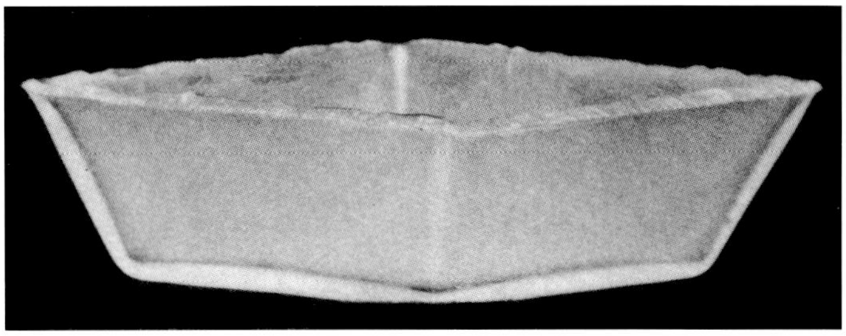

________ #A-229, 6.50" long. *Illustration from a Pairpoint catalog.*

________ #A-224, 5.50" long. *Illustration from a Pairpoint catalog.*

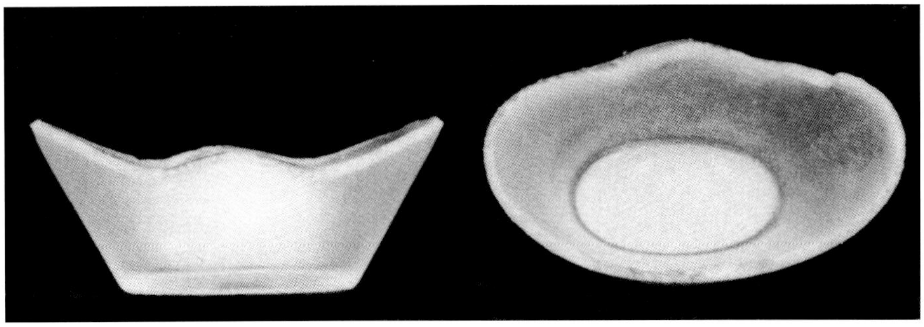

________ #A-225, 5.50" long. *Illustration from a Pairpoint catalog.*

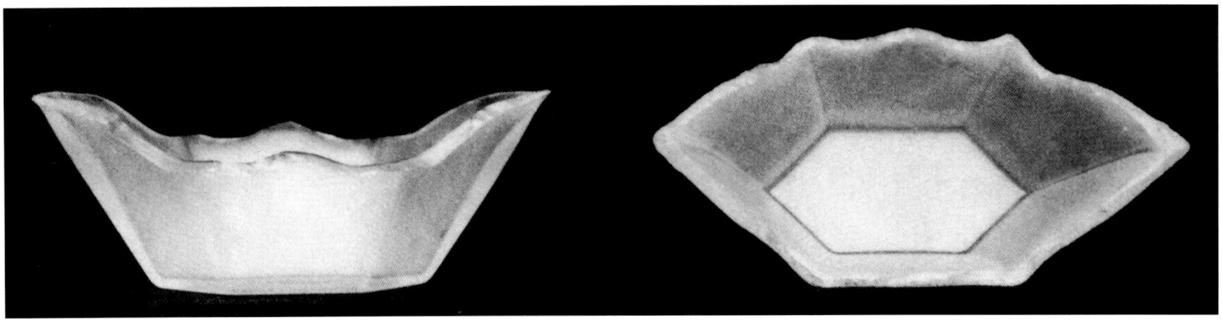

________ #A-226, 7.75" long. *Illustration from a Pairpoint catalog.*

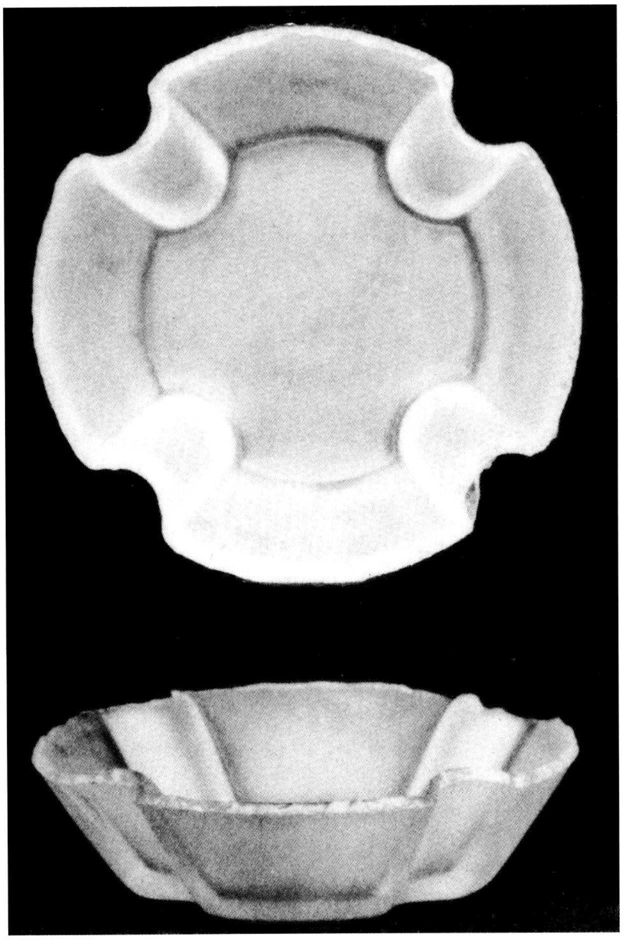

BON BON #A-230, 5"d, 6"d. *Illustration from a Pairpoint catalog.*

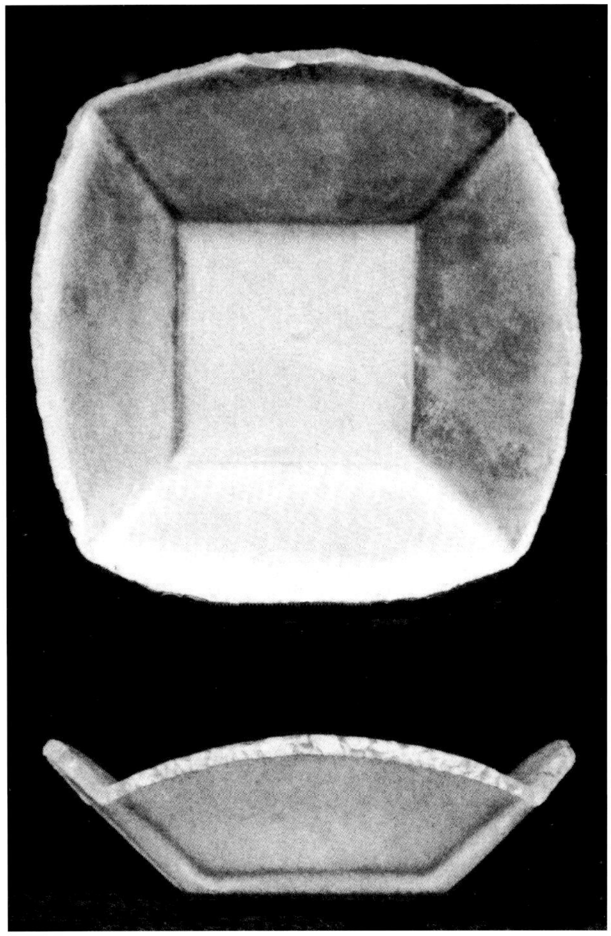

_______ #A-232, 5"d. *Illustration from a Pairpoint catalog.*

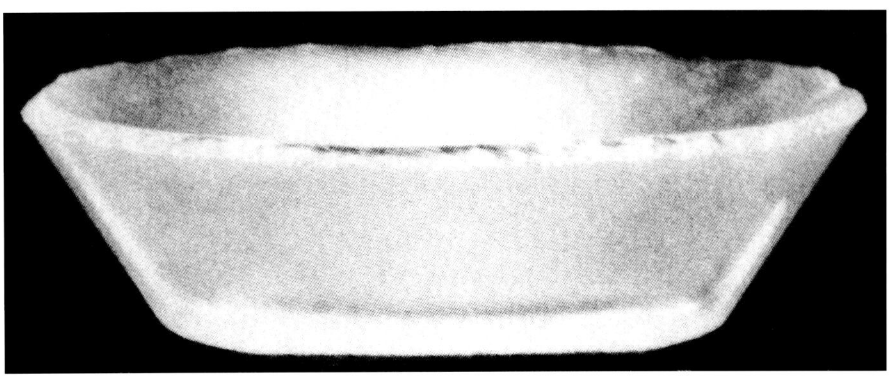

BON BON #A-231, 6"d. *Illustration from a Pairpoint catalog.*

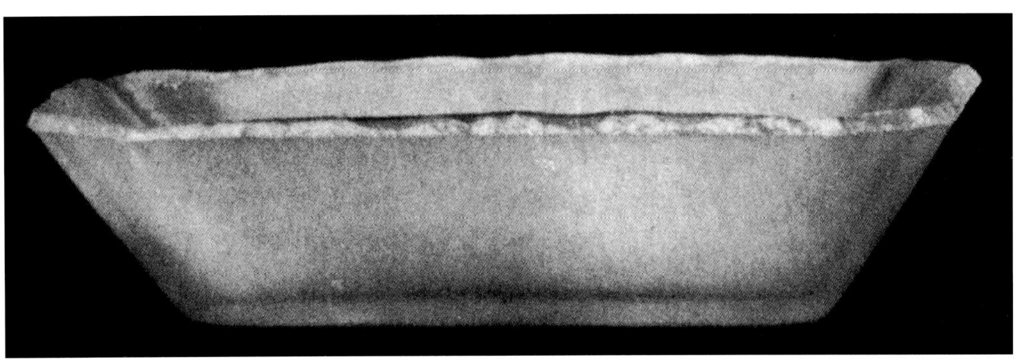

_______ #A-233, 7" long. *Illustration from a Pairpoint catalog.*

BON BON #234, 6.75" long x 4"wide x 2.75" high. *Illustration from a Pairpoint catalog.*

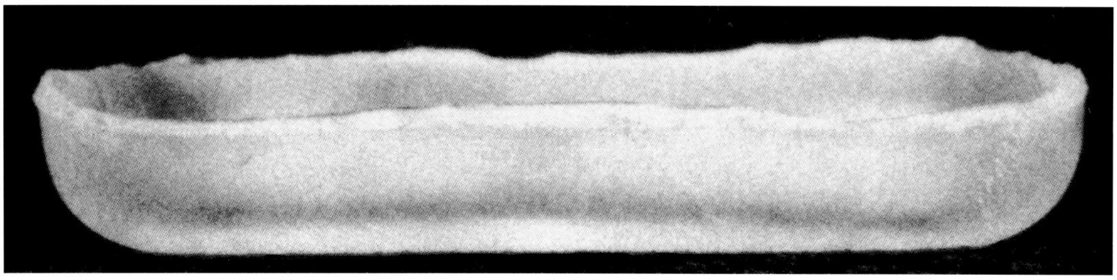

________ #238, 7.25" long. *Illustration from a Pairpoint catalog.*

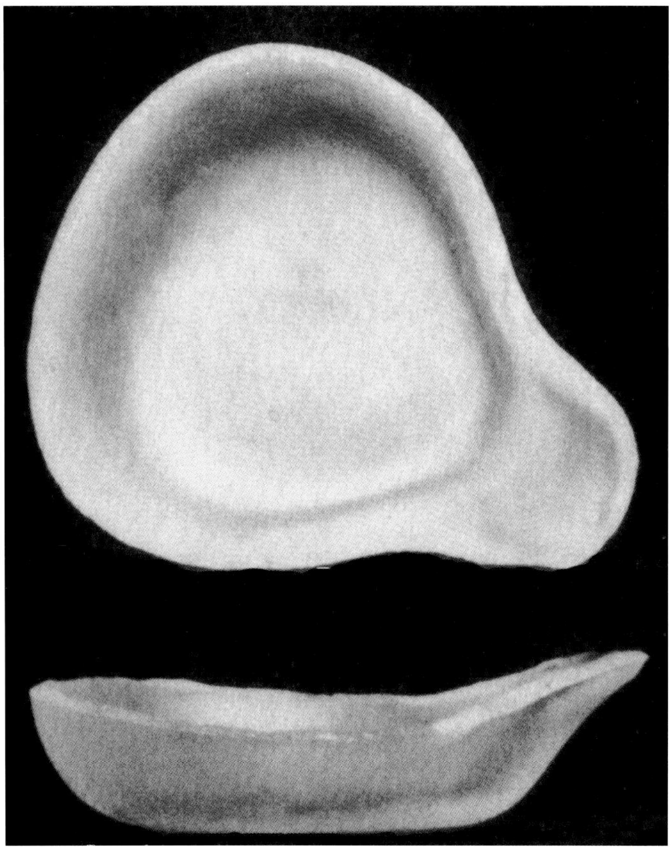

________ #243, 5", 6". *Illustration from a Pairpoint catalog.*

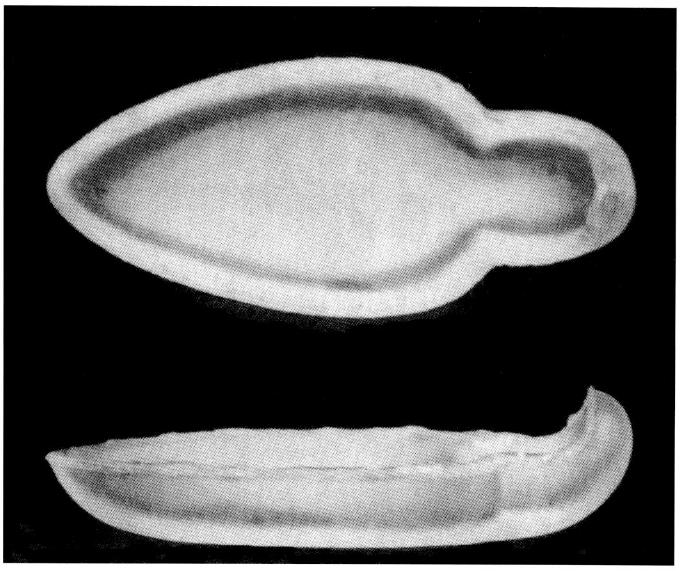

________ #244, 8" long x 3.50" wide. *Illustration from a Pairpoint catalog.*

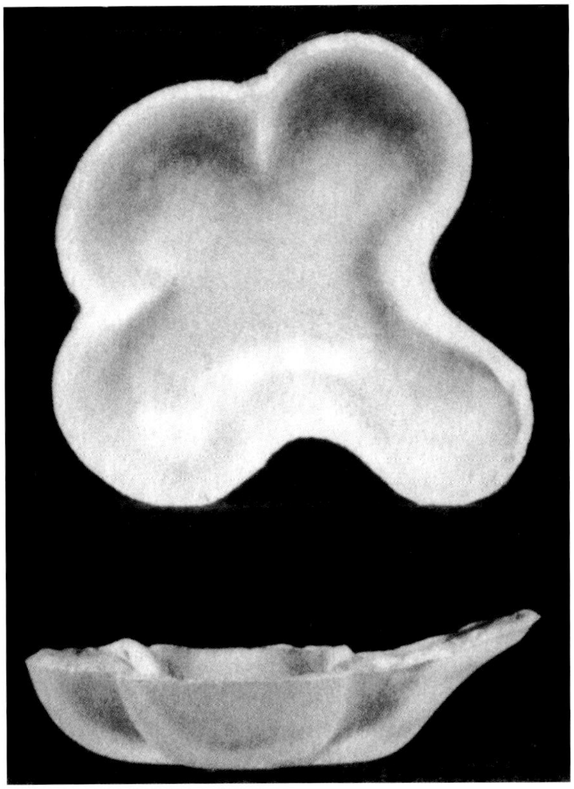

________ #246, 7" long x 7" wide. *Illustration from a Pairpoint catalog.*

BUTTER RECEIVER A-247, 6"d, 7.50"d. *Illustration from a Pairpoint catalog.*

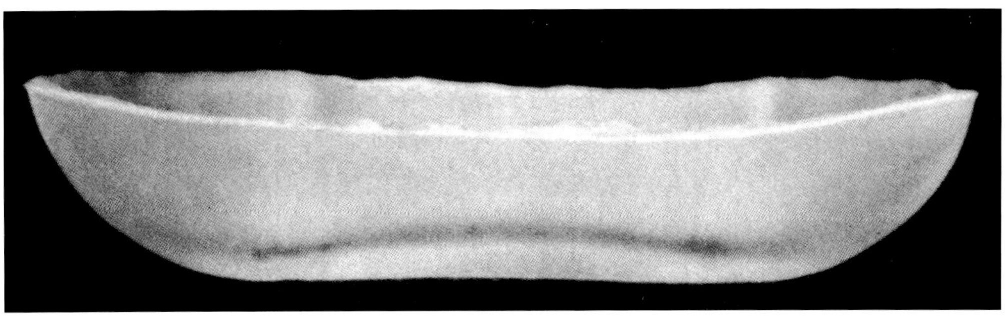

NAPPY #A-249, 8" long x 3.25" wide. *Illustration from a Pairpoint catalog.*

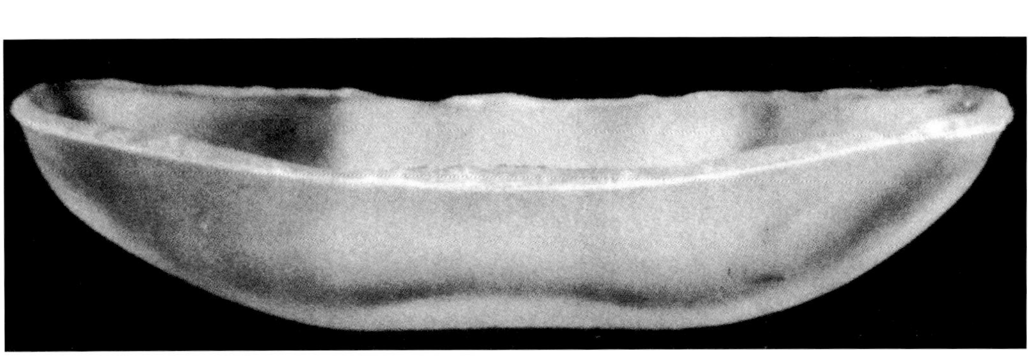

NAPPY #A-250, 8.25" long x 3.50" wide. *Illustration from a Pairpoint catalog.*

LOOP HANDLE NAPPY #250, 6"d. *Illustration from a Pairpoint catalog.*

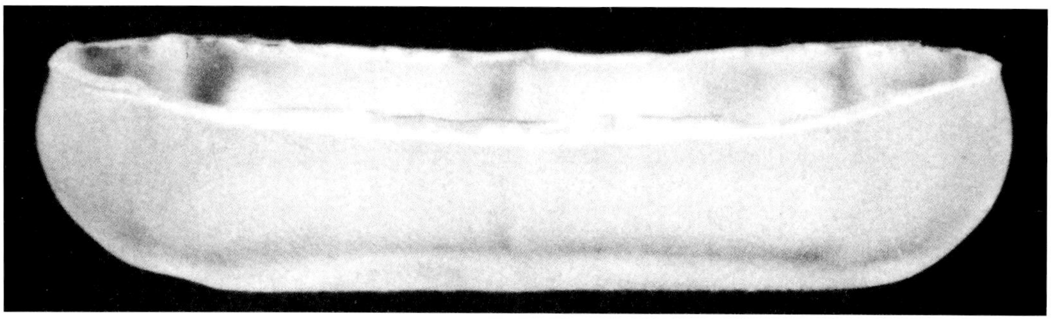

_______ #A-251, 8" long x 3.75" wide. *Illustration from a Pairpoint catalog.*

NAPPY #251, 5.50". *Illustration from a Pairpoint catalog.*

_______ #A-252, 8" long x 4" wide. *Illustration from a Pairpoint catalog.*

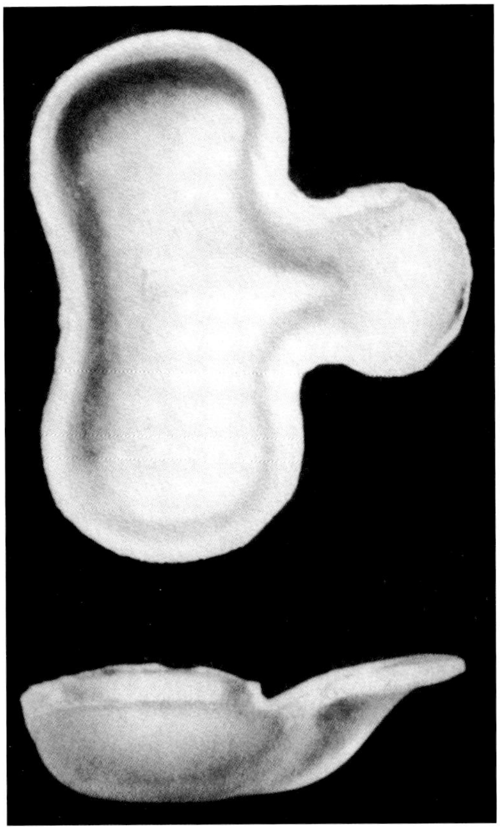

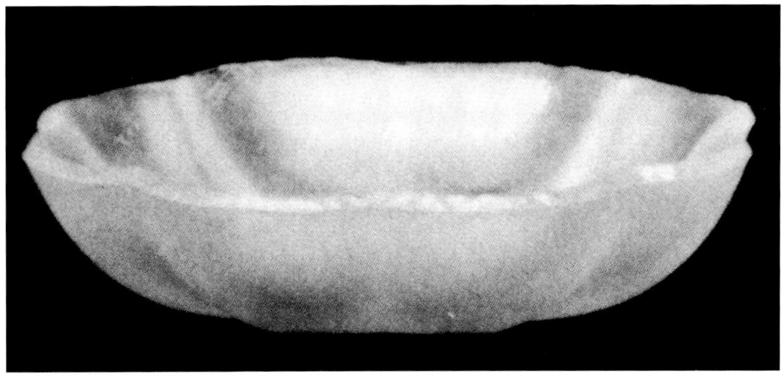

NAPPY #A-254, 6"d, 7"d, 8"d. *Illustration from a Pairpoint catalog.*

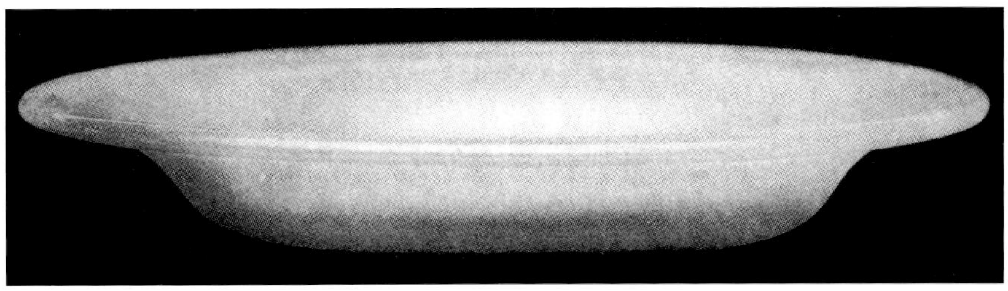

PLATE #A-257, 7"d. *Illustration from a Pairpoint catalog.*

________ #252, 6" long x 7.25" wide. *Illustration from a Pairpoint catalog.*

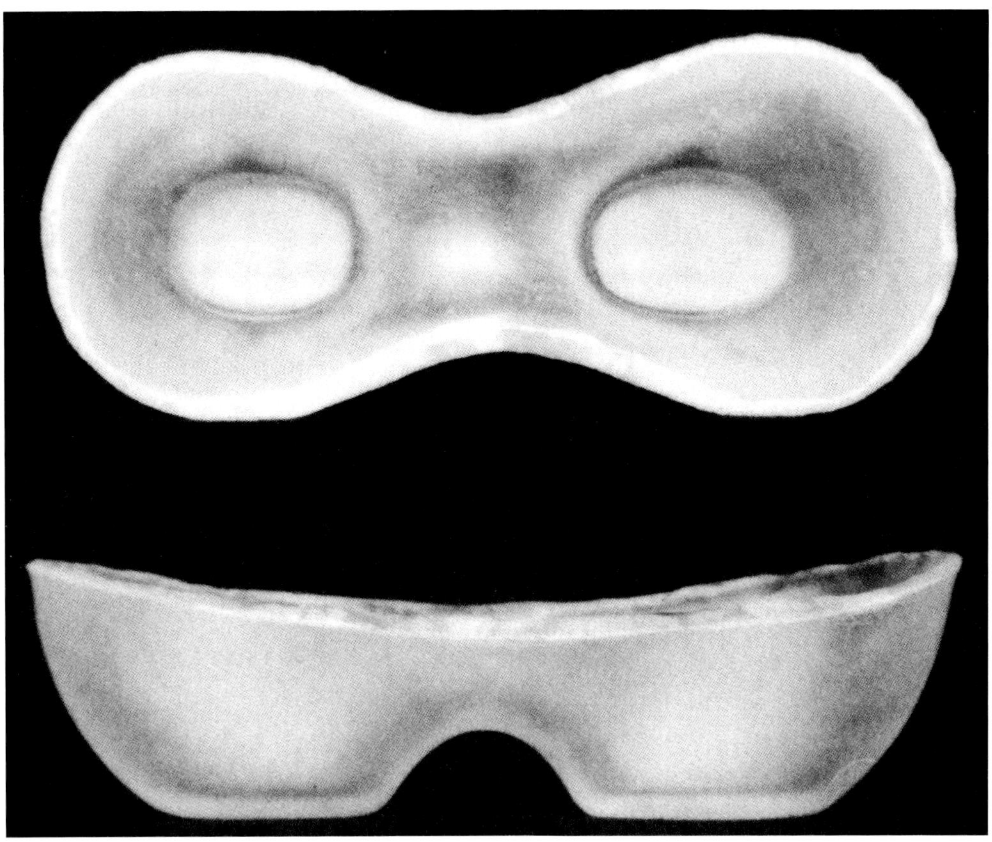

2-PART TRAY #A-253, 9" long. *Illustration from a Pairpoint catalog.*

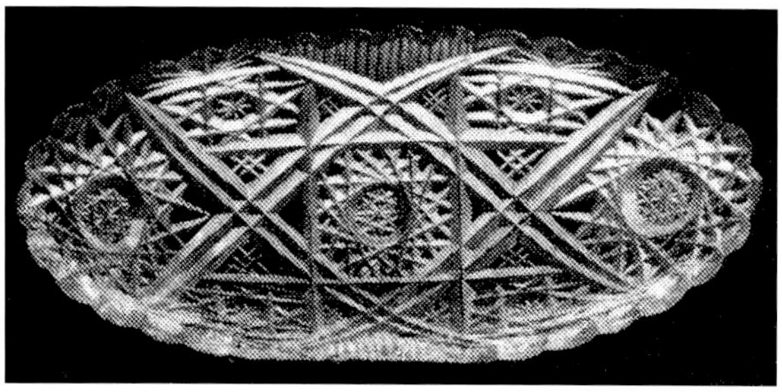

SPOON #259, 7.75" long. *Illustration from a Pairpoint catalog.*

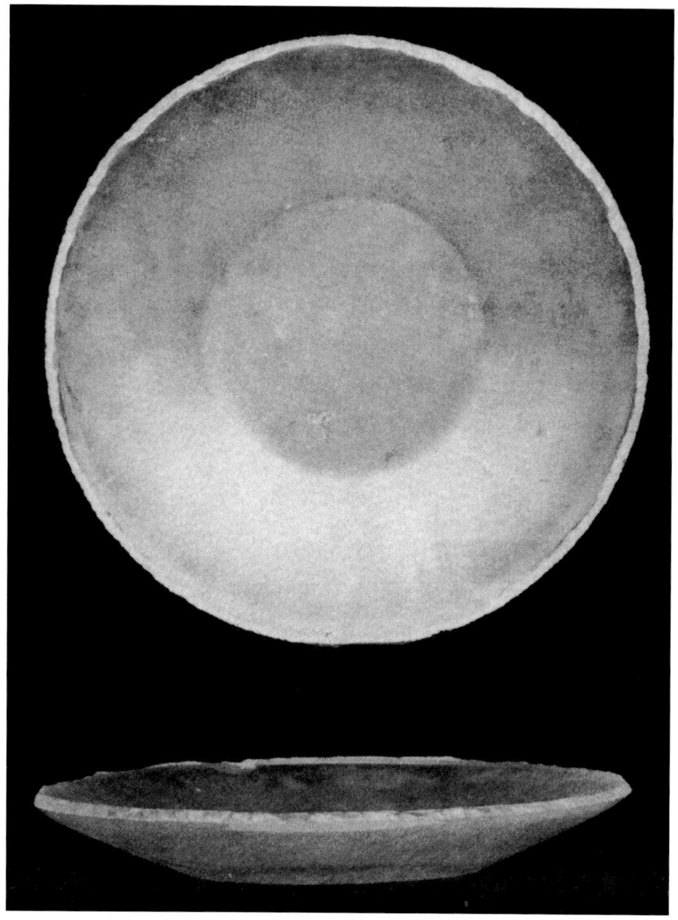

_______ #262, 6"d, 7"d. *Illustration from a Pairpoint catalog.*

LEMON DISH #A-261, 4.50"d. *Illustration from a Pairpoint catalog.*

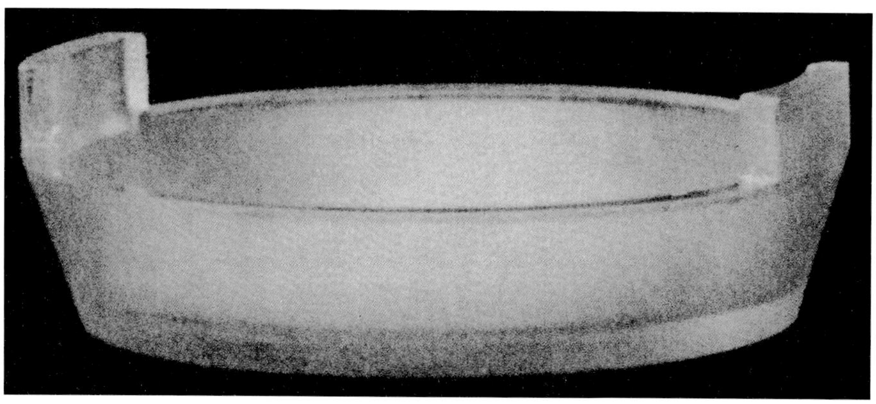

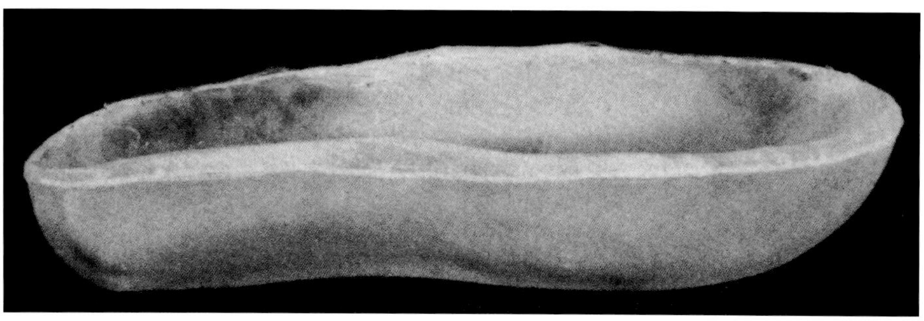

_______ #261, 6"d. *Illustration from a Pairpoint catalog.*

NAPPY #263. *Illustration from a Pairpoint catalog.*

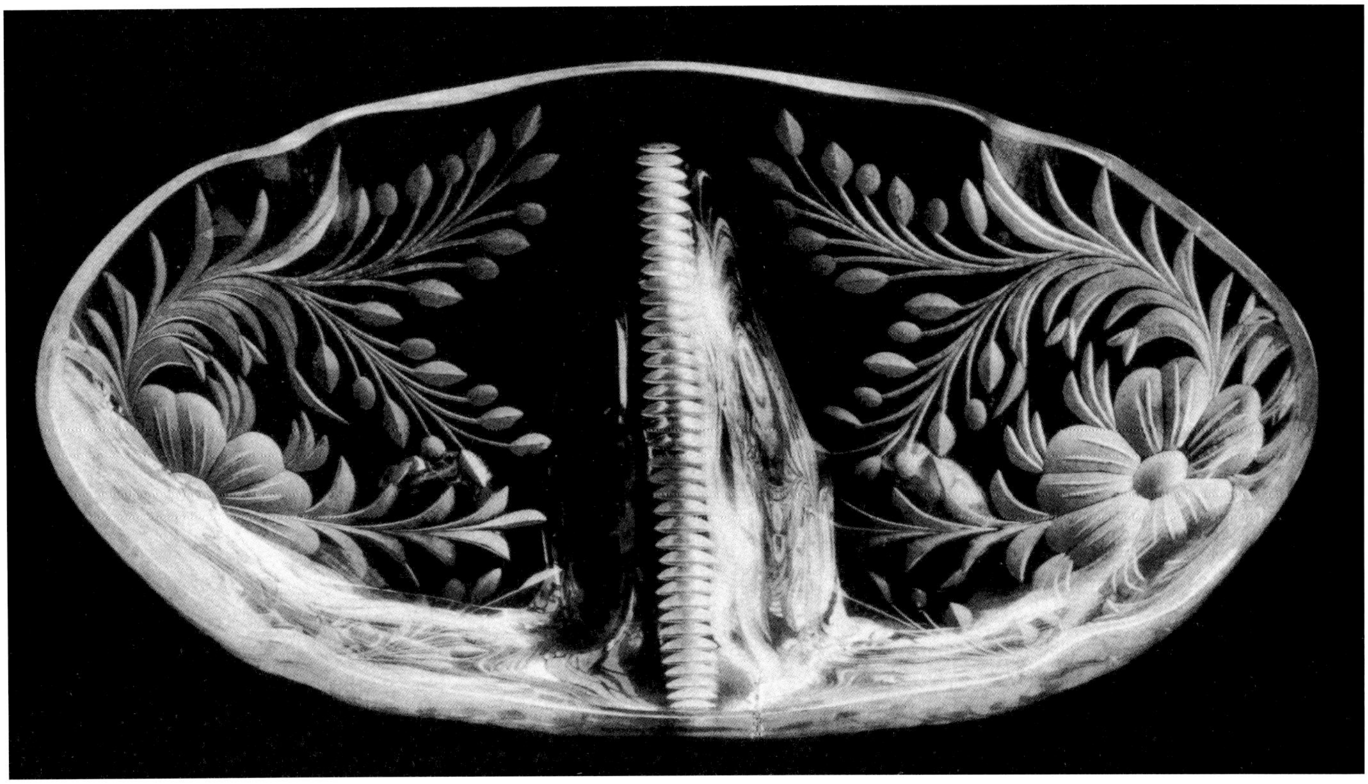

RELISH #A-265, 8.50" long, 2-Compartment. *Illustration from a Pairpoint catalog.*

BON BON #265. *Illustration from a Pairpoint catalog.*

PLATE #268, 7"d. The shape was round; the peripheral indentations were made at the time of cutting. *Illustration from a Pairpoint catalog.*

NAPPY #A-274, 8.50" long. *Illustration from a Pairpoint catalog.*

BON BON #A-275. *Illustration from a Pairpoint catalog.*

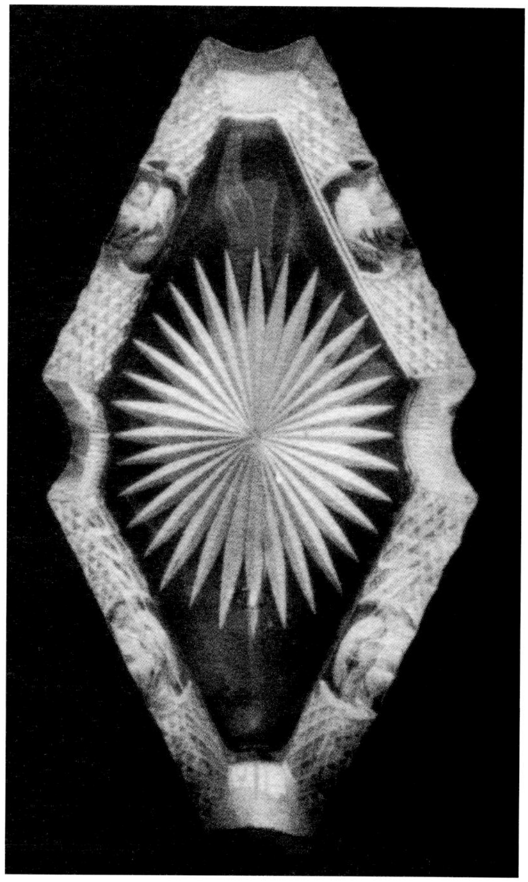

BON BON #A-277. *Illustration from a Pairpoint catalog.*

BON BON #A-276, 5" long. *Illustration from a Pairpoint catalog.*

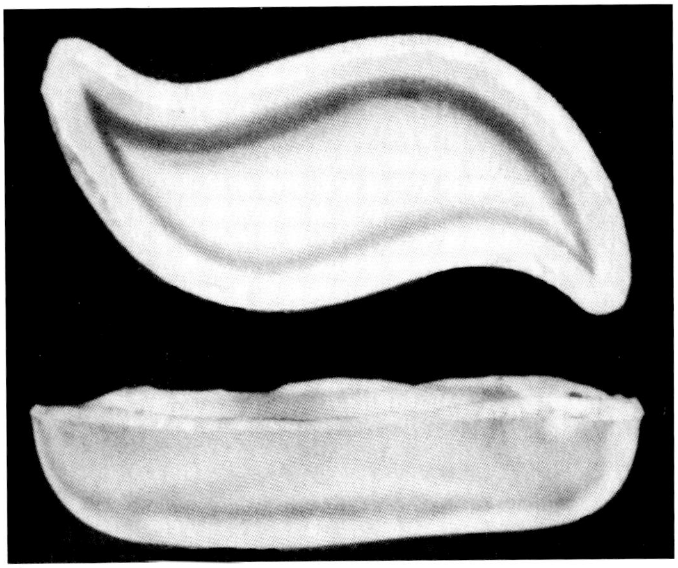

________ #278, 7" long x 2.75" wide. *Illustration from a Pairpoint catalog.*

PLATE #279, 7" x 7" square. *Illustration from a Pairpoint catalog.*

DOMINO SUGAR TRAY #A-280. *Illustration from a Pairpoint catalog.*

NAPPY #283. *Illustration from a Pairpoint catalog.*

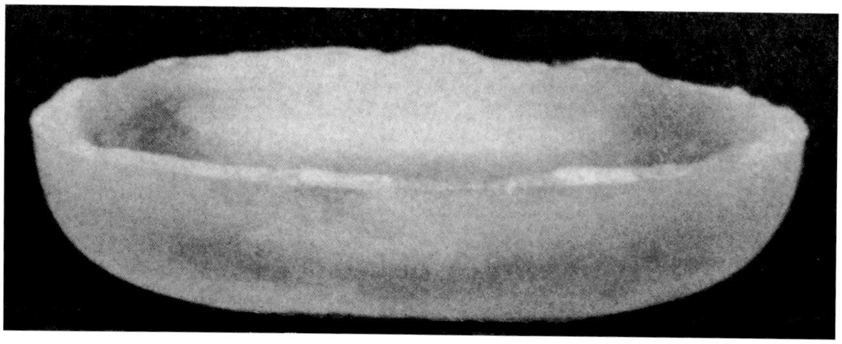

NAPPY #286, 5"d, 6"d, 7"d, 8"d. *Illustration from a Pairpoint catalog.*

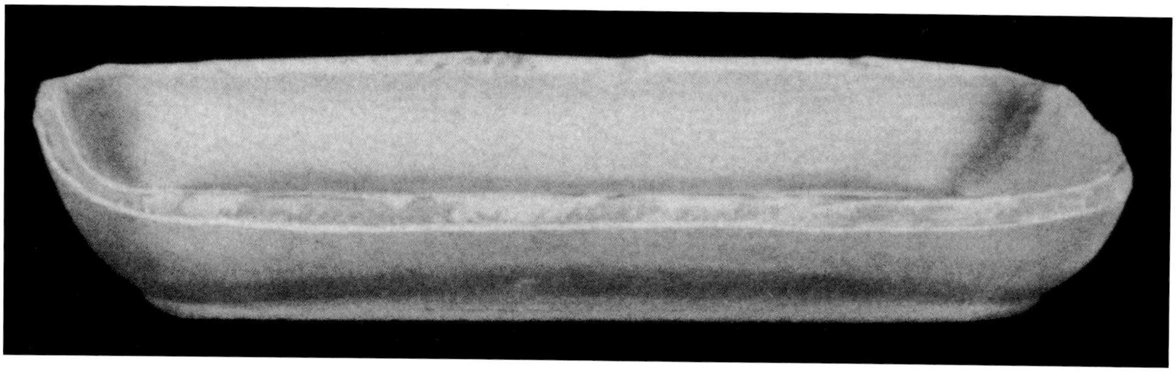

_______ #299, 8.25" long x 4" wide. *Illustration from a Pairpoint catalog.*

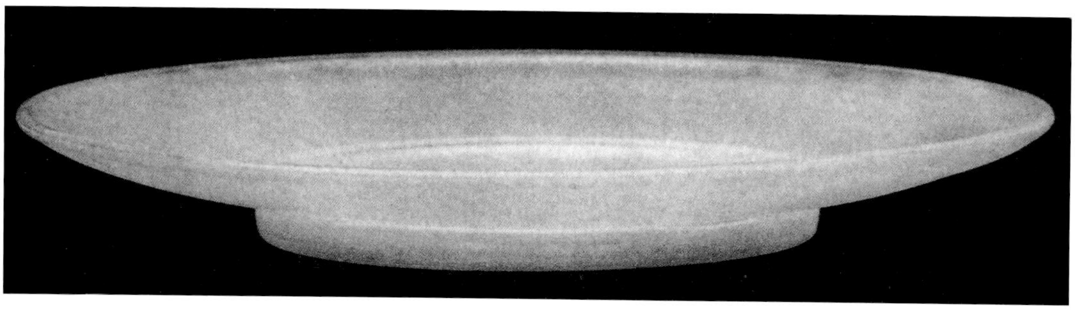

PLATE #319, 4.50"d, 5.25"d, 6"d, 7"d, 8"d, 9"d, 10"d, 12"d, 13"d, 14"d, 15"d, 16"d.
Illustration from a Pairpoint catalog.

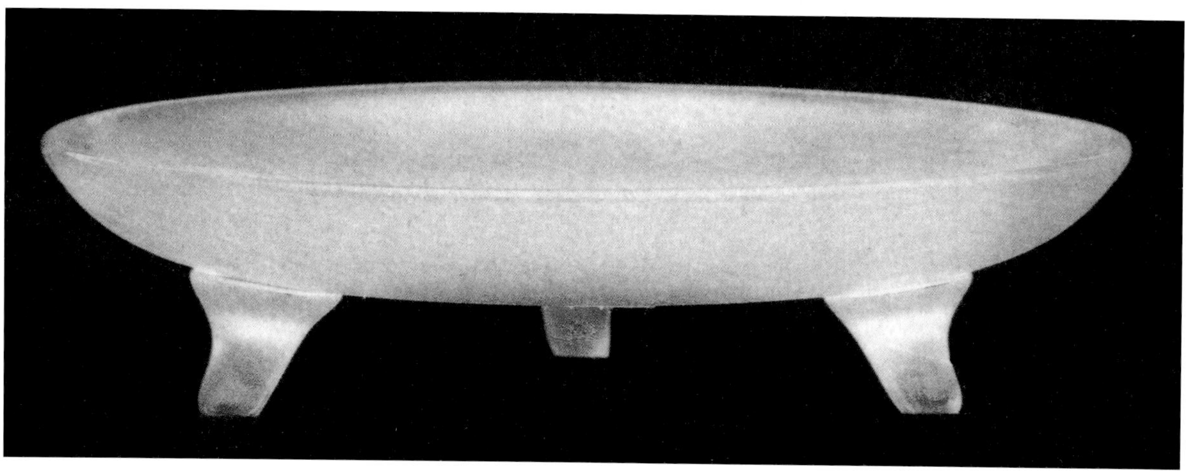

PLATE #321, 8"d, 9"d. *Illustration from a Pairpoint catalog.*

CRACKER & CHEESE PLATE #322, 9"d, 10"d. This shape has a heavy base projection underneath.

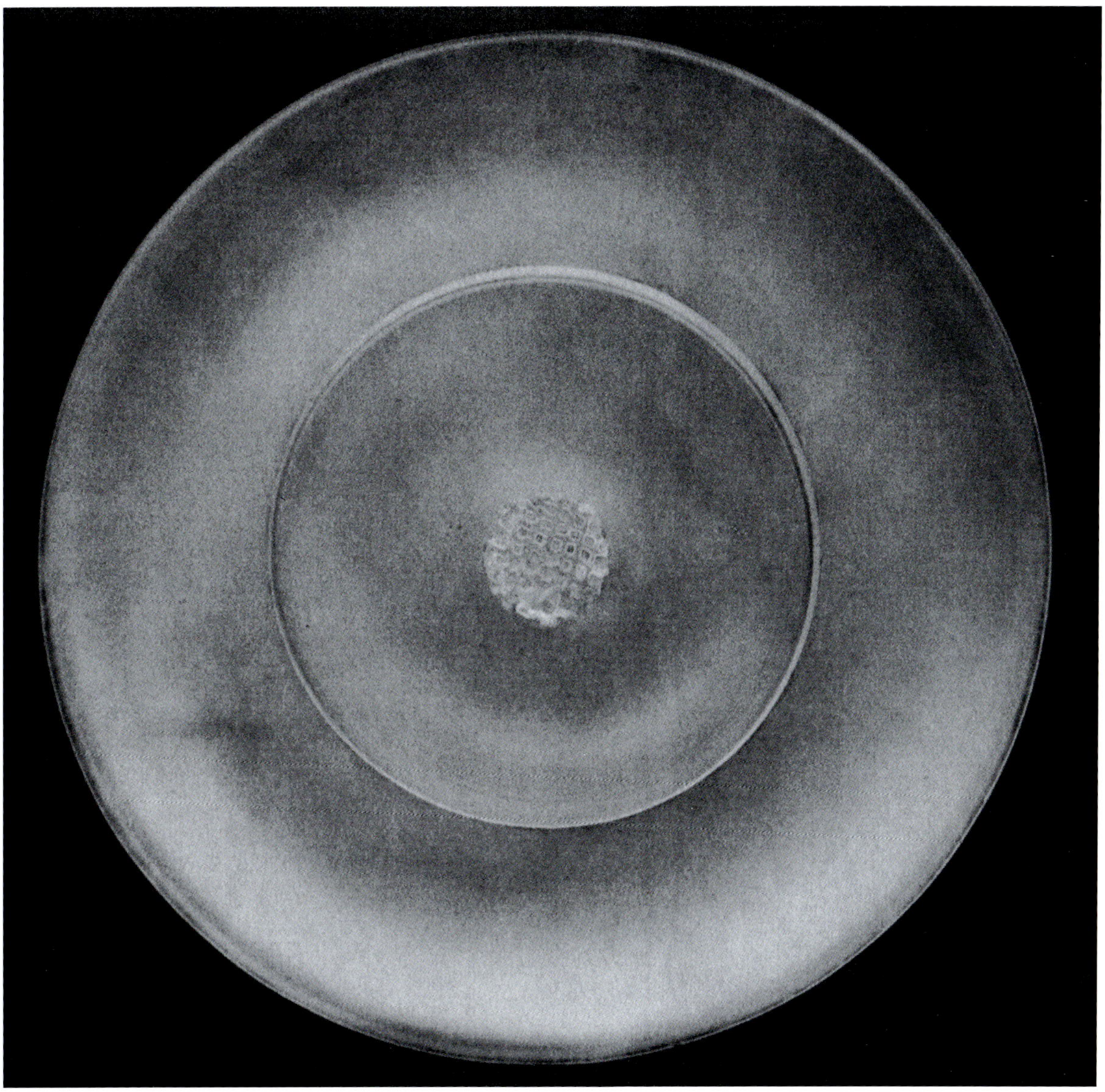

PLATE #329, 6"d, 6.50"d, 6.75"d, 7"d, 7.50"d, 8"d, 8.50"d, 9"d, 10"d, 10.75"d, 12"d, 14"d, 16"d.
Illustration from a Pairpoint catalog.

DISH #331, 9" long. *Illustration from a Pairpoint catalog.*

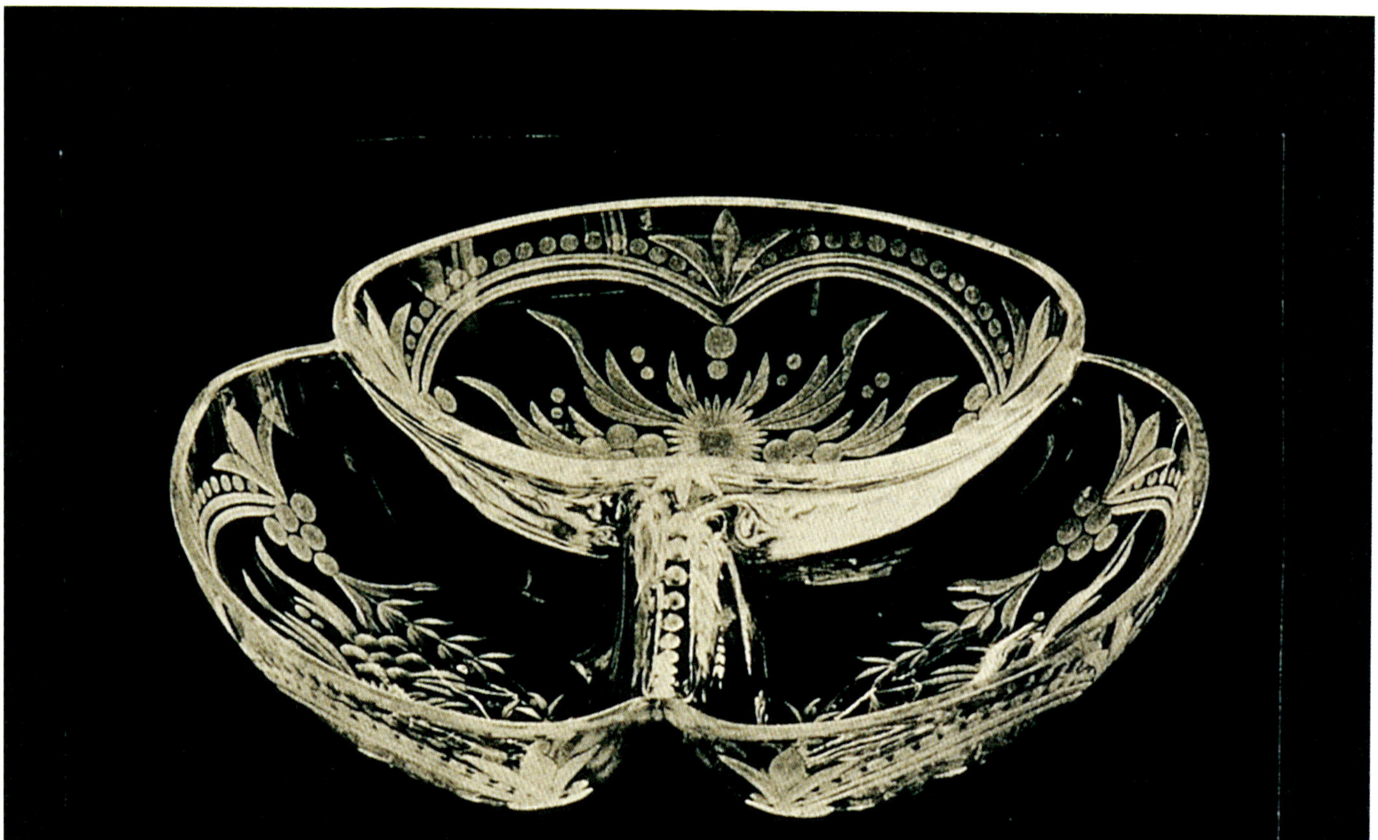

3-PART RELISH DISH #334. *Illustration from a Pairpoint catalog.*

HANDLED PLATE #336, 9.75"d, 10"d.

PLATE #336, 12"d, 14"d. The edges are upturned. *Illustration from a Pairpoint catalog.*

DISH #354, 6.50". *Illustration from a Pairpoint catalog.*

PLATE #395, 6"d, 8"d, 10"d, 12"d, 14"d, 16"d. This plate is formed with a flat resting base and does not have any extra glass projection underneath.

CRACKER & CHEESE PLATE #396, 10"d. This plate is based upon the #395 plate which has no extra projection of glass underneath.

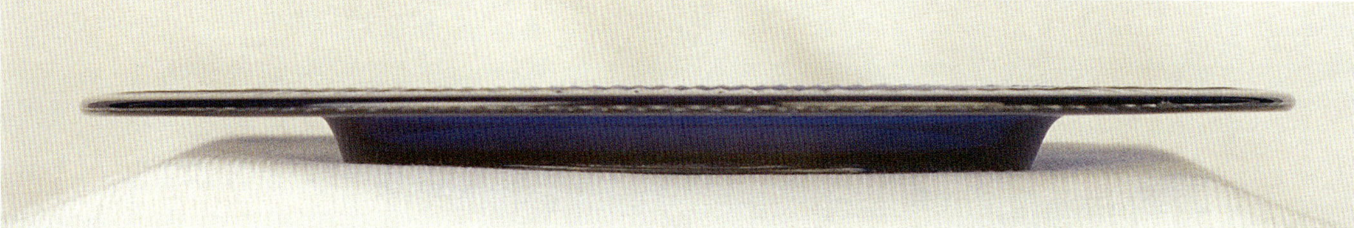

PLATE #397, 8.50"d, 9"d, 12"d, 14"d, 16"d.

JUG #400, 1/3-pint, 1/2-pint, 1-pint, 2-pint, 3-pint, 4-pint. *Illustration from a Pairpoint catalog.*

JUG #405, 3-pint. *Illustration from a Pairpoint catalog.*

JUG #406, 1/2-pint, 1-pint, 2-pint, 3-pint, 4-pint.

JUG #407, 2-pint, 3-pint, 4-pint. *Illustration from a Pairpoint catalog.*

JUG #417, 3-pint (14"h). *Illustration from a Pairpoint catalog.*

JUG #418, 3-pint, 4-pint.

JUG #425, 3-pint. *Illustration from a Pairpoint catalog.*

JUG #432, 4-pint. *Illustration from a Pairpoint catalog.*

JUG #427, 3-pint. *Illustration from a Pairpoint catalog.*

JUG #450, 1/2-pint, 1-pint, 2-pint, 3-pint, 4-pint. *Illustration from a Pairpoint catalog.*

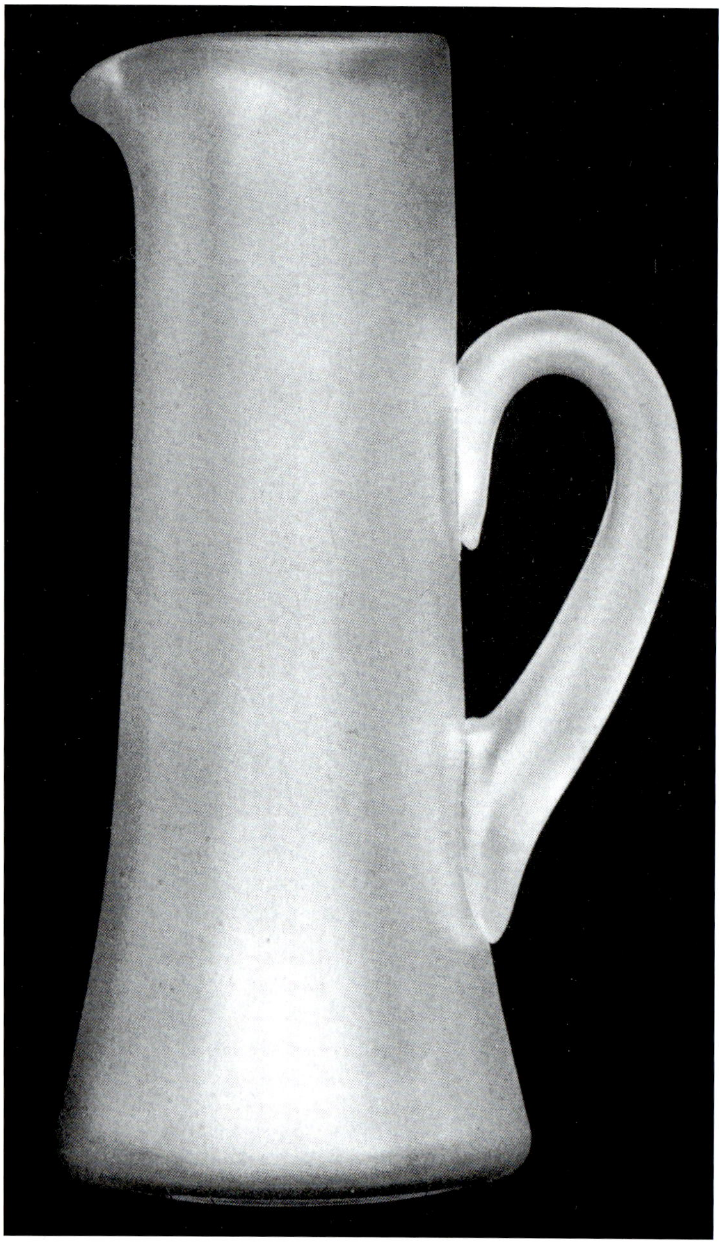

JUG #433, 11.50"h. *Illustration from a Pairpoint catalog.*

JUG #456. *Illustration from a Pairpoint catalog.*

JUG #457, 3-pint.

JUG #459. *Illustration from a Pairpoint catalog.*

ICED TEA JUG #458. *Illustration from a Pairpoint catalog.*

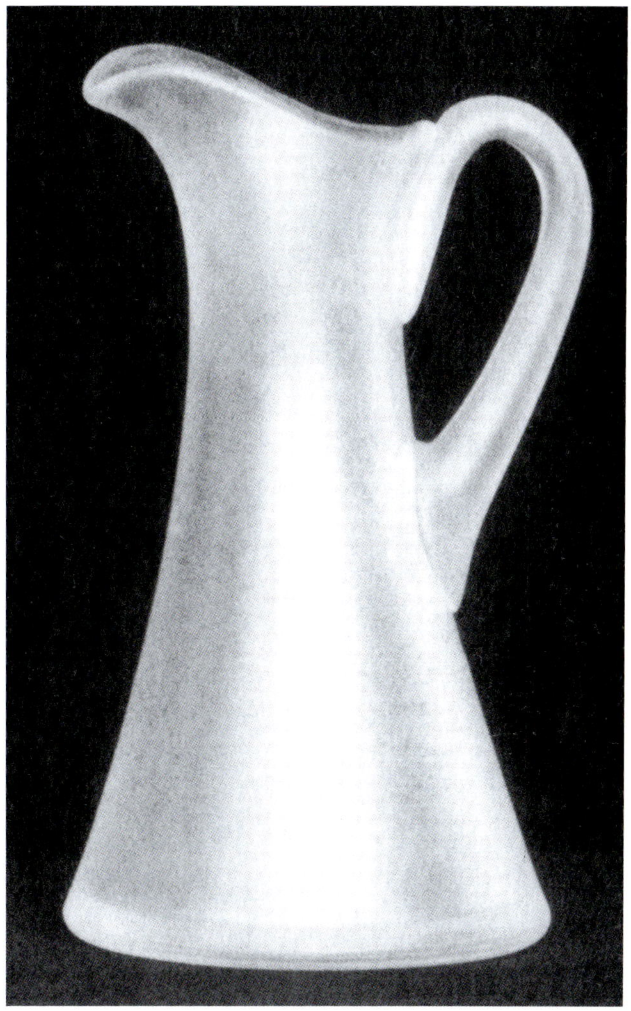

JUG #465, 2-pint (9.50"h). *Illustration from a Pairpoint catalog.*

JUG #466, 4-pint (12.50"h). *Illustration from a Pairpoint catalog.*

JUG #490, 1/2-pint, 1-pint, 2-pint, 3-pint, 4-pint. *Illustration from a Pairpoint catalog.*

OIL #502. *Illustration from a Pairpoint catalog.*

OIL #506, 5" body height. *Illustration from a Pairpoint catalog.*

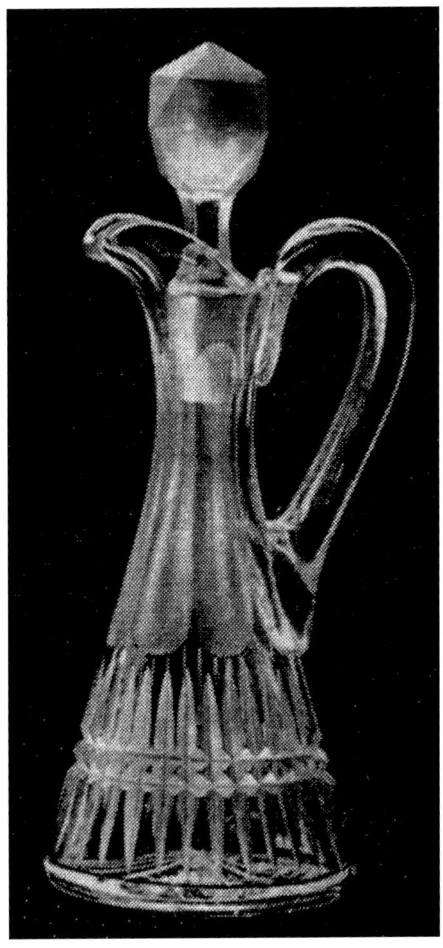

OIL #523, 5.75"h. *Illustration from a Pairpoint catalog.*

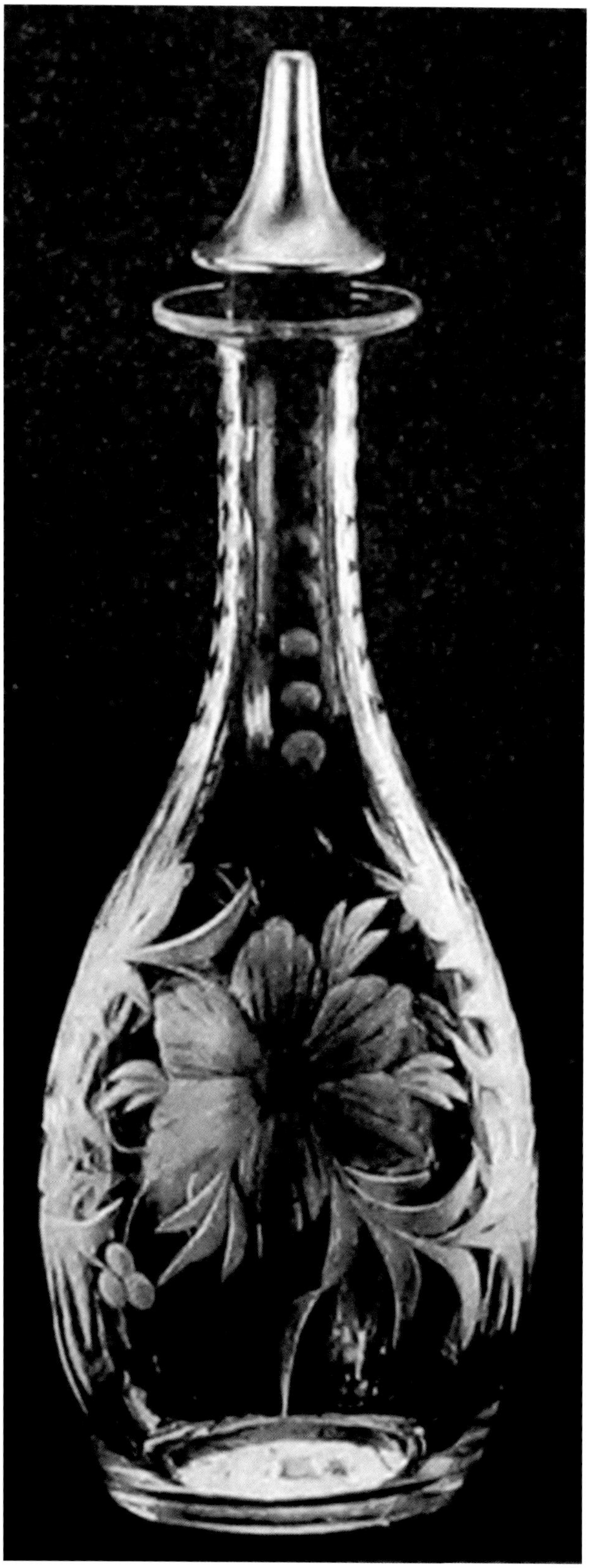

BITTERS BOTTLE #525. Sterling silver top. *Illustration from a Pairpoint catalog.*

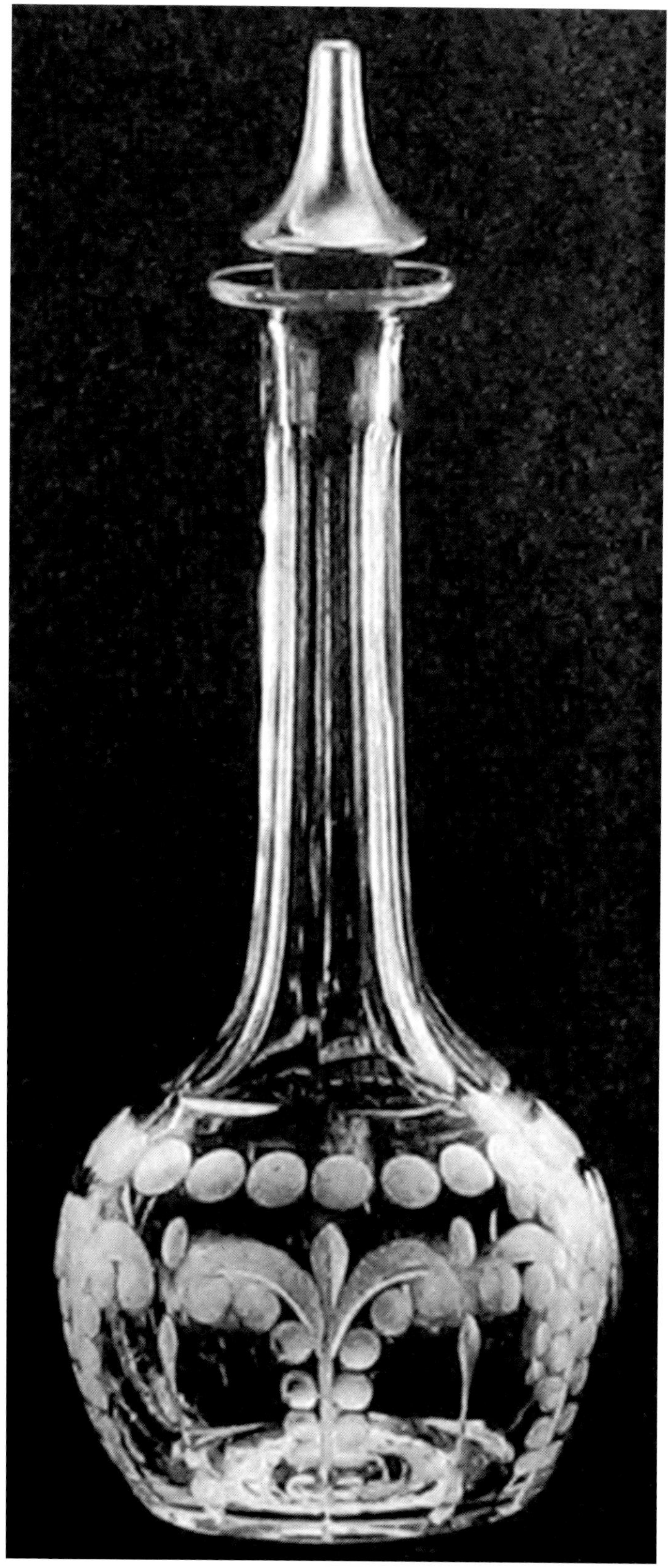

BITTERS BOTTLE #531. Sterling silver top. *Illustration from a Pairpoint catalog.*

OIL #535. *Illustration from a Pairpoint catalog.*

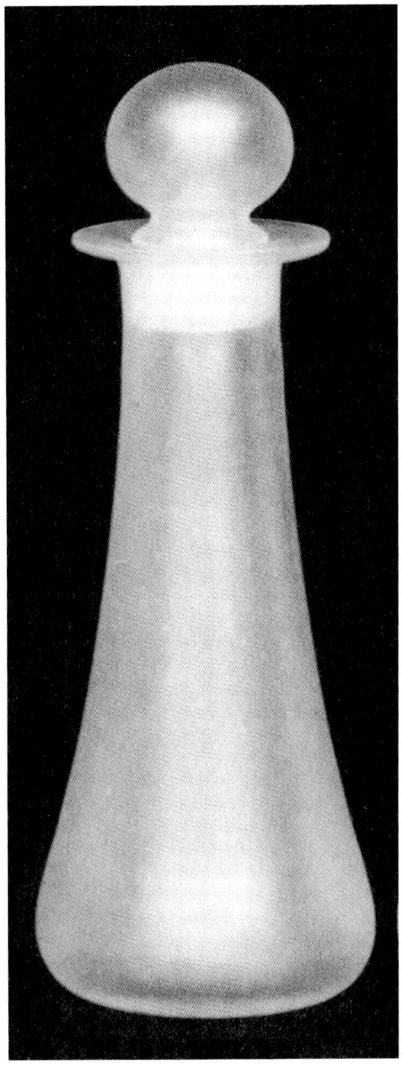

CATSUP #543, 7" body height. *Illustration from a Pairpoint catalog.*

OIL #544, 5.75" body height. *Illustration from a Pairpoint catalog.*

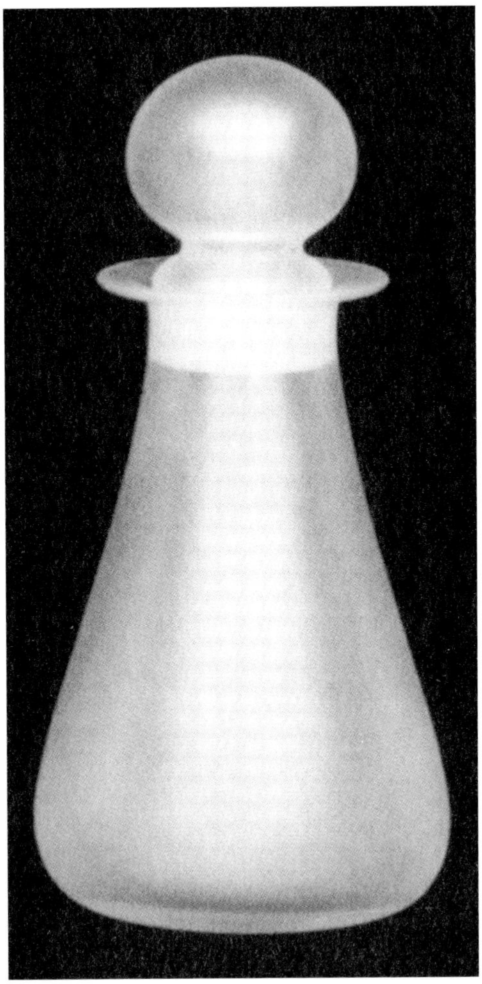

RADISH #542, 4.75" body height. *Illustration from a Pairpoint catalog.*

OIL #563. *Illustration from a Pairpoint catalog.*

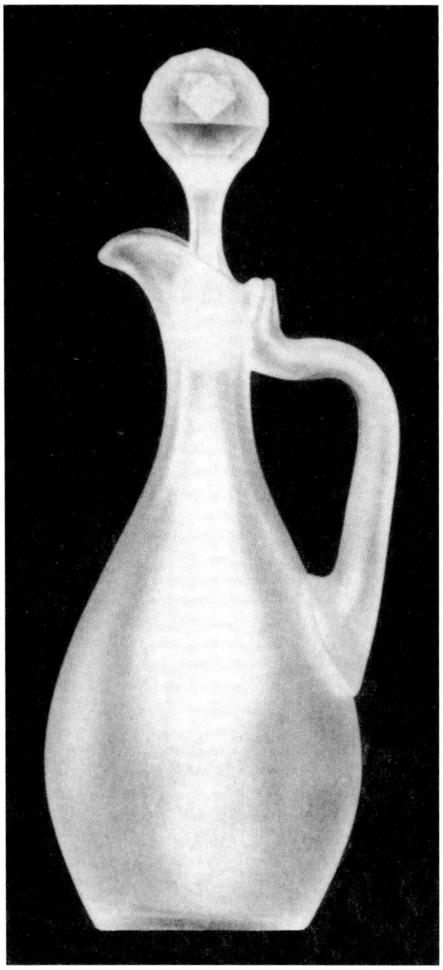

CLARET #604, 1-quart (13.25"h). The claret has a spout and handle. *Illustration from a Pairpoint catalog.*

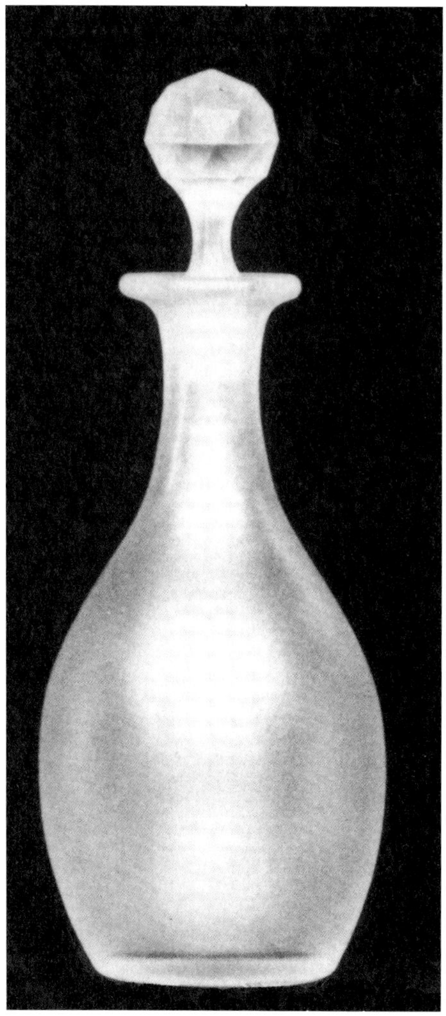

DECANTER #604, 1-quart (12.50"). The decanter has no spout or handle. *Illustration from a Pairpoint catalog.*

DECANTER #611, 15"h. *Illustration from a Pairpoint catalog.*

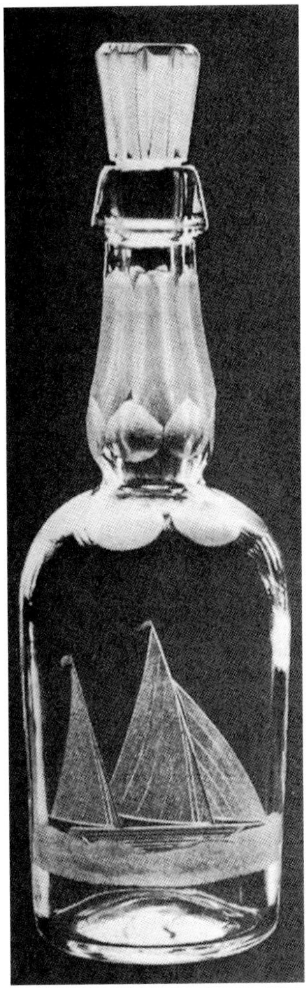

DECANTER #621. *Illustration from a Pairpoint catalog.*

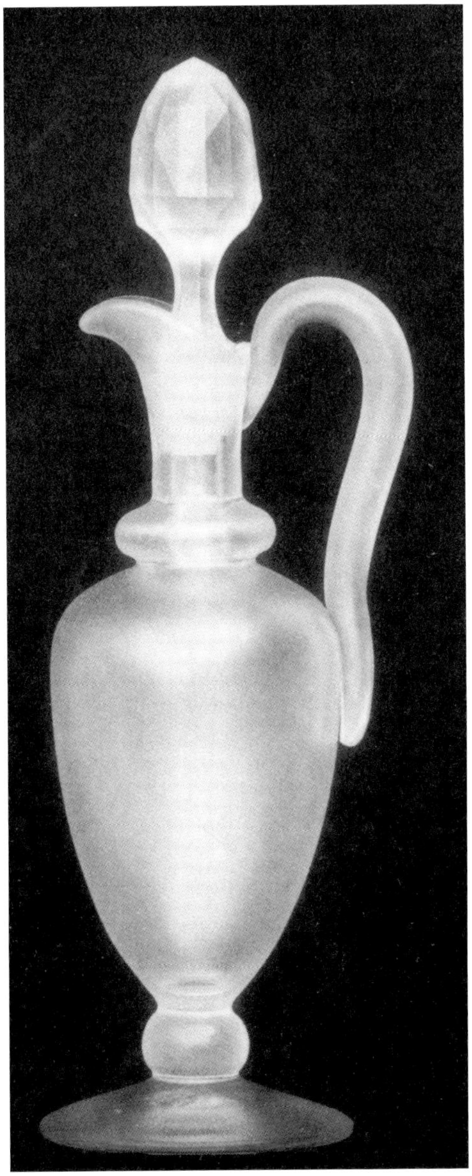

CLARET #622, 14.50" overall height. *Illustration from a Pairpoint catalog.*

OVAL DECANTER #624, 1-quart. (This shape was previously identified in The Essence of Pairpoint as Unknown 49.) *Illustration from a Pairpoint catalog.*

OVAL CLARET #627, 1.50-pint. The claret has a handle and spout. *Illustration from a Pairpoint catalog.*

OVAL DECANTER #627, 1.50-pint. The decanter has no spout or handle. *Illustration from a Pairpoint catalog.*

DECANTER #631, 9.75"h x 5"d.
Illustration from a Pairpoint catalog.

DONUT DECANTER #632, 9" overall height x 6" wide.

DECANTER #633, 14" overall height.

BOTTOMS UP GLASS. A Pairpoint catalog page shows these glasses with the #633 decanter, but they were used with various decanter and bar sets. As you can see, once filled with a favorite libation, they cannot be set down until finished.

BOTTLE #638, 14-oz. This bottle was used in the Fine Arts Line Liquor Set #1080. *Illustration from a Pairpoint catalog.*

BOTTLE #639, 16-oz. This bottle was used in the Fine Arts Line Liquor Set #1081. *Illustration from a Pairpoint catalog.*

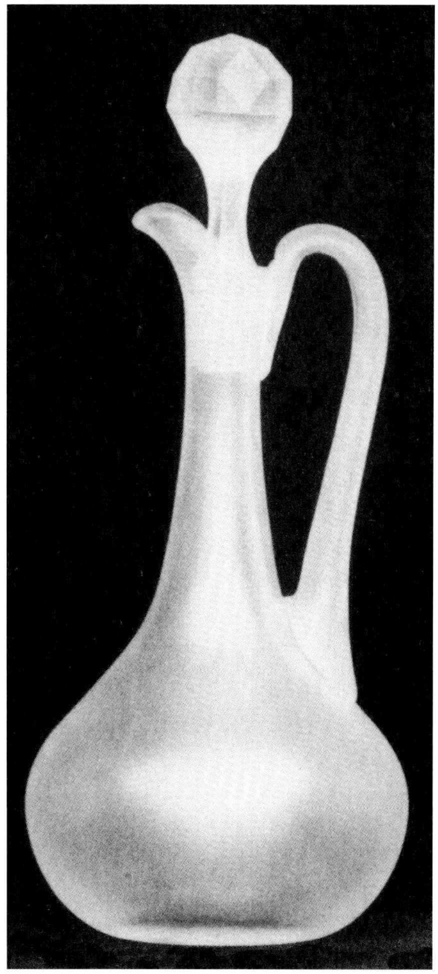

CLARET #650, 13" overall height. *Illustration from a Pairpoint catalog.*

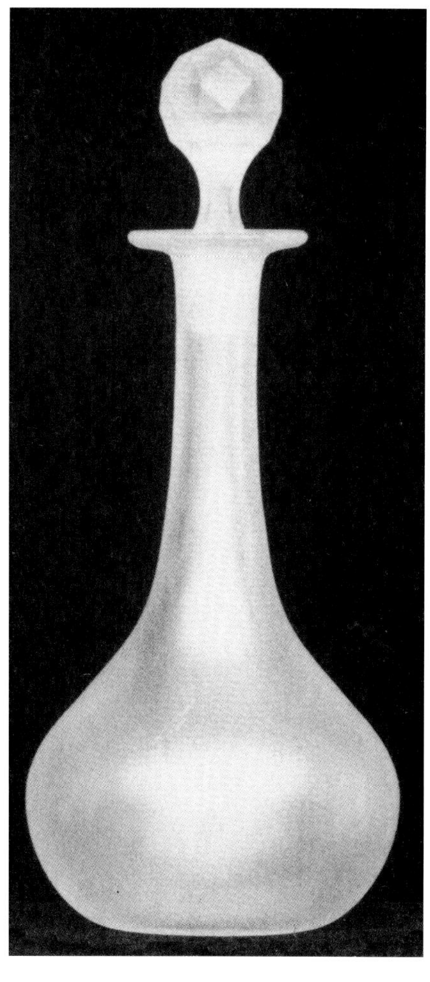

DECANTER #650, 13" overall height. *Illustration from a Pairpoint catalog.*

WHISKEY JUG #692, 10" overall height. *Illustration from a Pairpoint catalog.*

_______ #701, 1-quart. *Illustration from a Pairpoint catalog.*

CELERY #803, 7.75" long. *Illustration from a Pairpoint catalog.*

CELERY #809, 10.75" long x 4.50" wide. (This shape was previously identified in *The Essence of Pairpoint* as Unknown 68.) *Illustration from a Pairpoint catalog.*

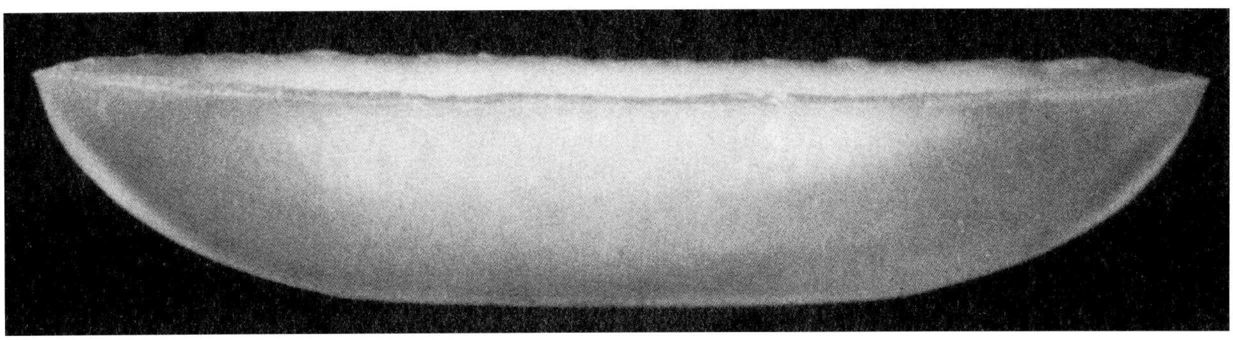

CELERY #814, 11.50" long. *Illustration from a Pairpoint catalog.*

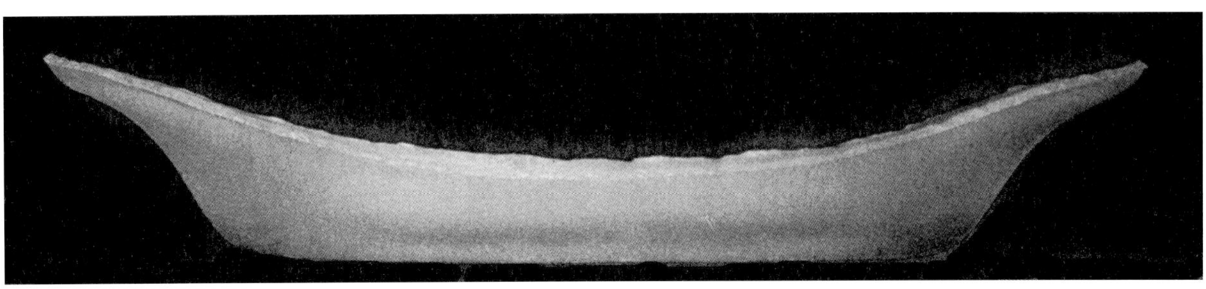

BREAD TRAY #815, 13" long x 6" wide. *Illustration from a Pairpoint catalog.*

CELERY TRAY #816, 12.25" long. *Illustration from a Pairpoint catalog.*

SPOON #873, 4.75"h.

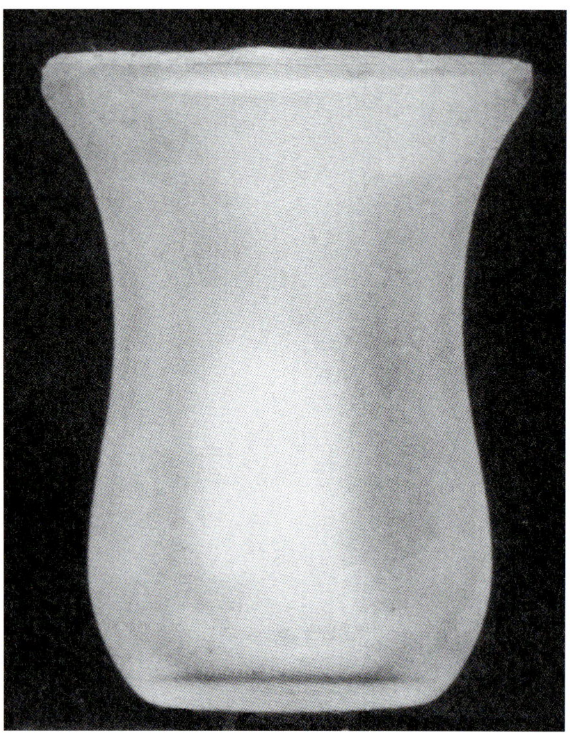

_______ #876, 5"h. *Illustration from a Pairpoint catalog.*

SPOON #877, 8.50" long. *Illustration from a Pairpoint catalog.*

SPOON TRAY #878, 9.25" long. *Illustration from a Pairpoint catalog.*

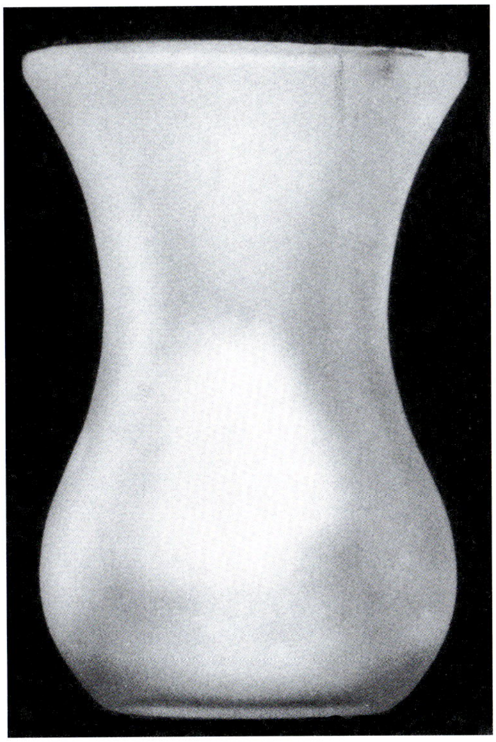

CELERY #882, 7.625" long. *Illustration from a Pairpoint catalog.*

JUICE GLASS #928, 4.50"h. These glasses were combined with #138 Grape Juice Bowl to make a Grape Juice Set.

CANDY JAR #B-915, 8.75" overall height. A 1926 Pairpoint engraving department cost book references two sizes, but does not specify where the measurements are taken: 6.50", 8". *Illustration from a Pairpoint catalog.*

PUNCH CUP #929. *Illustration from a Pairpoint catalog.*

CANDY BOX #951, 6"d x __"h, 6.50"d x 2.375"h, 7.75 (7.50)"d x 4"h, 8"d x __"h. *Illustration from a Pairpoint catalog.*

TOOTHPICK #1074, 3"h. *Illustration from a Pairpoint catalog.*

TOOTHPICK #1024. *Illustration from a Pairpoint catalog.*

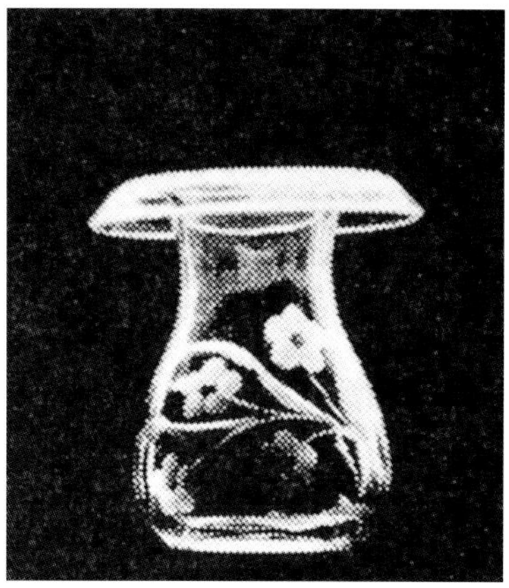

TOOTHPICK #1025. *Illustration from a Pairpoint catalog.*

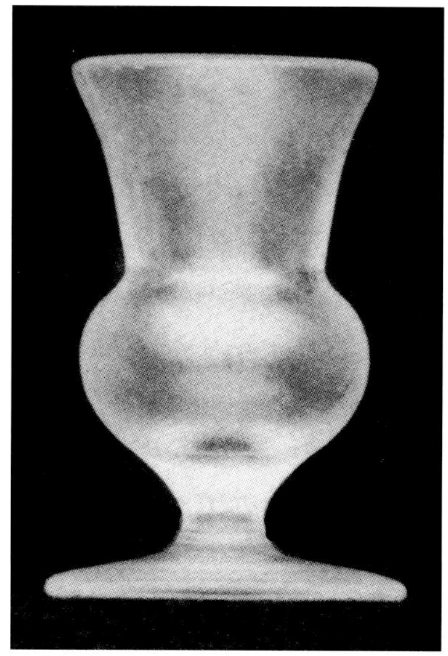

TOOTHPICK #1076, 3.25"h. (This shape was previously identified in *The Essence of Pairpoint* as #1077.) *Illustration from a Pairpoint catalog.*

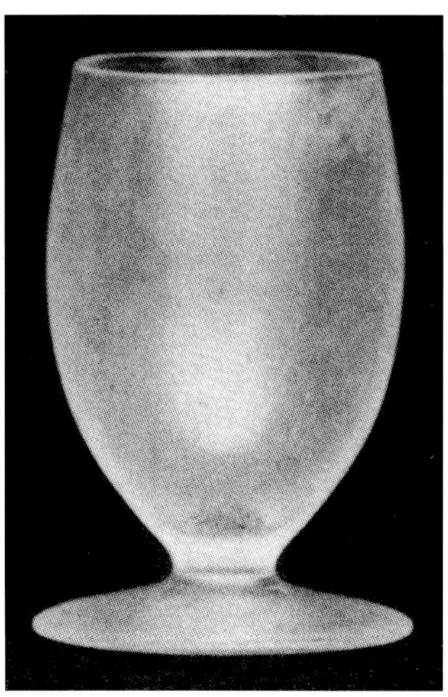

________ #1037, 4.25"h. *Illustration from a Pairpoint catalog.*

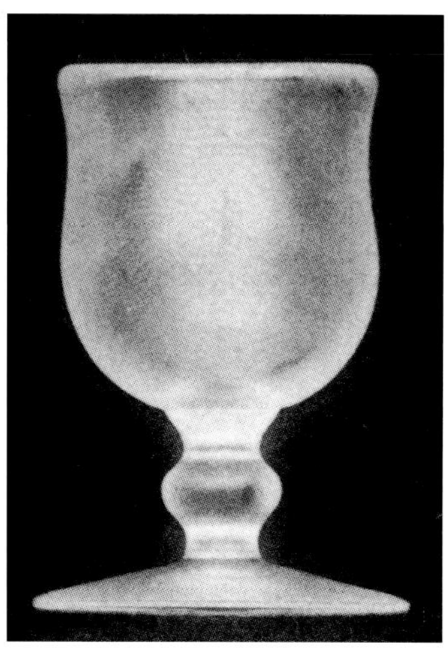

TOOTHPICK #1073, 3.25"h. *Illustration from a Pairpoint catalog.*

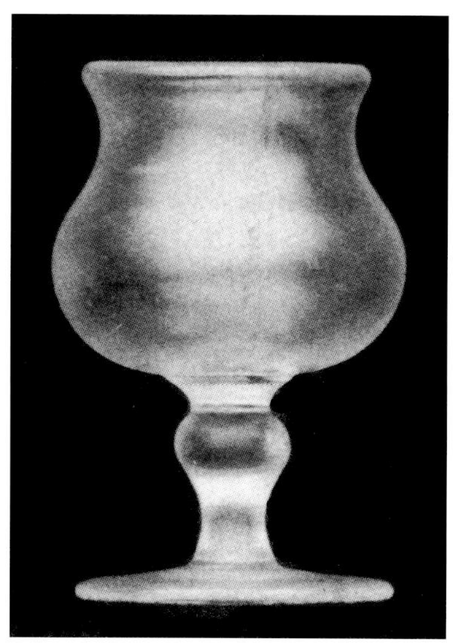

TOOTHPICK #1077, 3.25"h. *Illustration from a Pairpoint catalog.*

BUTTER #1126, Cover – 5"d, Plate – 7.25"d. *Illustration from a Pairpoint catalog.*

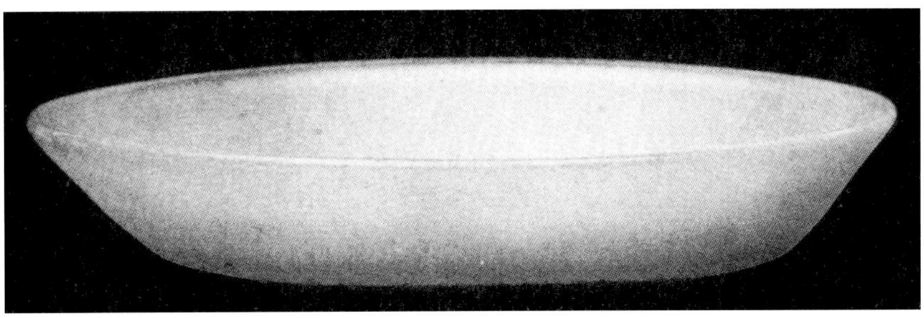

PLATE #1127, 6"d. *Illustration from a Pairpoint catalog.*

________ #1130, 4.50"d. *Illustration from a Pairpoint catalog.*

BUTTER(?) #1136, 5.50"d. *Illustration from a Pairpoint catalog.*

________ #1148, 5.50" x 8". *Illustration from a Pairpoint catalog.*

SPOON(?) #1140, 5.375" x 5.125". *Illustration from a Pairpoint catalog.*

ICE PAIL #1159, 5.50"h, 6.50"h, 7.50"h. This item comes with a perforated electro-plated nickel silver (EPNS) drainer disk that rests upon an internal ridge near the bottom.

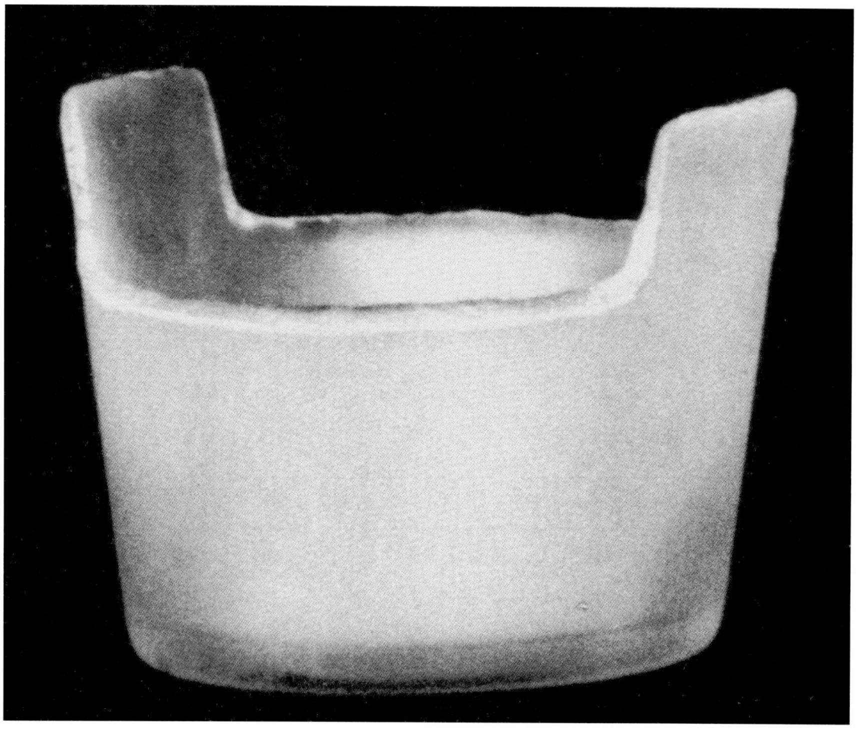

________ #1160, 5"d x 6"h, 7"d x 6"h. *Illustration from a Pairpoint catalog.*

BOWL and PLATE #1165, 6"d. *Illustration from a Pairpoint catalog.*

BOWL and PLATE #1166, 5"d. *Illustration from a Pairpoint catalog.*

BOWL and PLATE #1167, Bowl - 3.875"d x 3.75"h, Plate - 5.75"d. *Illustration from a Pairpoint catalog.*

MAYO BOWL & PLATE #1169. *Illustration from a Pairpoint catalog.*

_______ #1177, 5.25" x 6". *Illustration from a Pairpoint catalog.*

_______ #1178, 5.25" x 5.50". *Illustration from a Pairpoint catalog.*

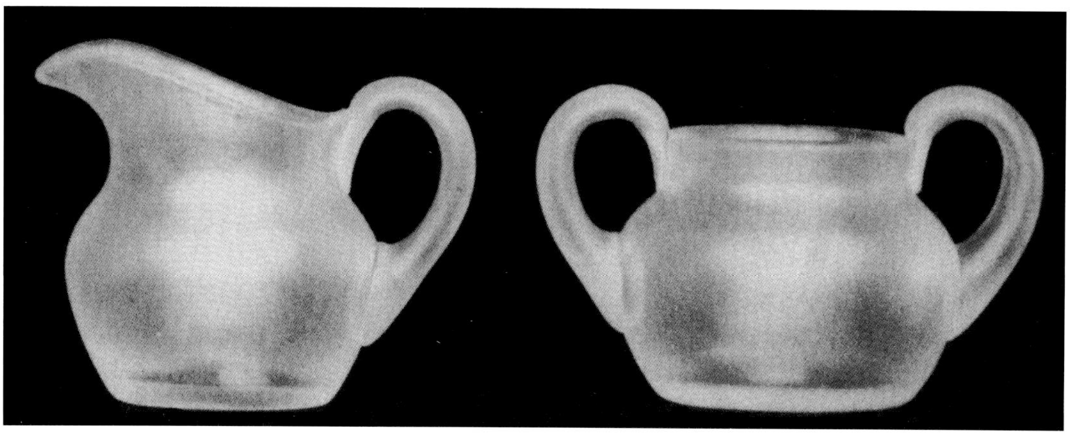

SUGAR and CREAM #1201, Sugar - 3.75"h, Cream - 4"h. *Illustration from a Pairpoint catalog.*

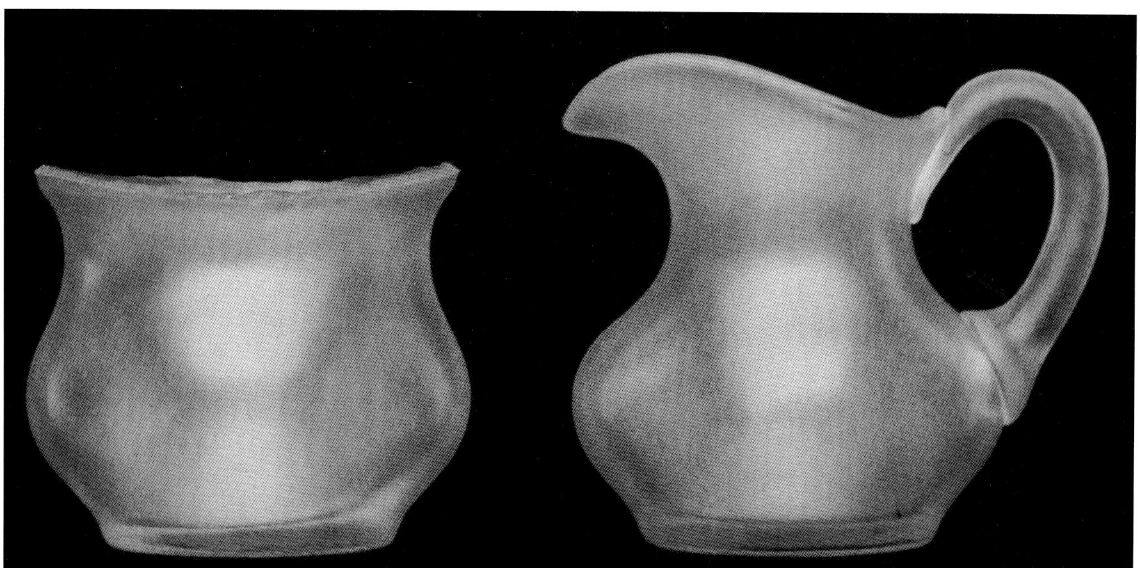

SUGAR and CREAM #1212, Sugar - 4"h, Cream - 4.50"h. *Illustration from a Pairpoint catalog.*

SUGAR & CREAM #1214. *Illustration from a Pairpoint catalog.*

SUGAR & CREAM #1217. *Illustration from a Pairpoint catalog.*

SUGAR and CREAM #1218. *Illustration from a Pairpoint catalog.*

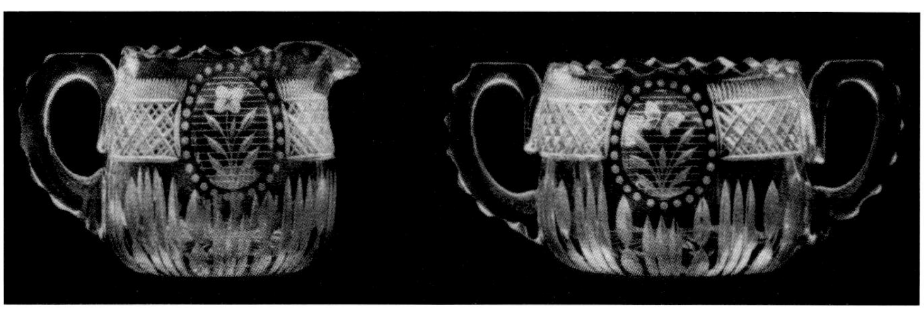

SUGAR & CREAM #1225. *Illustration from a Pairpoint catalog.*

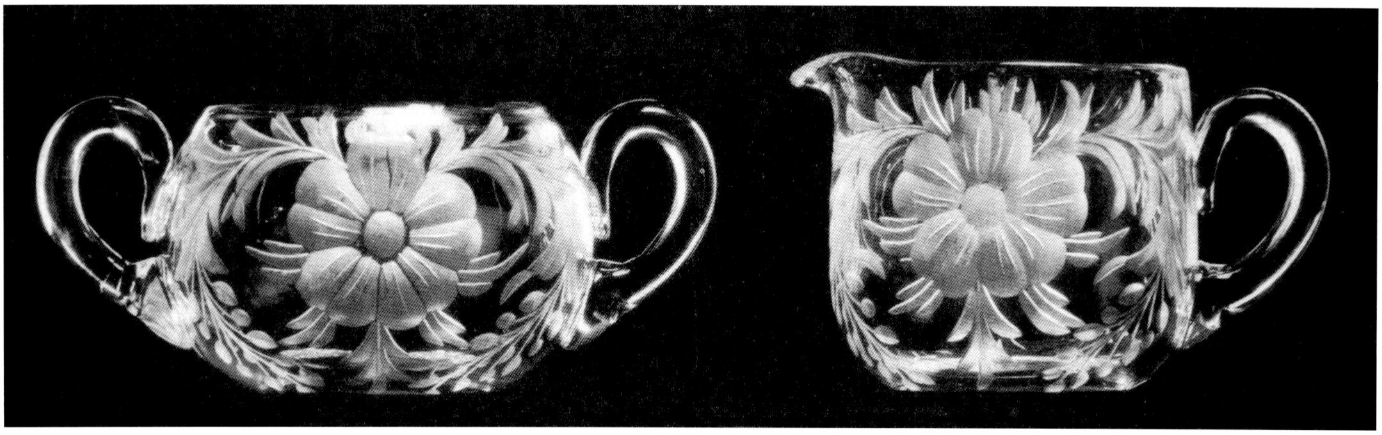

SUGAR & CREAM #1230. *Illustration from a Pairpoint catalog.*

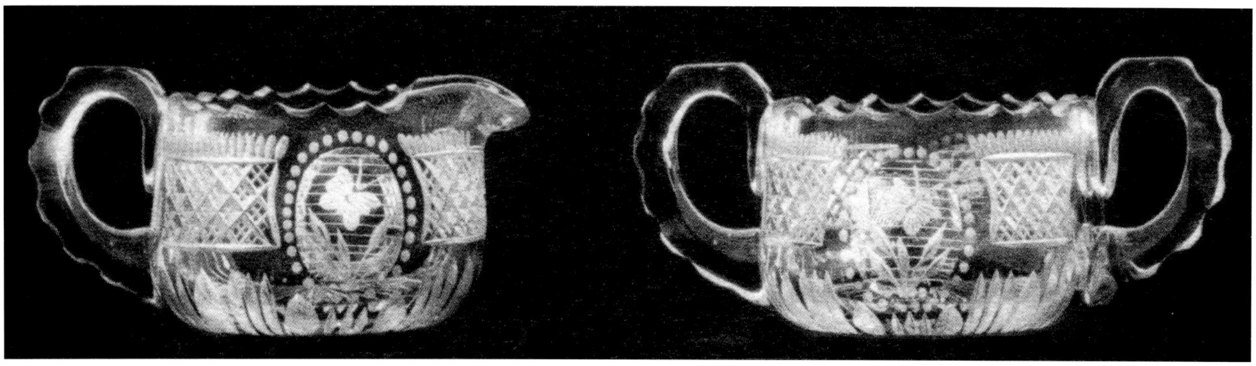

SUGAR & CREAM #1255. *Illustration from a Pairpoint catalog.*

SALT #1301. *Illustration from a Pairpoint catalog.*

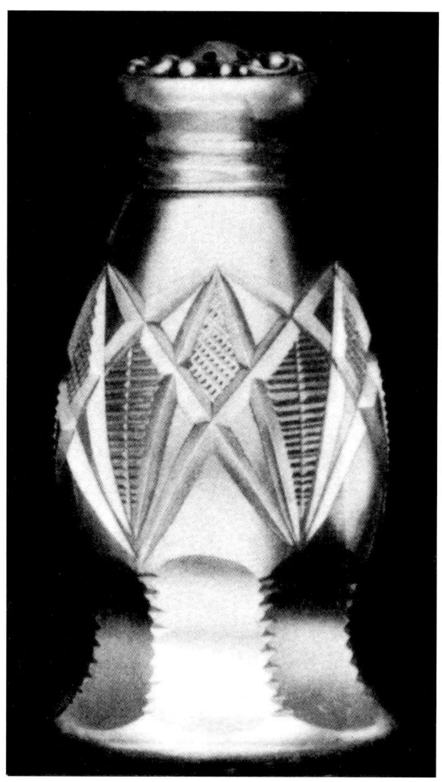

SALT #1302. *Illustration from a Pairpoint catalog.*

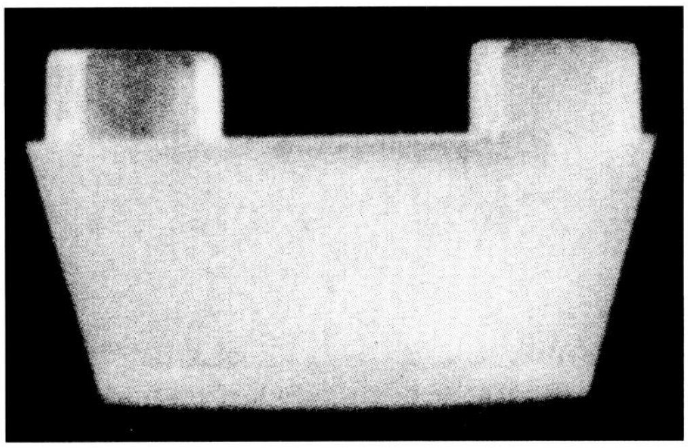

SALT #1303. *Illustration from a Pairpoint catalog.*

SALT #1313, 3.25"h. *Illustration from a Pairpoint catalog.*

SALT #1314, 3.25"h. *Illustration from a Pairpoint catalog.*

SALT #1315, 3.25"h. *Illustration from a Pairpoint catalog.*

SALT #1318. *Illustration from a Pairpoint catalog.*

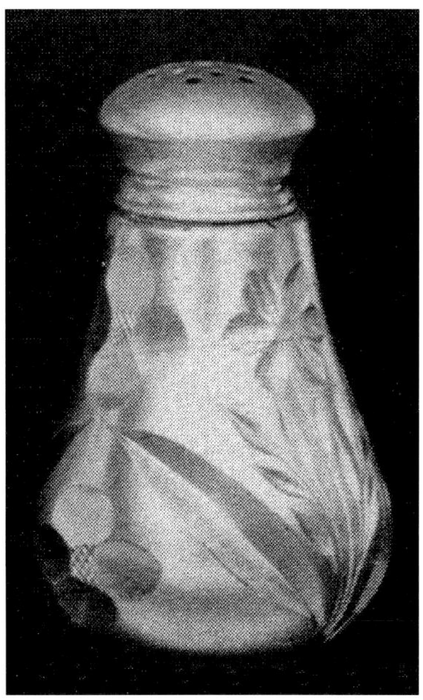

SALT #1319. *Illustration from a Pairpoint catalog.*

BOWL #1342, 5". *Illustration from a Pairpoint catalog.*

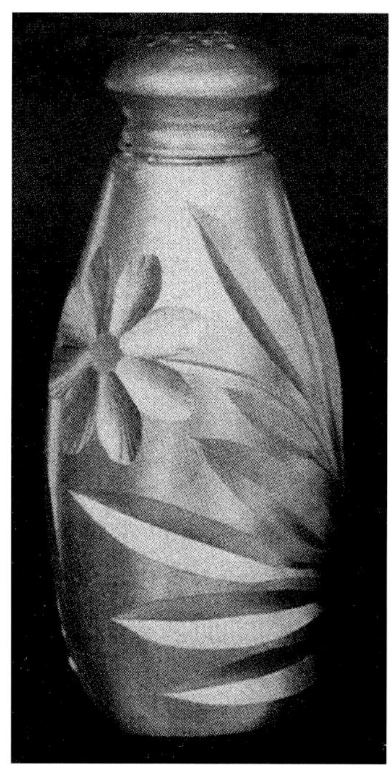

SALT #1369. *Illustration from a Pairpoint catalog.*

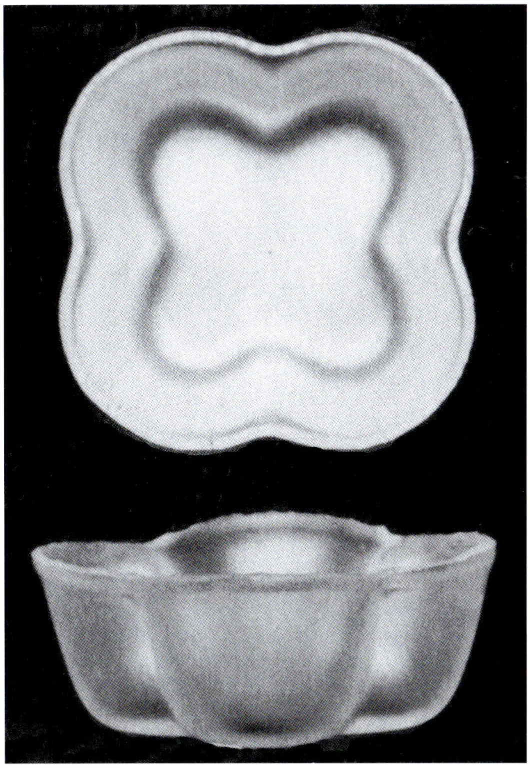

_______ #1387, 7"d x 2.50"h. *Illustration from a Pairpoint catalog.*

SMALL SYRUP #1502, The cap is silver-plated. There is a larger version available. *Illustration from a Pairpoint catalog.*

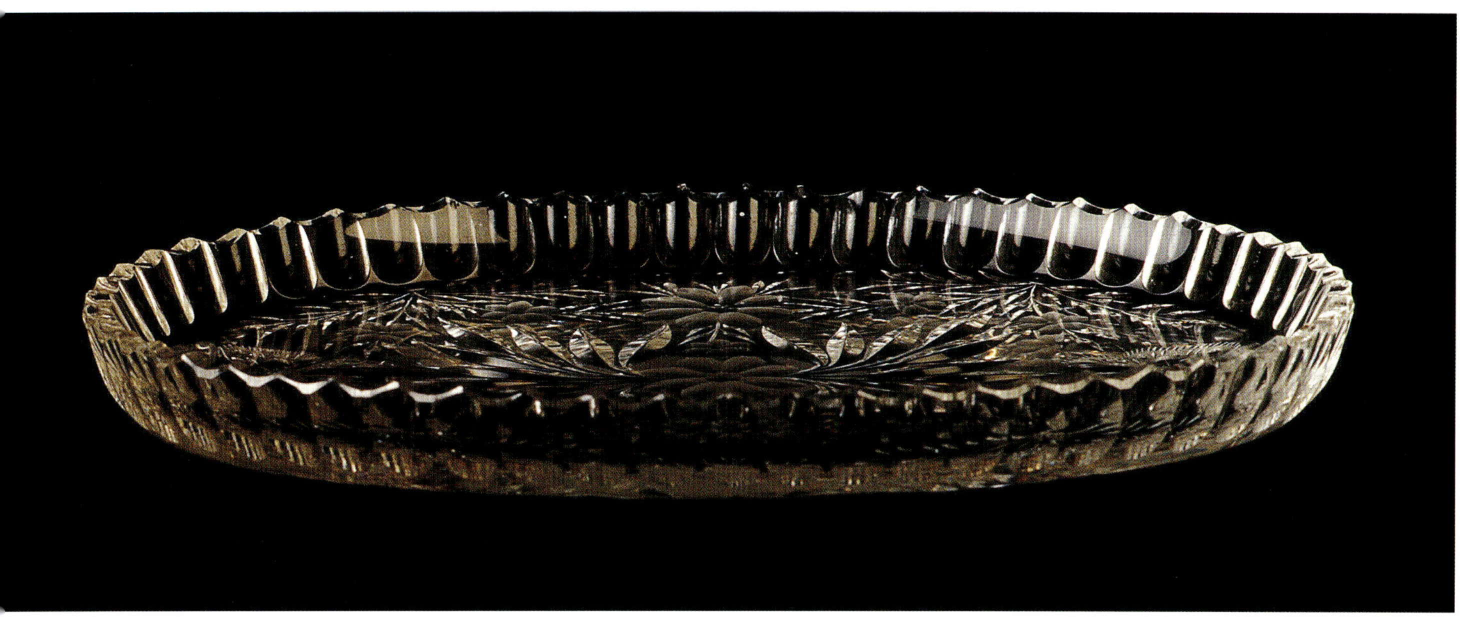

TRAY #1401, Oval, 10" long x 7" wide x 1" high. (This shape was previously identified in *The Essence of Pairpoint* as Unknown 71.)

SMALL CIGAR JAR #1650, 6"h x 4.50"d, 25-Cigar capacity. This is the same style as #1651. *Illustration from a Pairpoint catalog.*
LARGE CIGAR JAR #1651, 7"h x 5.50"d, 50-Cigar capacity. This is the same style as #1650. *Illustration from a Pairpoint catalog.*

JAM JAR #1653. *Illustration from a Pairpoint catalog.*

JAM JAR #1652. *Illustration from a Pairpoint catalog.*

JAM JAR #1654. *Illustration from a Pairpoint catalog.*

JAM JAR #1655. (This shape was previously identified in The Essence of Pairpoint as Unknown 48.) *Illustration from a Pairpoint catalog.*

ASH TRAY #1656. *Illustration from a Pairpoint catalog.*

MIXER #1726, 2-pint. This mixer was used in the Fine Arts Line #07938 frame. (This shape was previously identified in *The Essence of Pairpoint* as Unknown 61.) *Illustration from a Pairpoint catalog.*

MARTINI MIXER #1727, Small (1-pint), Large (1.75-pint). The top was silver-plated. *Illustration from a Pairpoint catalog.*

JUG #3858, 3-pint. (This shape was previously identified in *The Essence of Pairpoint* as Unknown 75.) *Illustration from a Pairpoint catalog.*

GRAPE FRUIT #1753, 7.50"d x 2.375"h.

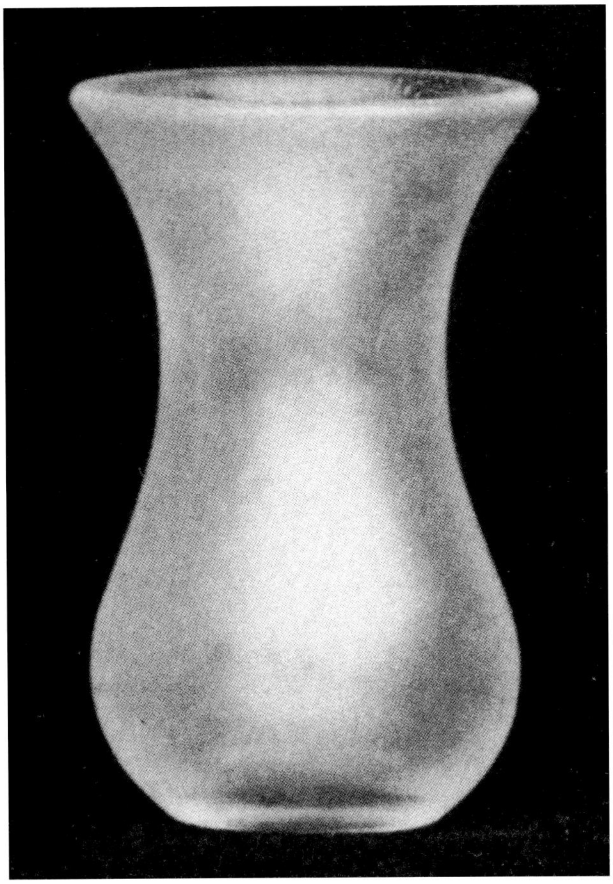

________ #4079, 4.50'h. *Illustration from a Pairpoint catalog.*

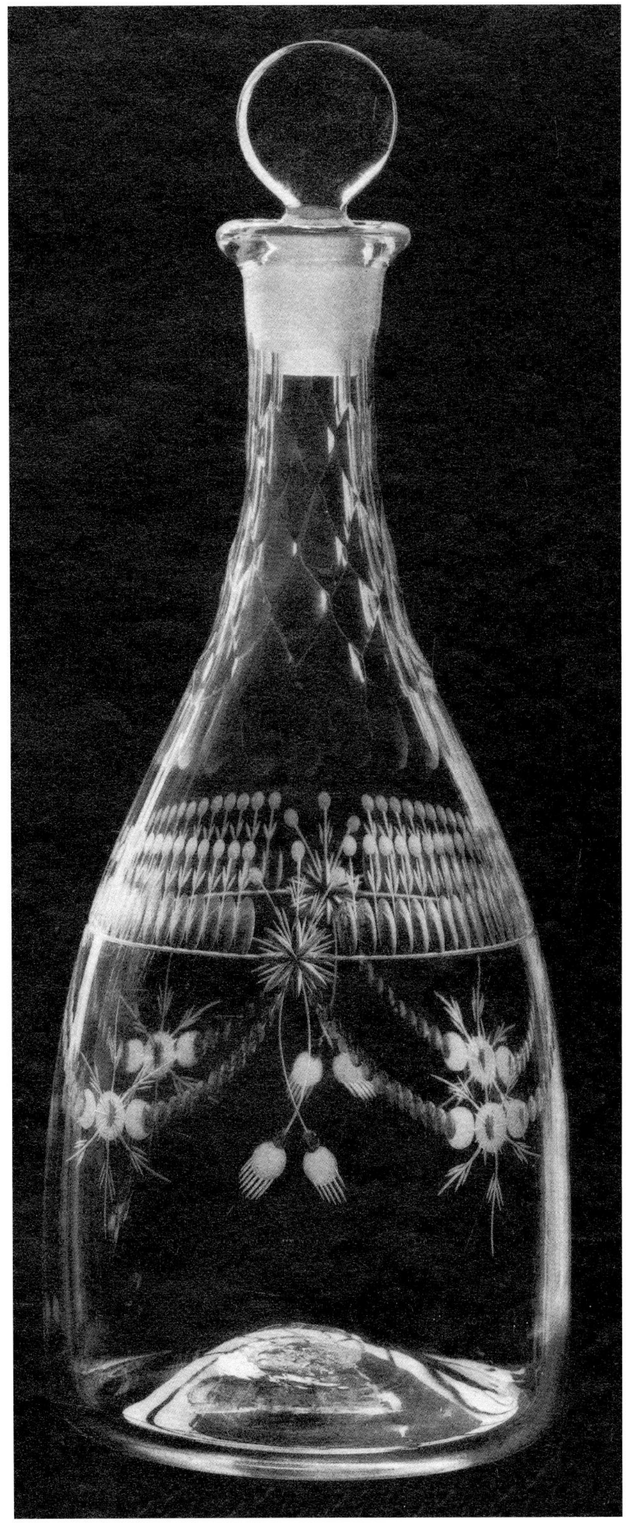

DECANTER #5014, 1-quart. *Illustration from a Pairpoint catalog.*

HANDLED JUG #Unknown 50. *Illustration from a Pairpoint catalog.*

DECANTER #Unknown 60. *Illustration from a Pairpoint catalog.*

COCKTAIL MIXER #Unknown 64, 2.50-pint. *Illustration from a Pairpoint catalog.*

SALAD PLATE #Unknown 65. *Illustration from a Pairpoint catalog.*

FINGER BOWL UNDERPLATE #Unknown 66.

OVAL BOWL #Unknown 70, 8"long x __"wide, 8.50"long x __"wide, 9"long x 6"wide x 1.75"high, 10"long x __"wide.

TUMBLER #Unknown 73, 1/2-pint.

SUGAR and CREAM #Unknown 76.

COVERED RELISH DISH #Unknown 77, 6"d x 3"h, 9"d x 4"h.

CIGARETTE HOLDER
#Unknown 84, 5"h.

OIL #Unknown 99, 6"h.

Cracker Jar #Unknown 114, 7"d x 5.50" to the top of the knob on the lid. *From the collection of Andrew Daniels.*

Handled Tray #Unknown 116, 10"d x 5.50" to top of handle. Expect to find the top of the bubble ball ground and polished where the pontil mark was. Also the bottom of the tray has a ground and polished pontil. *Previously in the collection of Ginny Griffith.*

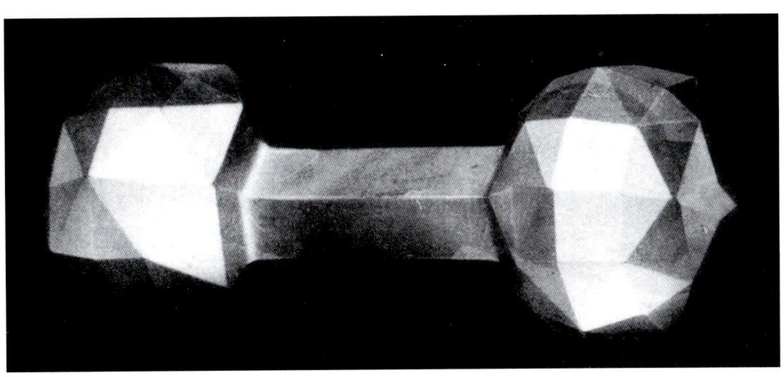

KNIFE REST, Large Size, Small Size, 3.50" Size. *Illustration from a Pairpoint catalog.*

CHEESE PLATE & COVER, 5" Cover w/8" Plate, 6" Cover w/9" Plate, 7" Cover w/10" Plate. *Illustration from a Pairpoint catalog.*

Stemware

GOBLET #130. *Illustration from a Pairpoint catalog.*

GOBLET #150. *Illustration from a Pairpoint catalog.*

GOBLET #140.5. *Illustration from a Pairpoint catalog.*

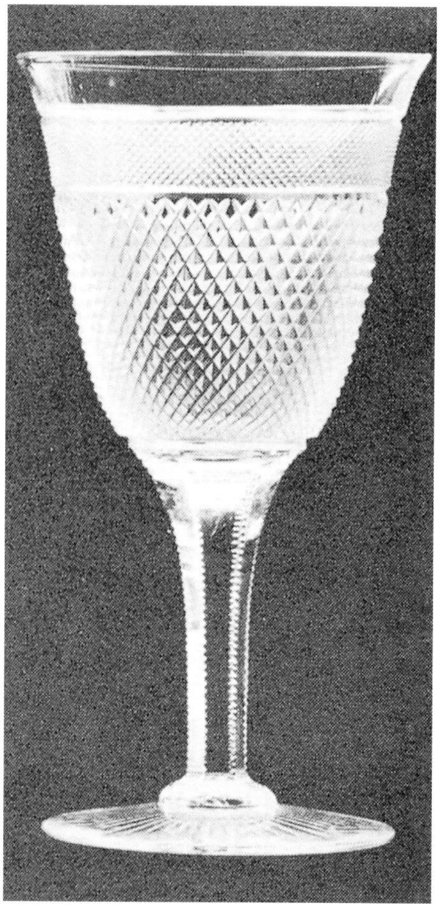

GOBLET #156. *Illustration from a Pairpoint catalog.*

SHERBET #161. *Illustration from a Pairpoint catalog.*

SAUCER CHAMPAGNE #175.

GOBLET #170. *Illustration from a Pairpoint catalog.*

GOBLET #184. *Illustration from a Pairpoint catalog.*

COCKTAIL #1072.

WINE #5015. *Illustration from a Pairpoint catalog.*

Left: GOBLET #5000 Nantucket-Style with round foot.
Right: GOBLET #5000 Yarmouth-Style with square foot.

GOBLET #Unknown 52.
Illustration from a Pairpoint catalog.

GOBLET #Unknown 55.
Illustration from a Pairpoint catalog.

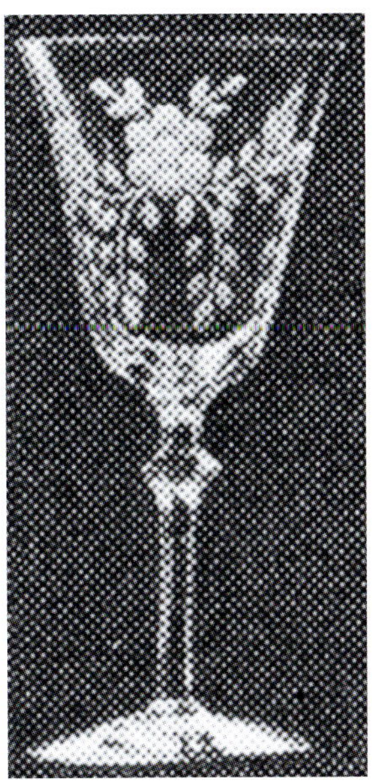

GOBLET #Unknown 54.
Illustration from a Pairpoint catalog.

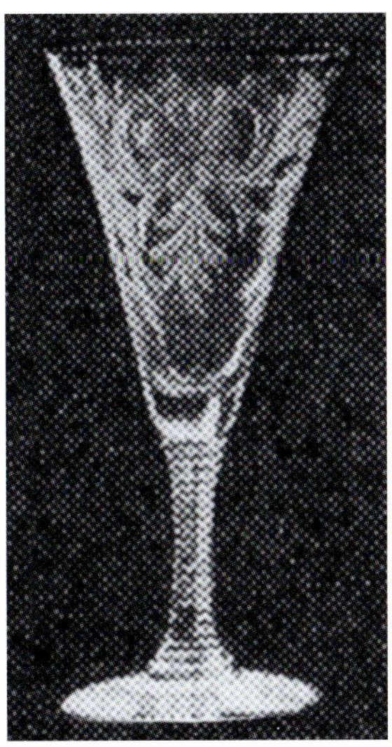

GOBLET #Unknown 56.
Illustration from a Pairpoint catalog.

BRANDY & SODA #Unknown 57.

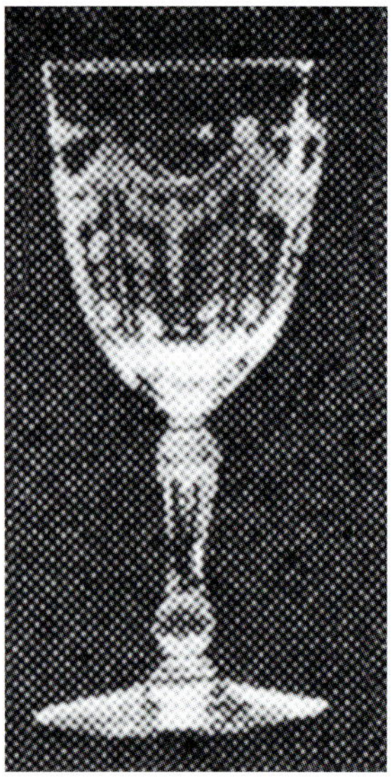

GOBLET #Unknown 58.
Illustration from a Pairpoint catalog.

GOBLET #Unknown 62.
Illustration from a Pairpoint catalog.

GOBLET #Unknown 72.

GOBLET #Unknown 59.
Illustration from a Pairpoint catalog.

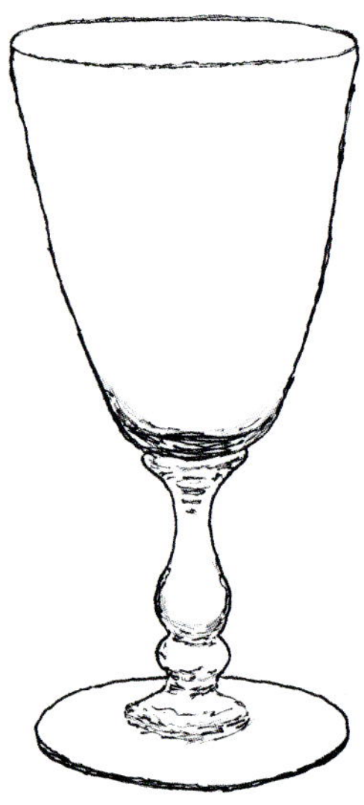

GOBLET #Unknown 74. Author's sketch.

Miscellaneous Items

SMALL CLOCK #946, 5"h x 4"w. *Illustration from a Pairpoint catalog.*

LARGE CLOCK #947, 8"h x 5.75"w. *Illustration from a Pairpoint catalog.*

DOOR KNOBS #Unknown 78.

Chapter 3
Pairpoint Decorating Patterns

The patterns that are presented within this chapter come primarily from the period of time after World War I. They are typically referred to as being of the lighter engraving style that became popular as the "Brilliant Era" drew to a close. While we are certain that more engraving patterns exist, we think that the majority are represented here. Some of these patterns, known to have been engraved/cut post-WWI, have their genesis in the few years preceding the war, a time frame often, but unofficially, referred to as the transitional period.

Our study does not include this transitional period, but the collector will occasionally find engraved items from this time. We believe that knowledge of the existence of this transitional period is necessary to explain that which

TRANSITIONAL PATTERN - SAMPLE #1

TRANSITIONAL PATTERN - SAMPLE #2

TRANSITIONAL PATTERN - SAMPLE #3

the collector will discover in his travels. As the "Brilliant Era" was coming to an end, the public interest in engraved decoration on glass was already forming. This new engraved form of decoration was generally focused upon natural subjects, primarily floral motifs. The use of butterflies was extremely popular also. Initially, Pairpoint (and other companies as well) incorporated engraved floral design elements within the deep cut geometrical patterns associated with the "Brilliant Era." As time passed, engraved designs became the predominant theme, and the geometric designs were all but discontinued. Eventually, except for perhaps special orders or matching work, the geometric designs were limited to the occasional starburst design under an item's foot.

The engraving designs and workmanship from this transitional period are unsurpassed in Pairpoint's history. Characterized by deep three-dimensional cutting/engraving on thick blanks in exquisite detail with magnificent polishing work, once seen, the collector will be able to recognize Pairpoint's work anywhere. These patterns are stunningly beautiful! The transitional patterns, with names such as "Butterfly and Daisy," "Silsbee," "Anemone," "Cactus," and "Thistle," to name a few, are clearly the prototypical ancestors of the engraving patterns that immediately followed the war. When one looks at patterns such as "Murillo," "Viscaria," "Garland," or "Arbutus," for example, the parentage cannot be denied.

SPECIAL NOTATION: Since the publication of *The Essence of Pairpoint*, we have reasonably determined that three of the engraving patterns we designated as "Unknown" are most likely not of Pairpoint origin. These patterns were identified as "Unknown G," "Unknown K," and "Unknown M." With regard to patterns "Unknown G" and "Unknown M," we do not believe the design elements to be consistent with Pairpoint's style of engraving. The pattern identified as "Unknown K" has been seen on other shapes that are clearly not of Pairpoint origin, but are of Pairpoint quality. Very similar to Pairpoint's Glenmore pattern, we think this design was done by one of Pairpoint's contemporaries.

TRANSITIONAL PATTERN - SAMPLE #4

ADELAIDE DESIGN.

ALBEMARLE. *Illustration from a Pairpoint catalog.*

ALBA. *Illustration from a Pairpoint catalog.*

ANNETTE

APPLES. Has also been designated as pattern No. 134. *Illustration from a Pairpoint catalog.*

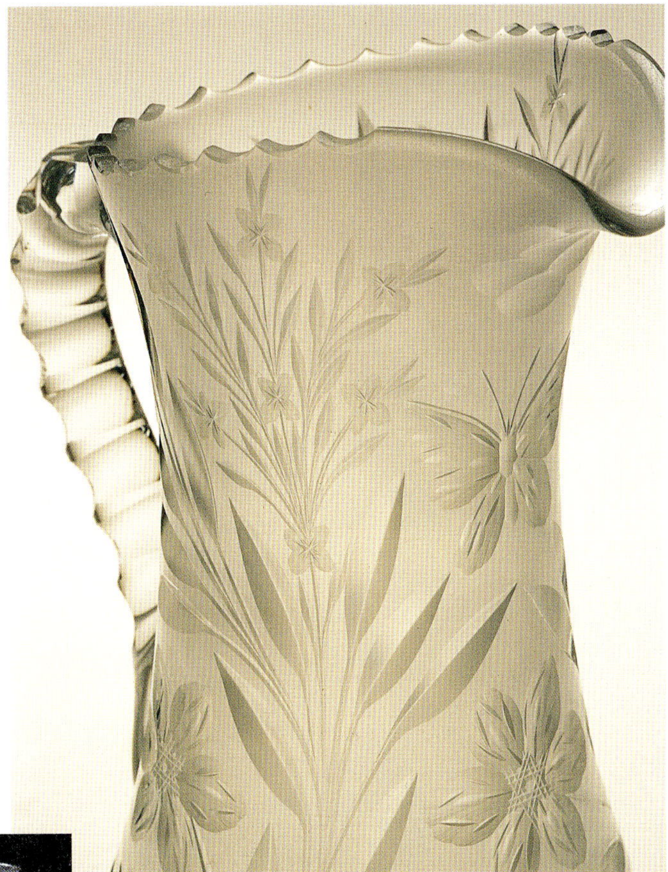

ARBUTUS

ARDSLEY. This is a very rare pattern and, from our observations, is only found on blanks that have been specifically blown with a spiraling optic in clear glass for this pattern. The combination of the complicated engraving over the spiral optic gives the appearance of elegant "carving." The look is unique and very elegant. *Illustration from a Pairpoint catalog.*

ASBURY

ASHLAND. *Illustration from a Pairpoint catalog.*

BARON

BALTIC

BARRINGTON DESIGN. *Illustration from a Pairpoint catalog.*

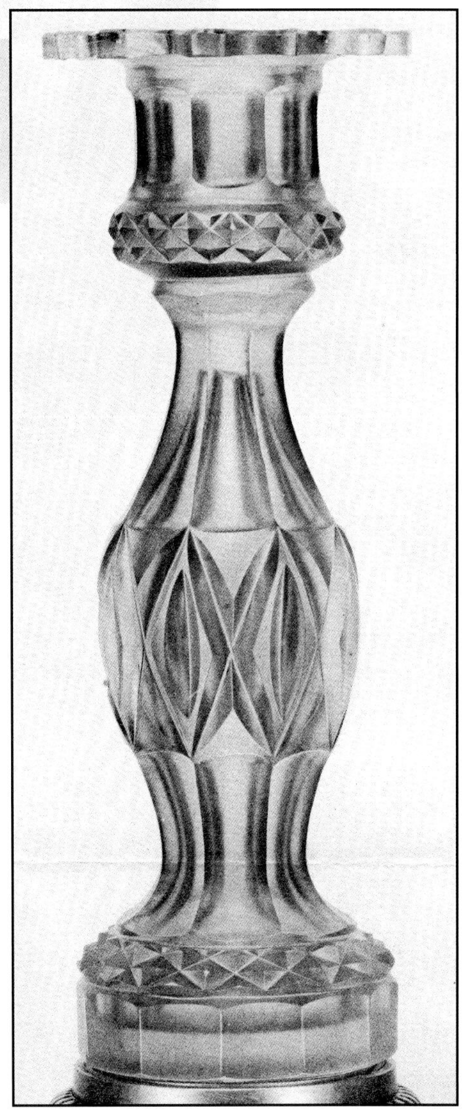

BEAUMONT DESIGN. *Illustration from a Pairpoint catalog.*

BEDMINSTER. No image has yet been matched to this documented pattern name.

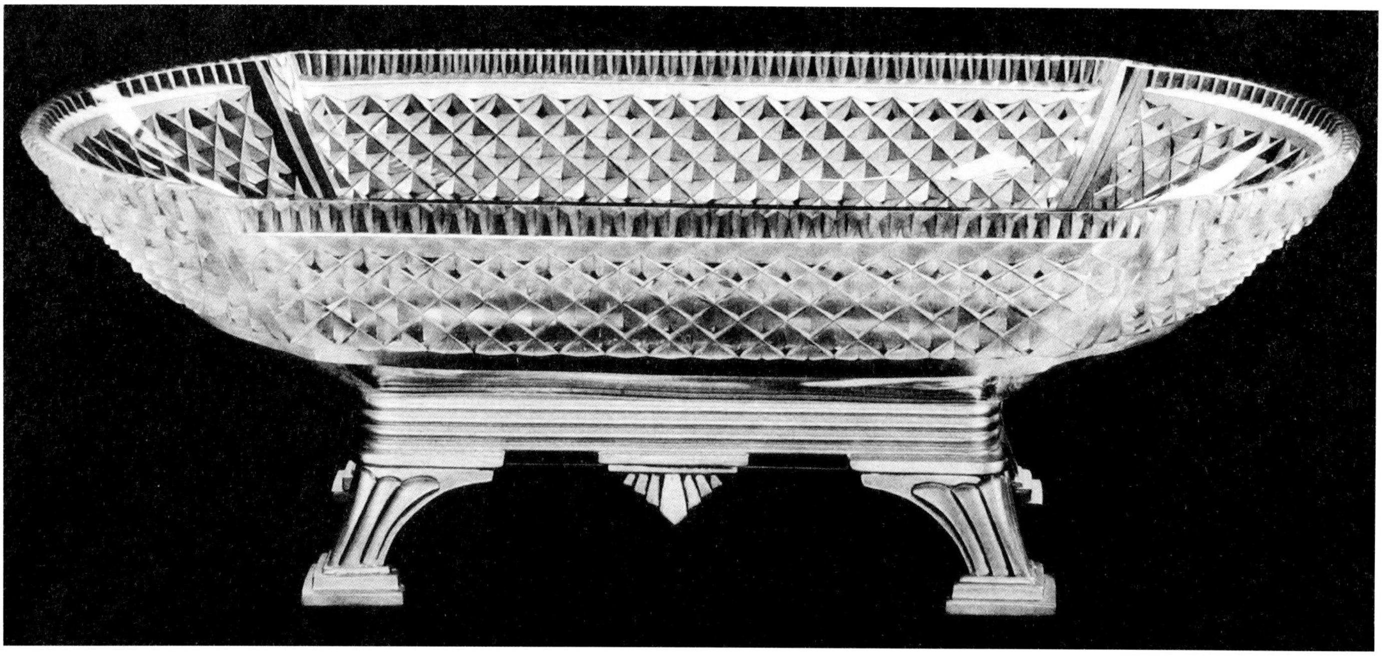

BELFAST. *Illustration from a Pairpoint catalog.*

BELLEVUE DESIGN. This pattern has only been identified with Rosaria-colored cut-to-clear items in factory documentation, but we have seen it in clear crystal. *Illustration from a Pairpoint catalog.*

BELVEDERE

BINGHAM. *Illustration from a Pairpoint catalog.*

BLOCK DIAMOND. *Illustration from a Pairpoint catalog.*

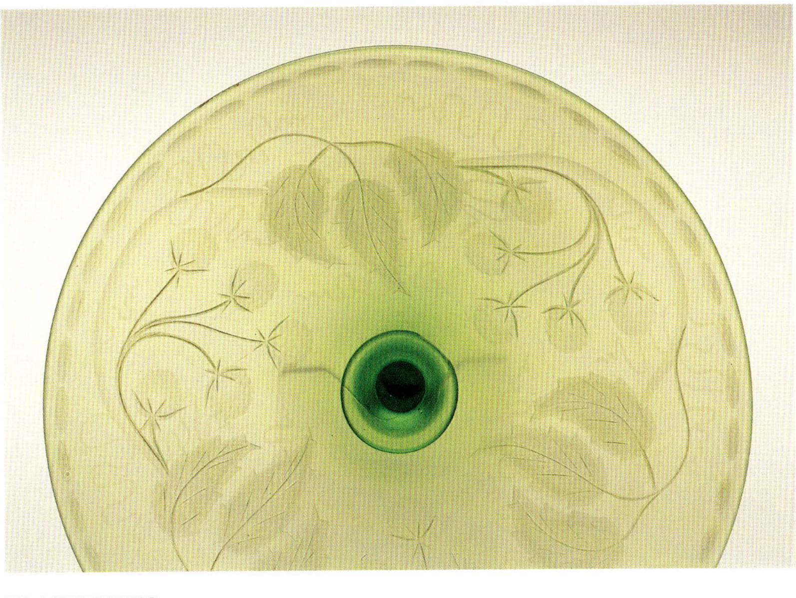

BLACKBERRY

BOMBAY. *Illustration from a Pairpoint catalog.*

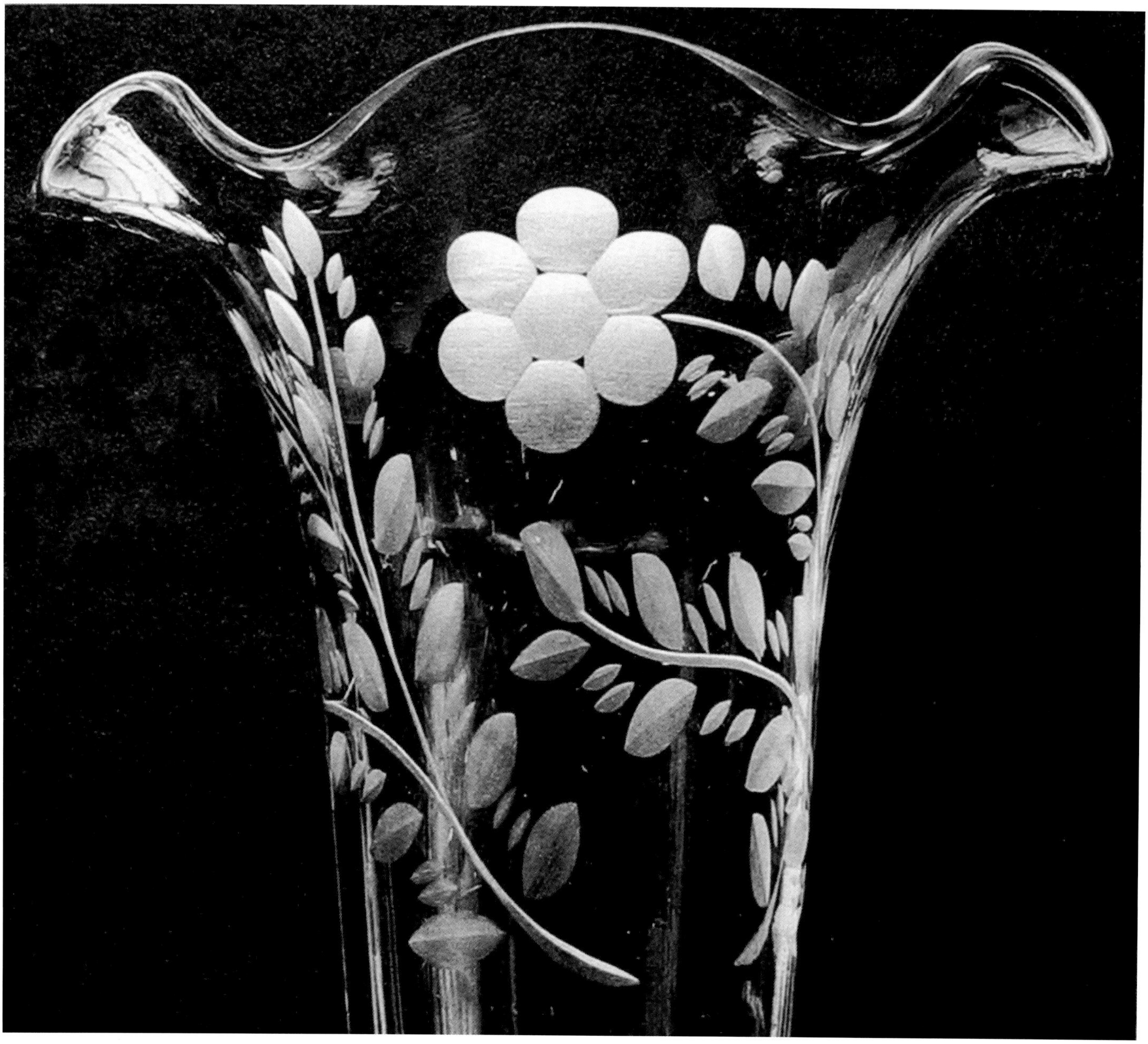

BOSWELL. *Illustration from a Pairpoint catalog.*

BRADFORD. *Illustration from a Pairpoint catalog.*

BRILLIANT

BUCKINGHAM DESIGN. *Illustration from a Pairpoint catalog.*

BUCHANAN

BURGOYNE. *Illustration from a Pairpoint catalog.*

CEDAR. *Illustration from a Pairpoint catalog.*

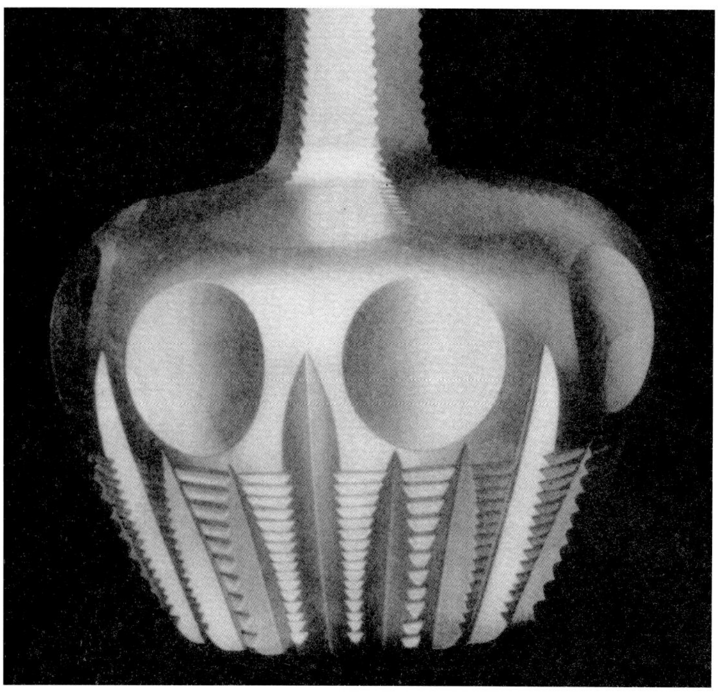

CAMBRIDGE. *Illustration from a Pairpoint catalog.*

CHELSEA. *Illustration from a Pairpoint catalog.*

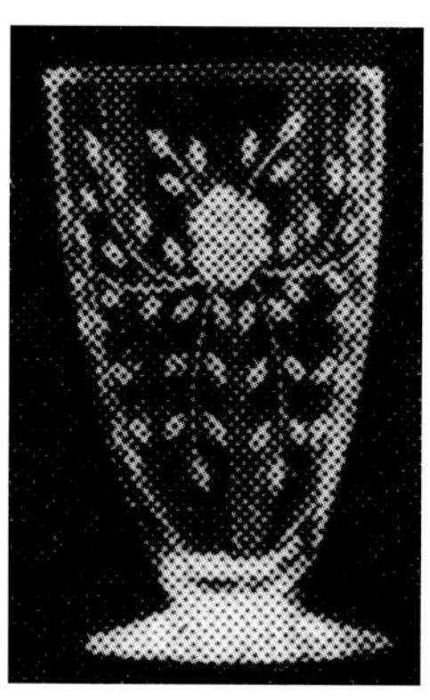

CAROL. *Illustration from a Pairpoint catalog.*

CLARINA

CLARKSON. *Illustration from a Pairpoint catalog.*

CLEVELAND. *Illustration from a Pairpoint catalog.*

COLERIDGE. *Illustration from a Pairpoint catalog.*

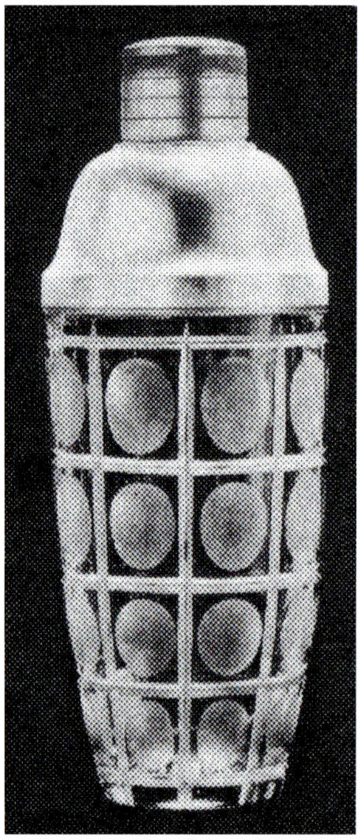

CLYDE. *Illustration from a Pairpoint catalog.*

COLIAS. Occasionally this pattern will be found on Pairpoint blanks with the spider web omitted.

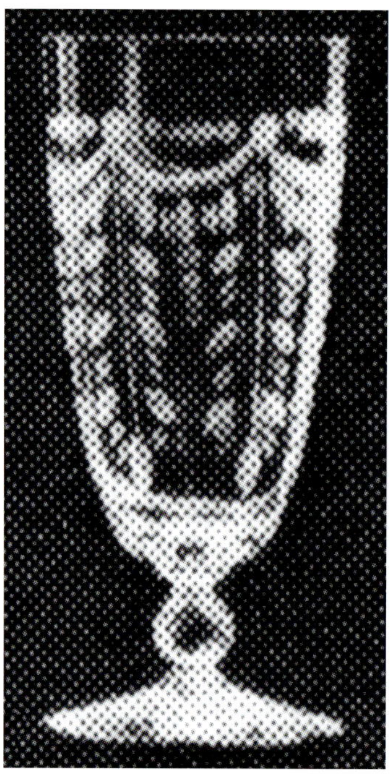

COBURN. *Illustration from a Pairpoint catalog.*

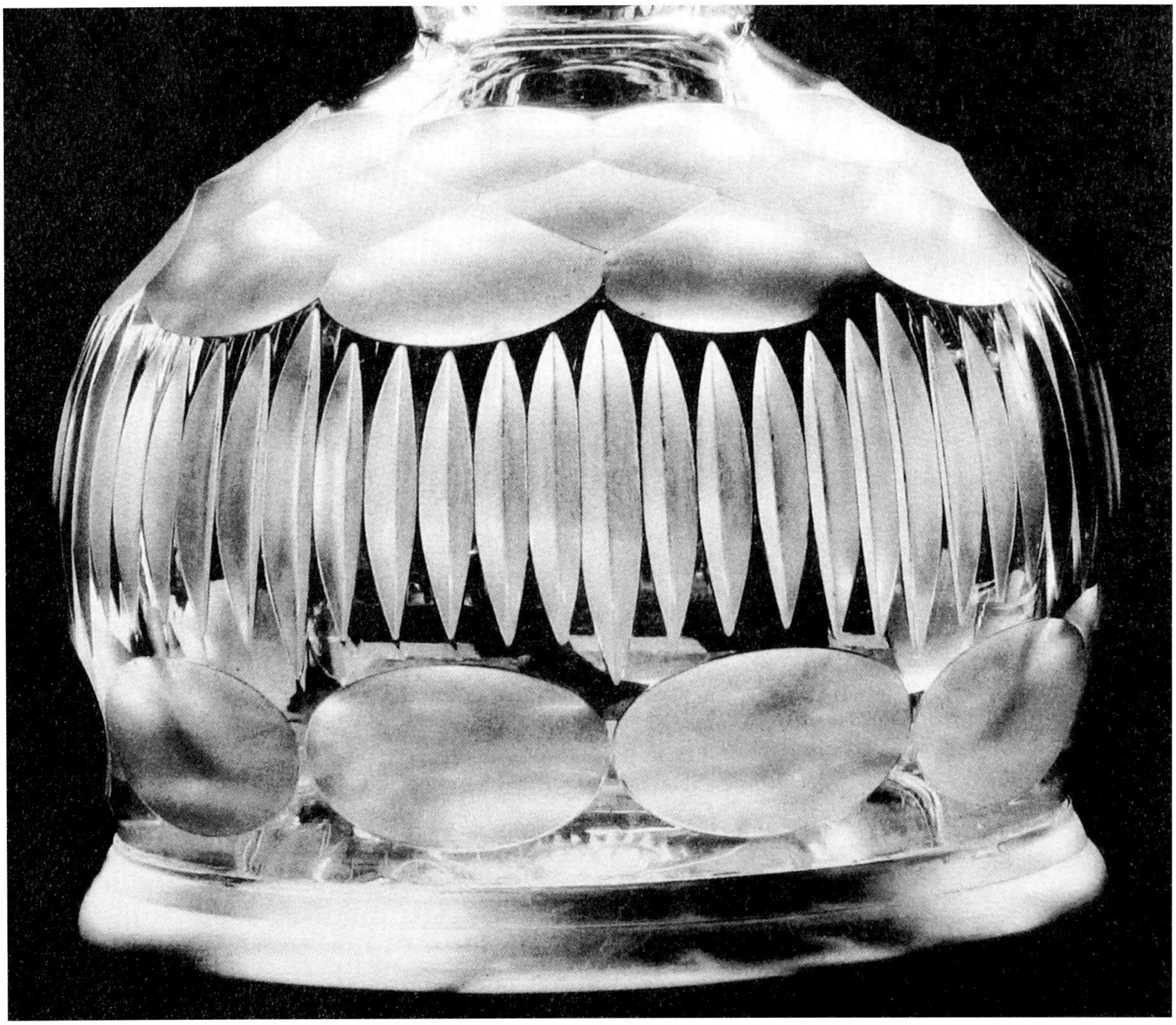

COLONEL. *Illustration from a Pairpoint catalog.*

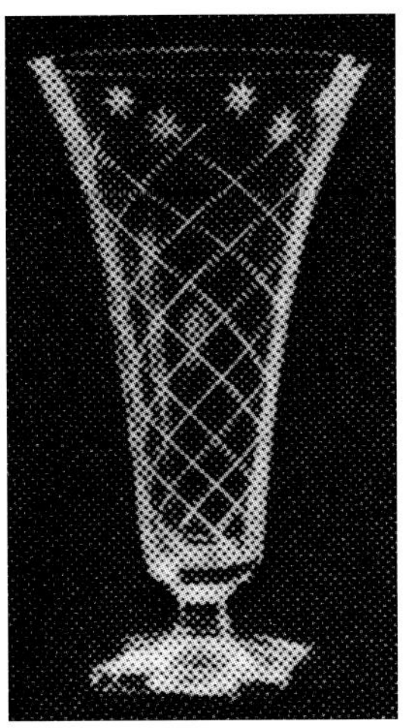

COMET. *Illustration from a Pairpoint catalog.*

CORNWALL. *Illustration from a Pairpoint catalog.*

CORONAL (with festooning)

CUT. *Illustration from a Pairpoint catalog.*

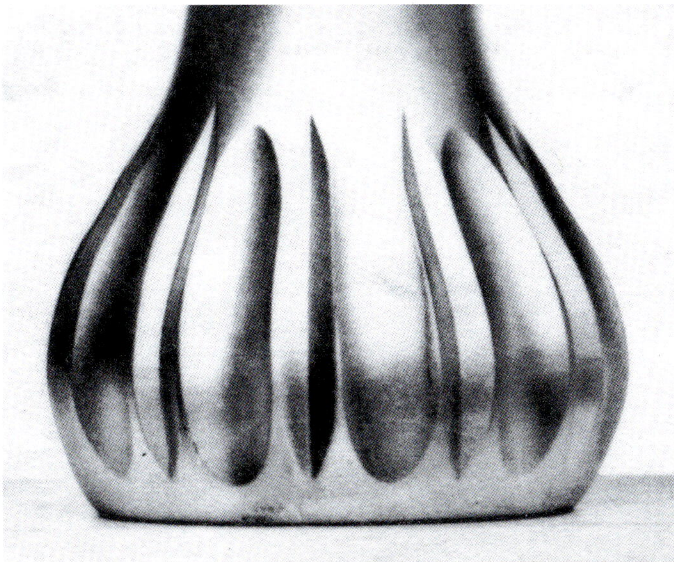

DAISY. *Illustration from a Pairpoint catalog.*

DARLINGTON. This pattern is virtually identical to Gladstone except it incorporates a Rosaria cut-to-clear cross-hatch band.

DELDEN DESIGN. This pattern is very complicated and contains many design elements. It will be most commonly found on the Fine Arts Line #4970 cigarette holder, which has a small cylindrical glass cup mounted atop a silver-plated cherub base. When applied to this small item, most of the design elements will be omitted. *Illustration from a Pairpoint catalog.*

DENMARK

DERBYSHIRE. *Illustration from a Pairpoint catalog.*

DEW DROP DESIGN No. 218

DUNMORE DESIGN. *Illustration from a Pairpoint catalog.*

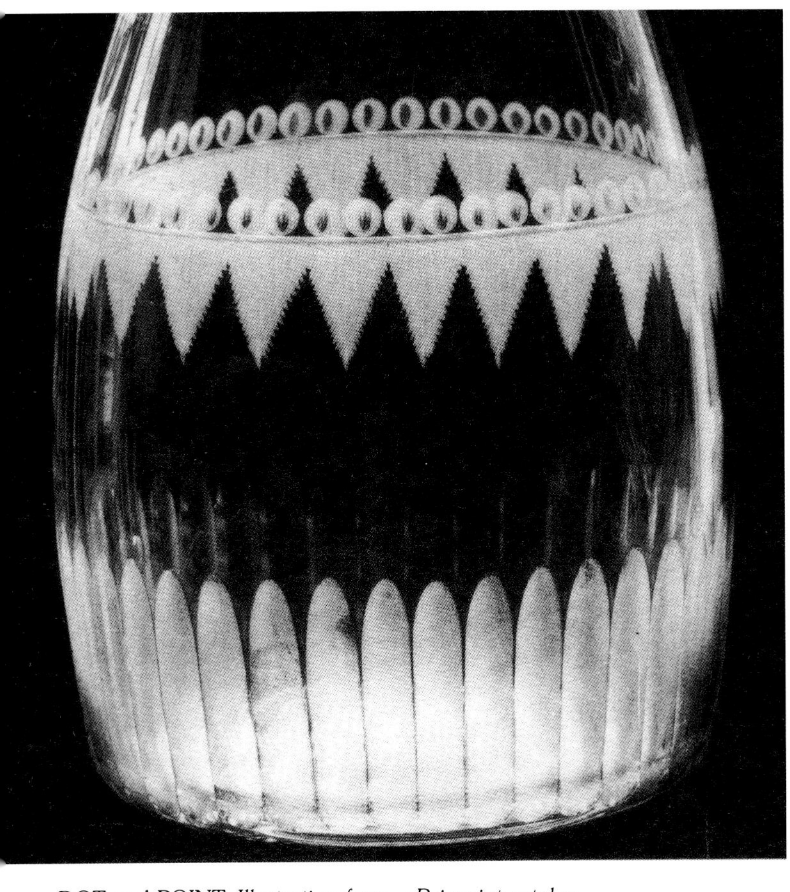

DOT and POINT. *Illustration from a Pairpoint catalog.*

DUXBURY. *Illustration from a Pairpoint catalog.*

ENGLISH DESIGN. *Illustration from a Pairpoint catalog.*

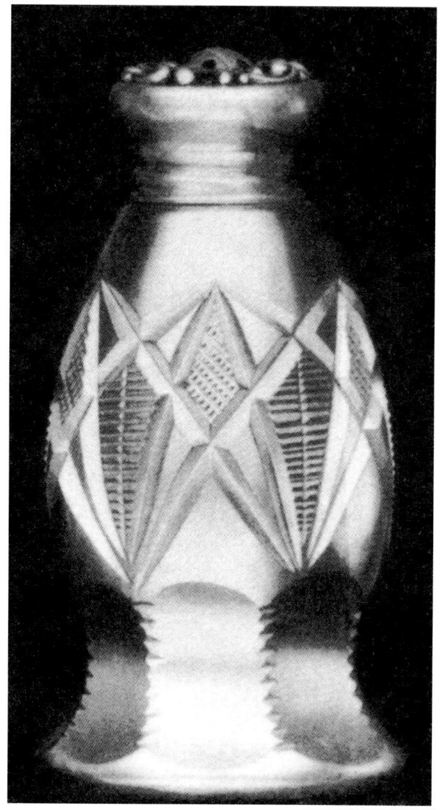

FANCY. *Illustration from a Pairpoint catalog.*

ENGRAVED WREATH. *Illustration from a Pairpoint catalog.*

FLORENTINE. (This shape was previously identified in *The Essence of Pairpoint* as Unknown J.) The Florentine pattern will almost always be seen on the colored edge and trim pieces, but has been seen on solid-color Canaria items from the 1920s and 1930s. When this pattern is engraved on some of the smaller blanks, the "fern" component may be omitted. This pattern name was recycled by Pairpoint, because it was originally used to name a heavy cut pattern from the "Brilliant Era." *Illustration from a Pairpoint catalog.*

FLUTE and RINGS. *Illustration from a Pairpoint catalog.*

GAINSBOROUGH. *Illustration from a Pairpoint catalog.*

FLUTES & MITRE

GARDENIA. Upon first glance this pattern could easily be mistaken for Clarina. *Illustration from a Pairpoint catalog.*

GARLAND

GEM. *Illustration from a Pairpoint catalog.*

GEORGIAN. *Illustration from a Pairpoint catalog.*

GLADSTONE. This pattern is virtually identical to the Darlington pattern except that it does not utilize the Rosaria cut-to-clear rim band.

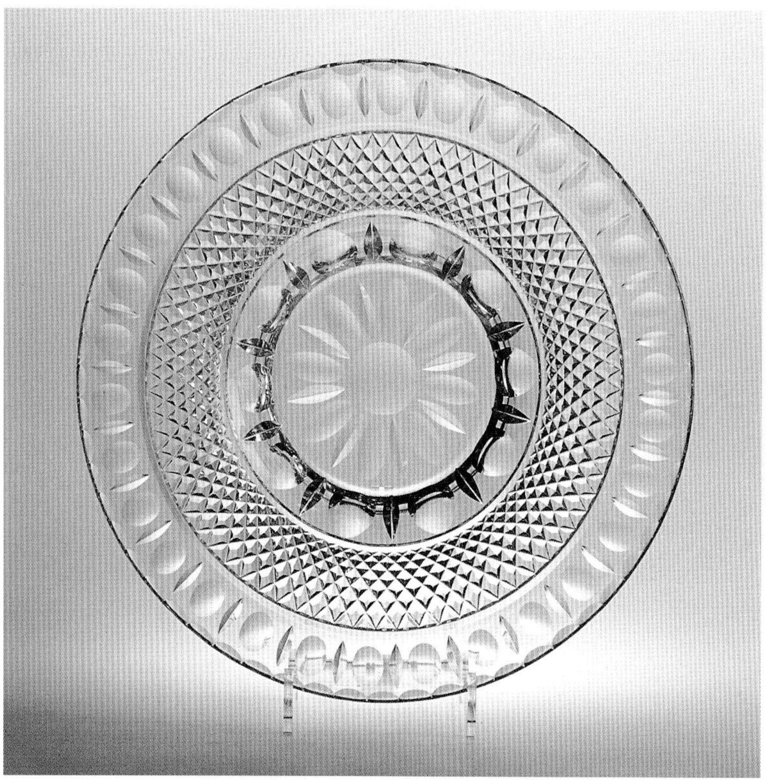

GLENMORE

GLOUCESTER. *Illustration from a Pairpoint catalog.*

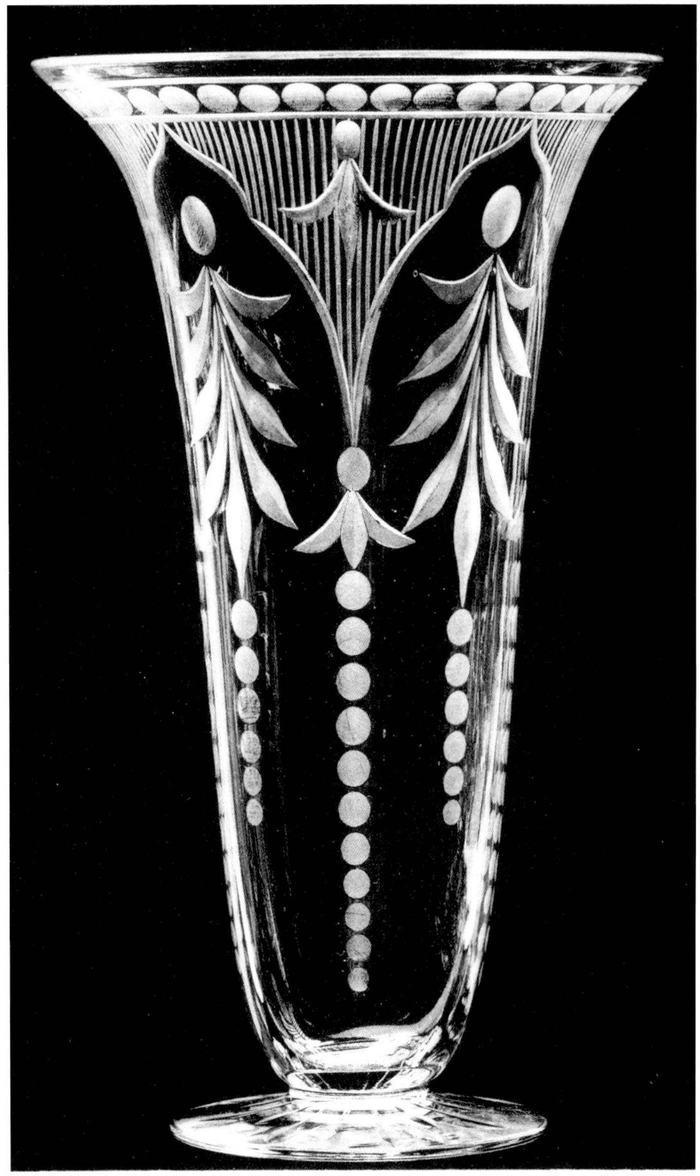

GOODWIN. *Illustration from a Pairpoint catalog.*

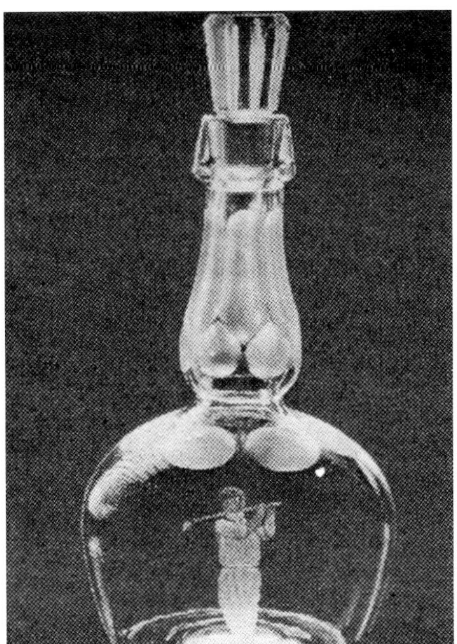

GOLFER. *Illustration from a Pairpoint catalog.*

GOTHIC. *Illustration from a Pairpoint catalog.*

GRAHAM. *Illustration from a Pairpoint catalog.*

GRAPE DESIGN. On multiple occasions, we have seen this Pairpoint pattern on various Fostoria shapes. However, in each and every instance, the grape "stems" were omitted. *Illustration from a Pairpoint catalog.*

GRECIAN. *Illustration from a Pairpoint catalog.*

GREGORY. *Illustration from a Pairpoint catalog.*

GREYLOCK. *Illustration from a Pairpoint catalog.*

GUILFORD. *Illustration from a Pairpoint catalog.*

HAMPTON

HANOVER. *Illustration from a Pairpoint catalog.*

HARWICH. *Illustration from a Pairpoint catalog.*

HIBISCUS. *Illustration from a Pairpoint catalog.*

HEMPSTEAD DESIGN. (This shape was previously identified in *The Essence of Pairpoint* as Unknown C.) *Illustration from a Pairpoint catalog.*

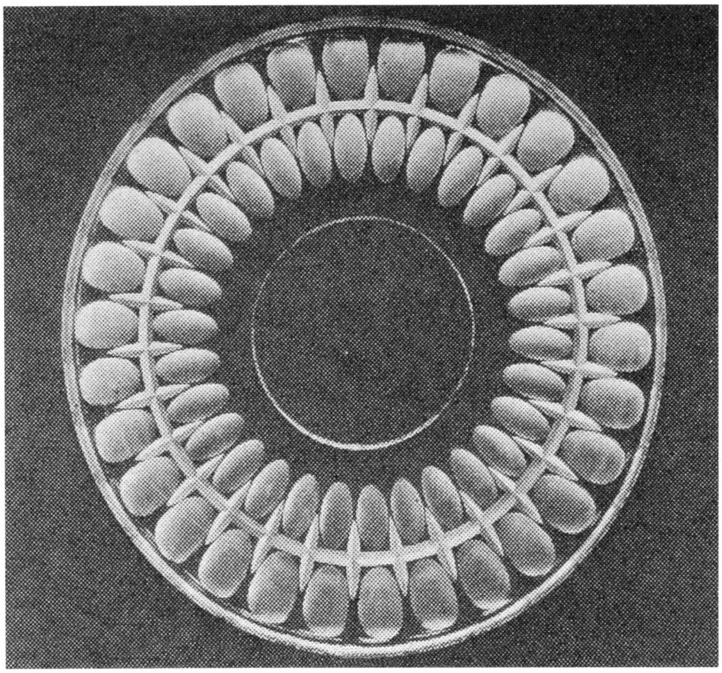

HOLLOW & SPLIT. *Illustration from a Pairpoint catalog.*

KENTWOOD DESIGN. *Illustration from a Pairpoint catalog.*

KENT. *Illustration from a Pairpoint catalog.*

LAPIDARY. *Illustration from a Pairpoint catalog.*

LEXINGTON. *Illustration from a Pairpoint catalog.*

LINCOLN

LINDFIELD. *Illustration from a Pairpoint catalog.*

MALDEN ("recycled" name from the "Brilliant Era") *Illustration from a Pairpoint catalog.*

MANSFIELD DESIGN. *Illustration from a Pairpoint catalog.*

MALDEN (early heavy-cut pattern from the "Brilliant Era")

MARQUIS. *Illustration from a Pairpoint catalog.*

MAYFAIR

MELROSE. *Illustration from a Pairpoint catalog.*

MITRE. *Illustration from a Pairpoint catalog.*

MODERNE. *Illustration from a Pairpoint catalog.*

MONROE. *Illustration from a Pairpoint catalog.*

MORGAN. (This shape was previously identified in *The Essence of Pairpoint* as Unknown N.)

MURILLO

NO.33

NO.35. No image has yet been matched to this documented pattern name.

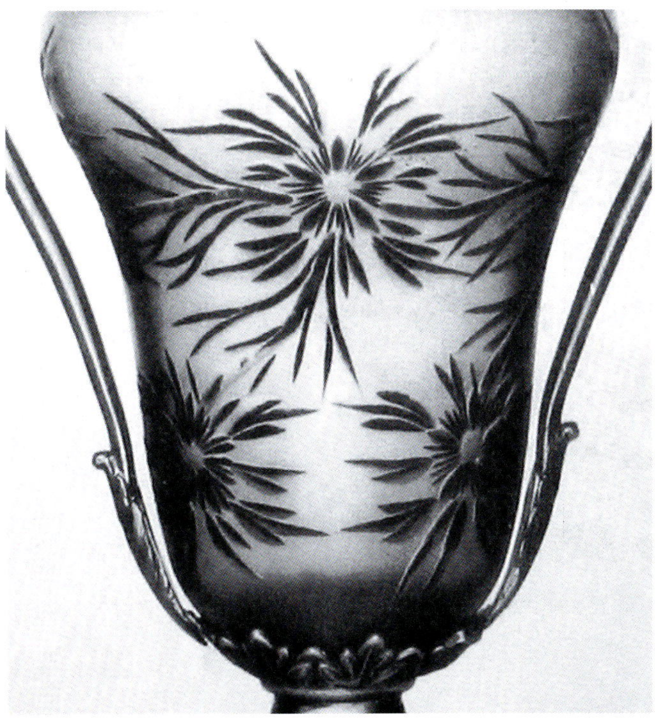

NO.81. Do not confuse with patterns Unknown 0 or Unknown AG. *Illustration from a Pairpoint catalog.*

NO.136

NO.129. *Illustration from a Pairpoint catalog.*

NO.137 (?). Identical to No. 137, but with added scalloped border feature. (This shape was previously identified in *The Essence of Pairpoint* as Unknown D.)

NO.151. *Illustration from a Pairpoint catalog.*

NO.154

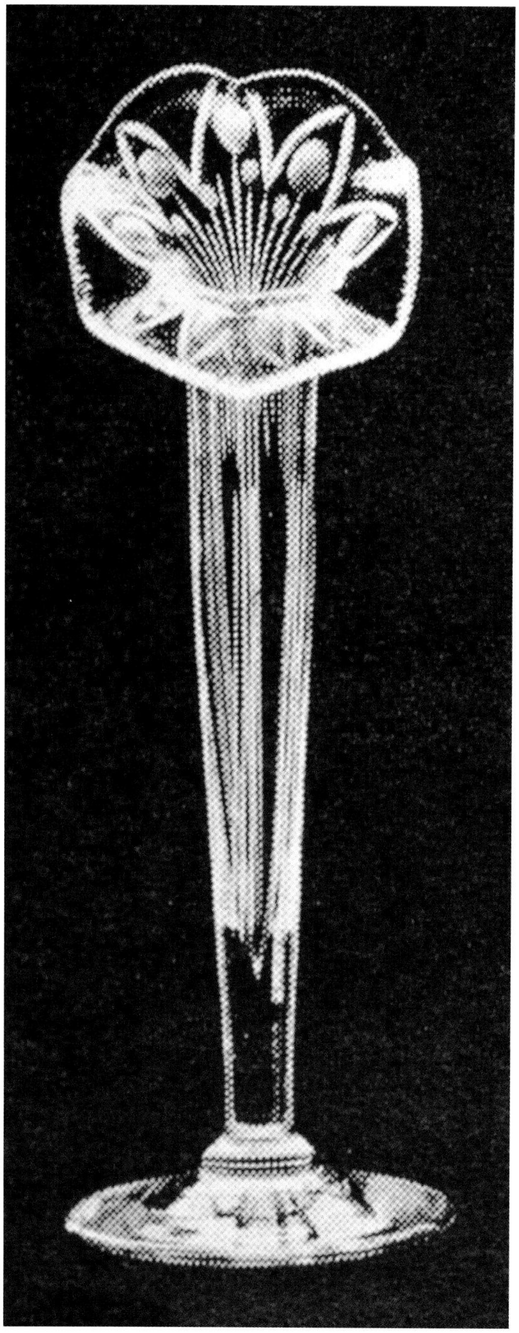

NO.160. *Illustration from a Pairpoint catalog.*

NO.192. *Illustration from a Pairpoint catalog.*

NO.195. *Illustration from a Pairpoint catalog.*

NO.187. *Illustration from a Pairpoint catalog.*

NO.246. *Illustration from a Pairpoint catalog.*

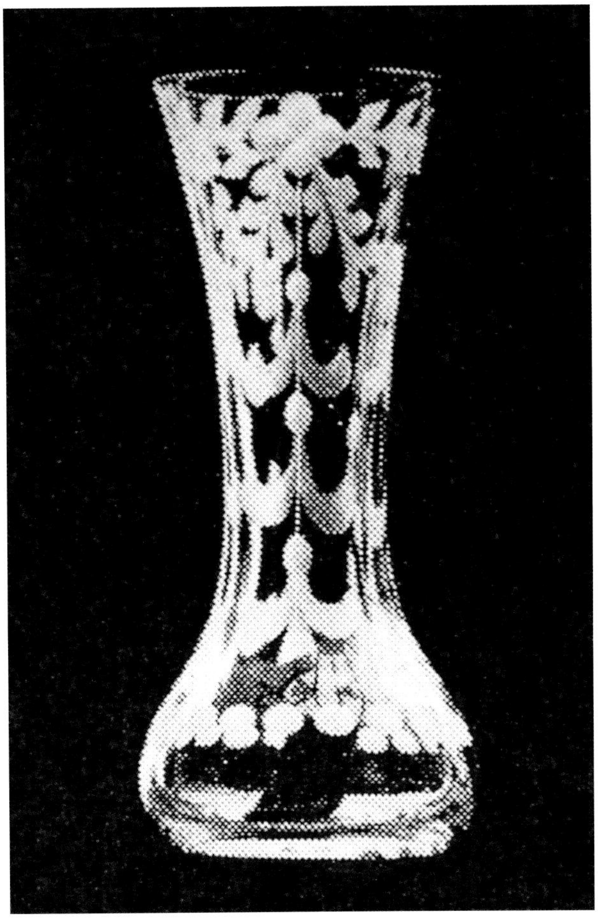

NO.196. *Illustration from a Pairpoint catalog.*

NO.247. *Illustration from a Pairpoint* catalog.

NO.218. No image has yet been matched to this documented pattern name.

NO.235. No image has yet been matched to this documented pattern name.

NO.258. *Illustration from a Pairpoint catalog.*

NO.259. *Illustration from a Pairpoint catalog.*

NO.6280. *Illustration from a Pairpoint catalog.*

NO.263 No image has yet been matched to this documented pattern name.

NO.264. No image has yet been matched to this documented pattern name.

NORFOLK. Upon occasion this pattern will be legitimately found with the tulip component omitted. *Illustration from a Pairpoint catalog.*

OLD COLONY. *Illustration from a Pairpoint catalog.*

OPERA. *Illustration from a Pairpoint catalog.*

NOTTINGHAM

OSIRIS DESIGN. *Illustration from a Pairpoint catalog.*

PATCH DIAMOND. *Illustration from a Pairpoint catalog.*

PLAIN (or CUT) FLUTES.

PLYMOUTH. *Illustration from a Pairpoint catalog.*

POLAR BEAR

PRINCESS. *Illustration from a Pairpoint catalog.*

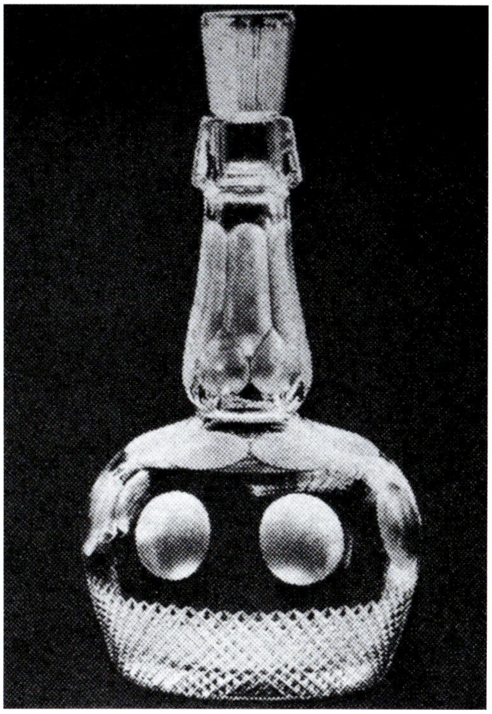

PUNTY & RAISED DIAMOND. *Illustration from a Pairpoint catalog.*

PORTSMOUTH. *Illustration from a Pairpoint catalog.*

RICHMOND DESIGN. *Illustration from a Pairpoint catalog.*

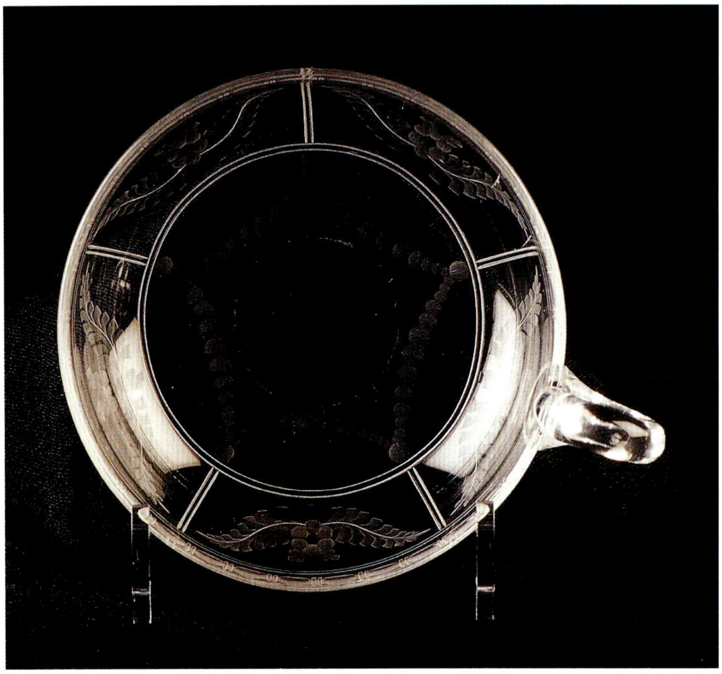

ROCKFORD (This pattern is alternatively known as No.245.)

ROYAL FERN

ROOSTER DESIGN. *Illustration from a Pairpoint catalog.*

SCHOONER. *Illustration from a Pairpoint catalog.*

SIRIUS. *Illustration from a Pairpoint catalog.*

SHELL DESIGN. *Illustration from a Pairpoint catalog.*

SMILAX. *Illustration from a Pairpoint catalog.*

SPANISH GALLEON. *Illustration from a Pairpoint catalog.*

STAFFORDSHIRE. *Illustration from a Pairpoint catalog.*

STRAWBERRY. *Illustration from a Pairpoint catalog.*

STAMFORD. *Illustration from a Pairpoint catalog.*

STRAWBERRY DIAMOND & FAN. *Illustration from a Pairpoint catalog.*

TASSEL. *Illustration from a Pairpoint catalog.*

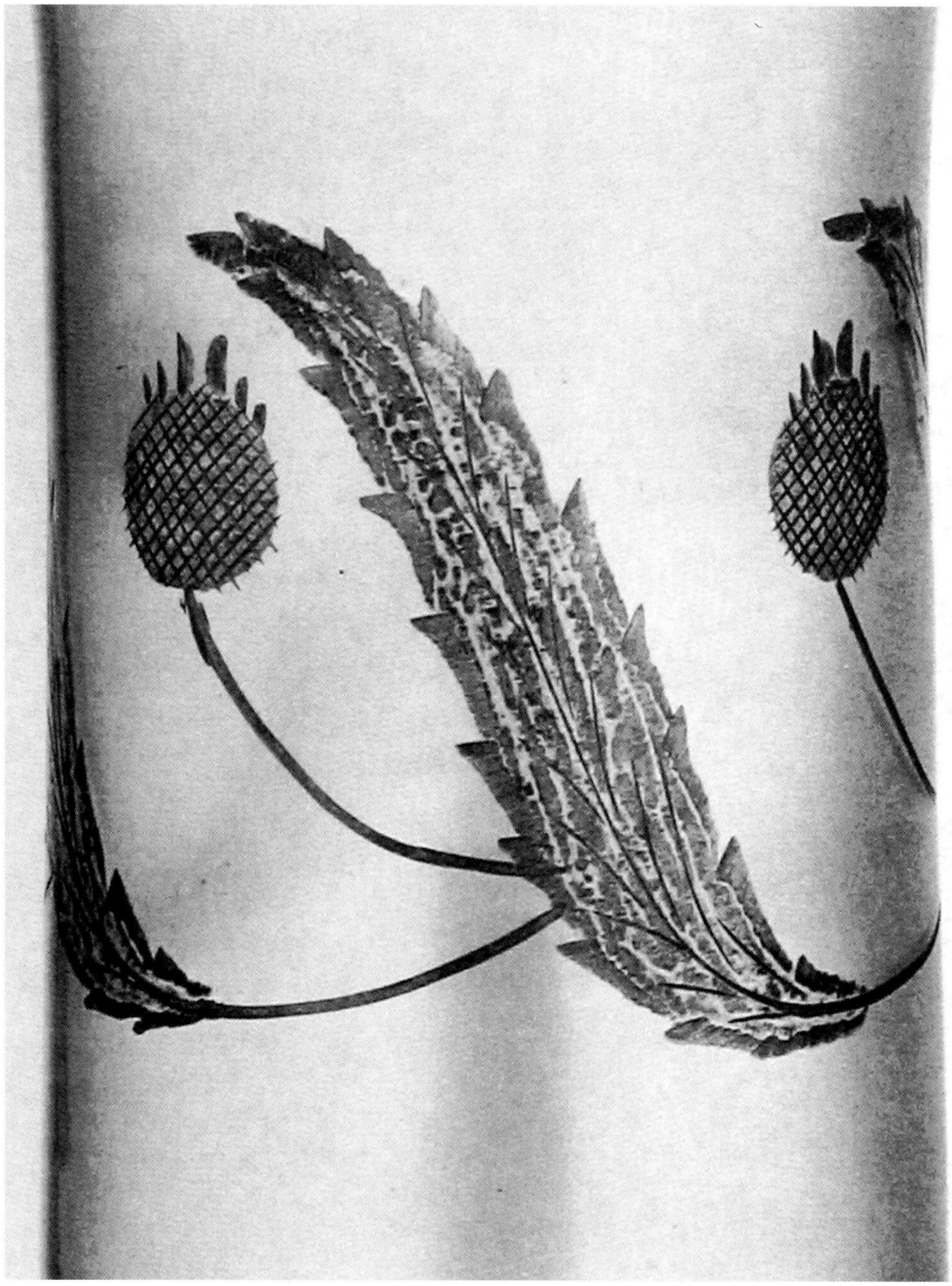

THISTLE. *Illustration from a Pairpoint catalog.*

TRIANON. No image has yet been matched to this documented pattern name.
This pattern has only been identified in factory documents with Cobalt-colored cut-to-clear items.

TYRONE

URN & FLAME

VERNON. *Illustration from a Pairpoint catalog.*

VICEROY. *Illustration from a Pairpoint catalog.*

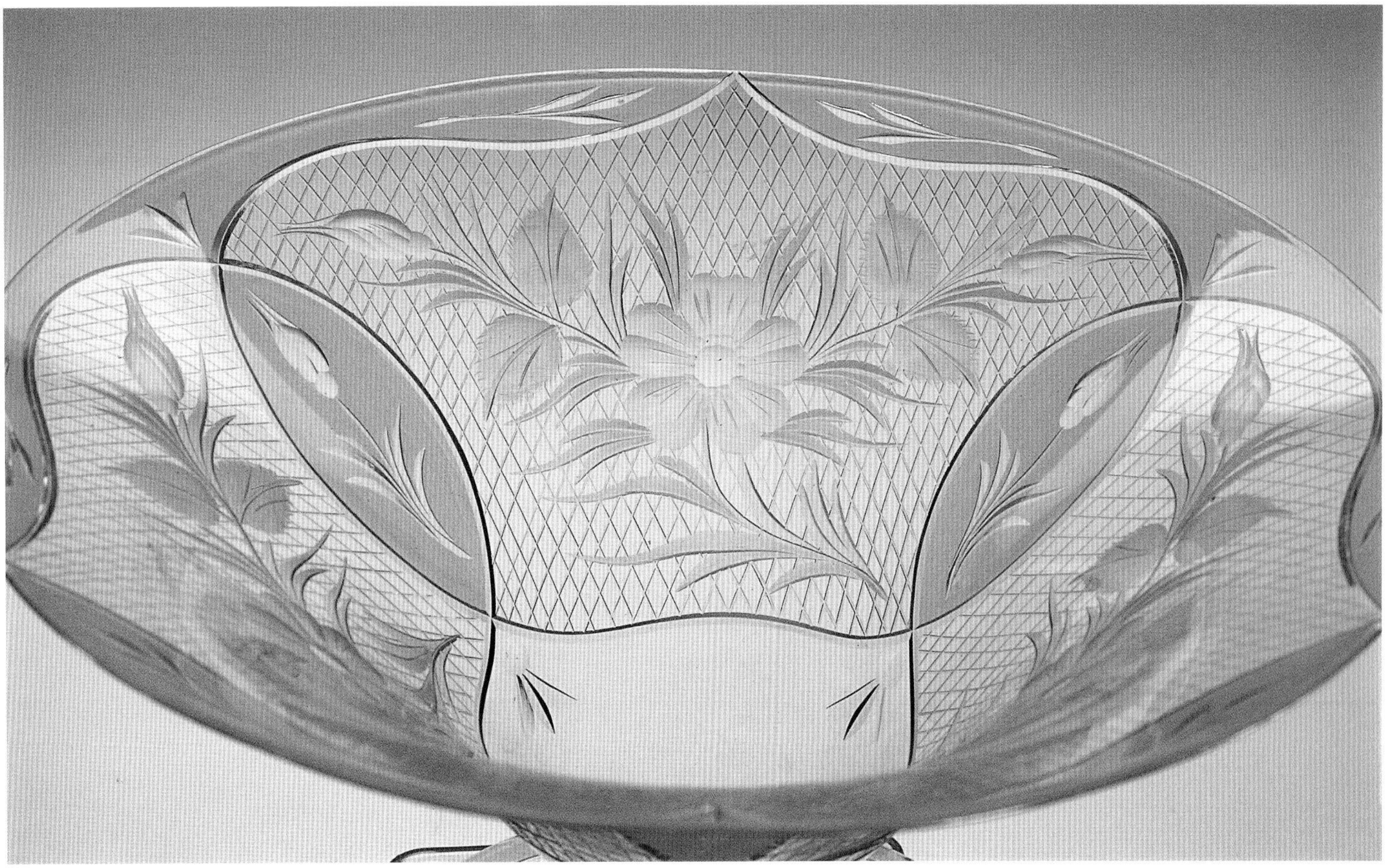

VICTORIA

VISCARIA. *Illustration from a Pairpoint catalog.*

WATERFORD. *Illustration from a Pairpoint catalog.*

WELLINGTON

WEXFORD. *Illustration from a Pairpoint catalog.*

WICKHAM DESIGN. *Illustration from a Pairpoint catalog.*

WILLARD. *Illustration from a Pairpoint catalog.*

WILTON. *Illustration from a Pairpoint catalog.*

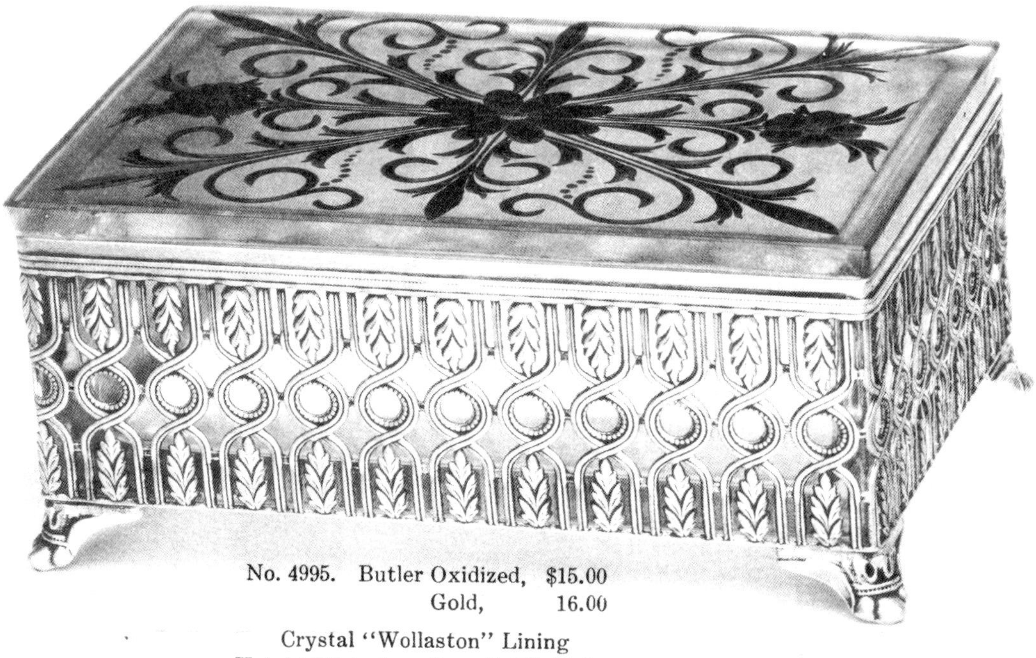

No. 4995. Butler Oxidized, $15.00
Gold, 16.00

Crystal "Wollaston" Lining
Height 2¼ inches, Length 5¾ inches

WOLLASTON. *Illustration from a Pairpoint catalog.*

WOLVERTON. No image has yet been matched to this documented pattern name.

WREN. *Illustration from a Pairpoint catalog.*

UNKNOWN A. *Illustration from a Pairpoint catalog.*

UNKNOWN AA

UNKNOWN AB

UNKNOWN AC

UNKNOWN AD. *Illustration from a Pairpoint catalog.*

UNKNOWN AE. *Sketch from the Pairpoint engraving department cost book.*

UNKNOWN AF

UNKNOWN AG. This pattern is similar to UNKNOWN O, except the flower has six (6) petals.

UNKNOWN AH. This pattern was found on a Pairpoint Fine Arts Line glass insert and bears many similarities to the engraving pattern called Albemarle. *Courtesy of Andrew Daniels.*

UNKNOWN B

UNKNOWN E. *Courtesy of Ruth A. Frost.*

UNKNOWN F

UNKNOWN I

UNKNOWN H

UNKNOWN L

UNKNOWN O. This pattern is similar to UNKNOWN AG, except the flower has eight (8) petals.

UNKNOWN P

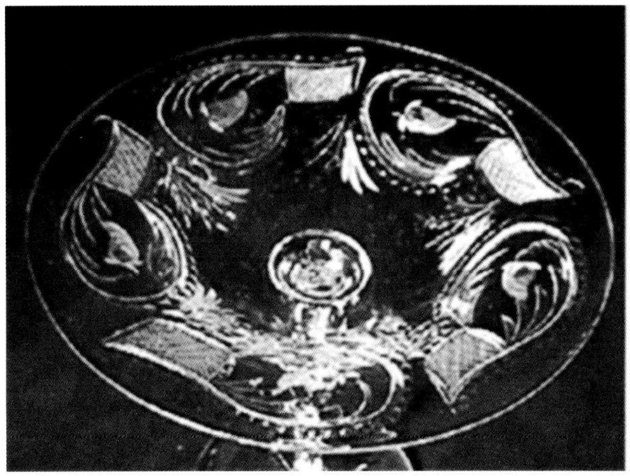

UNKNOWN S

UNKNOWN R

UNKNOWN U

UNKNOWN V

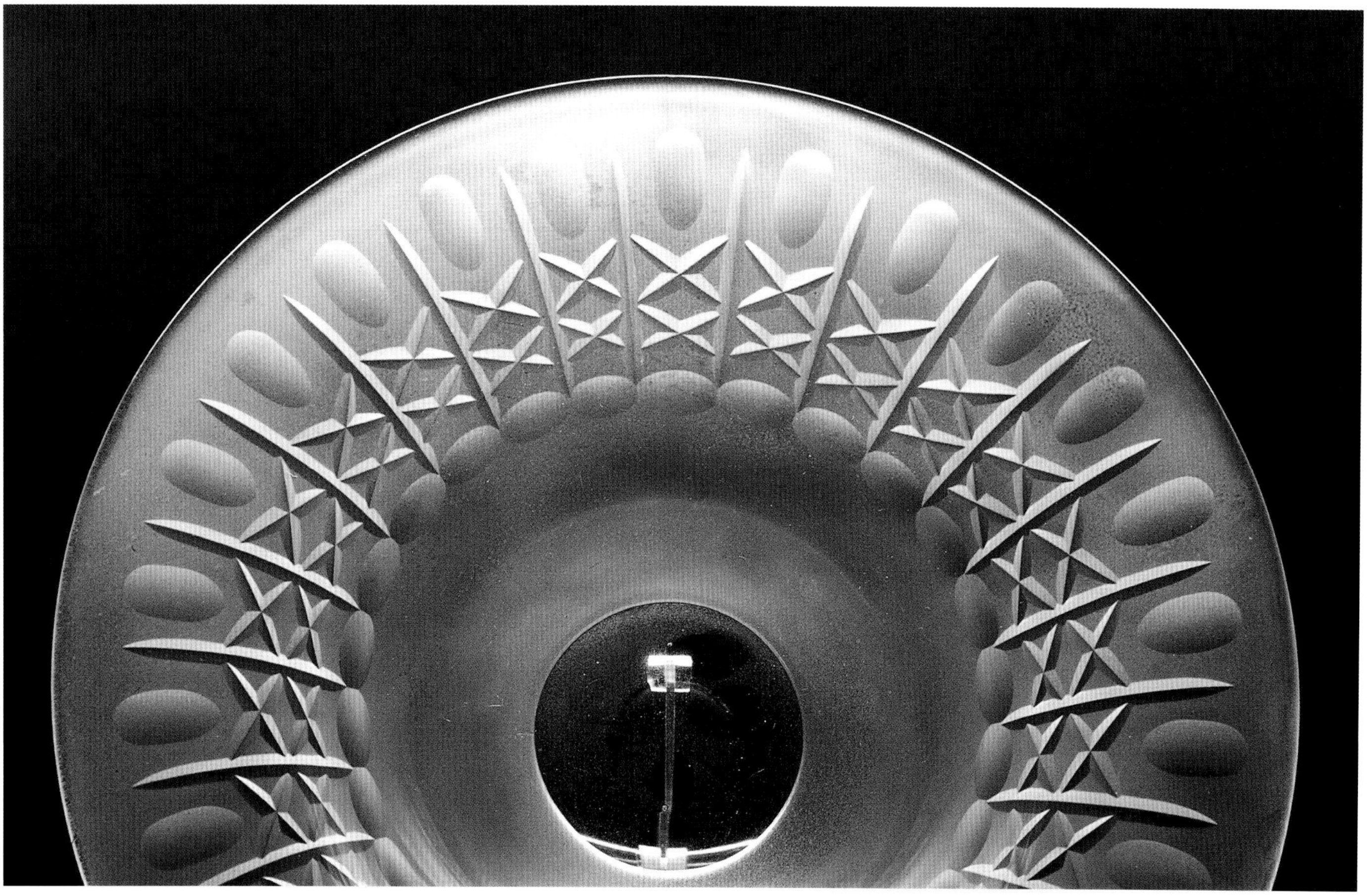

UNKNOWN X

UNKNOWN Y. *Illustration from a Pairpoint catalog.*

UNKNOWN Z

Chapter 4

Information Updates

Following the publication of *The Essence of Pairpoint* in 2001, we discovered a little more information about some of the special products that were showcased in Chapter 5 of that book. This information is outlined below and has been taken directly from Pairpoint documents. We have also included other updated information when we thought it would clarify issues or improve accuracy.

Colored Edge and Trim Products

Decorative glass items with the colored trim were actually part of a product line. The official name for these products, as shown on Pairpoint catalog pages, was "Crystal Glass with Trimmings of Blue, Amethyst and Chrysopos." As shown in the catalog pages, the only engraving patterns associated with this product line were Waterford and Florentine. From all our observations, this would be true, however, we do have a vase that is not engraved. It is worth mentioning that while the Florentine pattern is mostly found on these color-trimmed items, it will occasionally be found on Canaria colored pieces from the same production period. The Waterford pattern will regularly be found throughout the Pairpoint product lines.

The Florentine pattern shown on a solid Canaria A-104 Comport. This pattern is almost exclusively found on the Colored Edge and Trim pieces.

We recently acquired an example of the A-215 Comport from this product line that supports our belief that you should always expect the unexpected. Instead of the comport having the connecting wafer above the foot in the Chrysopos color, the entire foot was Chrysopos, and the wafer was clear. This product line would have been produced during the 1920s and 1930s.

A variant of the Colored Edge and Trim A-215 comport, this example has a colored foot and clear connecting wafer.

Colors

We have discovered a difference in the spelling of one of the colors. Previously, in all reference materials published to date, including our own, the golden-brown color was identified as "Chrysopras." According to published Pairpoint catalog pages, the correct spelling is "Chrysopos."

Chrysopos, a medium brown color.

EPNS with Cobalt Blue

We have determined through catalog pages that decorative items combining blue (or clear) glass with EPNS (electro-plated nickel silver) metal parts are part of Pairpoint's Fine Arts Line of products. Many of these items will be shown in our upcoming book on the Fine Arts Line.

An example of a beautiful silver and blue glass centerpiece bowl from Pairpoint's Fine Arts Line.

Tavern Glass

This well-crafted and fascinating product line was also called "Seeded Ware" by the lamp department which assumed responsibility for this line. Once the glass blanks were made, they went to the lamp department where they were decorated by hand and sold using the lamp department discount structures. Unlike any other Pairpoint glass product at the time, Tavern Glass or Seeded Ware was signed in enamel with the item number followed by the decoration number. The number D1507/281 would designate a 6" Vase (D1507) with the Whale decoration (281). Listed below are as many shapes and decorating patterns as we could verify from price lists and lamp department internal documents, all of which date from 1926. Note that all shapes use the prefix "D" before the number. While we cannot be certain, of course, the documents in our possession lead us to believe that the following list is fairly complete.

Examples of Pairpoint's Tavern Glass (Seeded Ware).

Items

D1507 Vase 6"
D1508 Vase 5-1/2"
D1509 Round Vase 5"
D1510 Vase 6-1/2"
D1511 Vase 8"
D1512 Vase 7"
D1513 Vase 8"
D1514 Flip Glass 6"
D1515 Flip Glass 5-1/4"
D1516 Hi Ball 5-1/2"
D1517 Tumbler 4"
D1518 Cocktail 3-7/8"
D1519 Centerpiece Bowl 11" diameter
D1520 Princess Candle
D1521 Plate 8-1/2"
D1522 Plate 12"
D1523 Plate 14"
D1524 Jam Jar
D1525 Candy Box

Decorating Patterns

#11 Waiter & Coach
#12 Indian
#13 Mounted Police
#14 Racketeers
#15 Golfer
#16 Coast Guard Patrol
#17 Satan
#281 Whale
#282 Galleon (Various configurations)
#283 Grapes
#284 Polar Bear
#285 Urn & Flowers
#286 Flowers
#287 Spray of Flowers
#288 Rooster
Giraffe
Pig
Duck
Parrot
Camel
Dog
Elephant
Monkey
Fox & Grapes
Donkey

Venetti Design

On Page 206, in *The Essence of Pairpoint*, we draw your attention to Vase #1818. While we have only seen this form in the Venetti Design, we have learned from information provided in the 1926 engraving department cost book that this shape was engraved with other patterns..

We have also acquired more dimensional information on some of the other shapes within this product line: #1813 Candlestick, 6.25" high; #1817 Vase, 12" high with a 5.75" flare diameter.

Chapter 5

An Engraving Department Cost Book

Within this chapter we have included a real treat for Pairpoint enthusiasts…a reproduction of a portion of the notebook used by an engraving department superintendent. In the possession of engraver Carl Silva long after he left Pairpoint, this notebook, which measures 3-1/2" wide by 6" high, is dated 1926, and was used to keep track of the labor cost associated with applying the many different engraving patterns to the many different blank shapes. The portion we have selected to reproduce is that portion containing hand sketches of the various shapes. This portion is extremely enlightening, and shows some shapes not shown in the "Shapes" chapter earlier in this book. This extremely valuable document was generously given to us by Myldred Costa.

You will observe, as you examine these sketches, a numbering system that has no relationship to the actual catalog numbers Pairpoint used to identify their products in their catalog pages. This numbering system was internal to the engraving department and was used by them to identify the various shapes. It is anyone's guess why a dual numbering system was employed.

Following the pages containing the sketches, you will find a cross-reference chart that we created to assist you in converting the internal numbering system over to the numbers Pairpoint actually used in their catalogs. Additionally, we have included other information extracted from the portion of the cost book that we did not reproduce. Most of this additional information has already been integrated into the photograph captions within the "Shapes" chapter. Where a shape was ambiguous or questionable in its identification, we chose not to attempt a cross-over match.

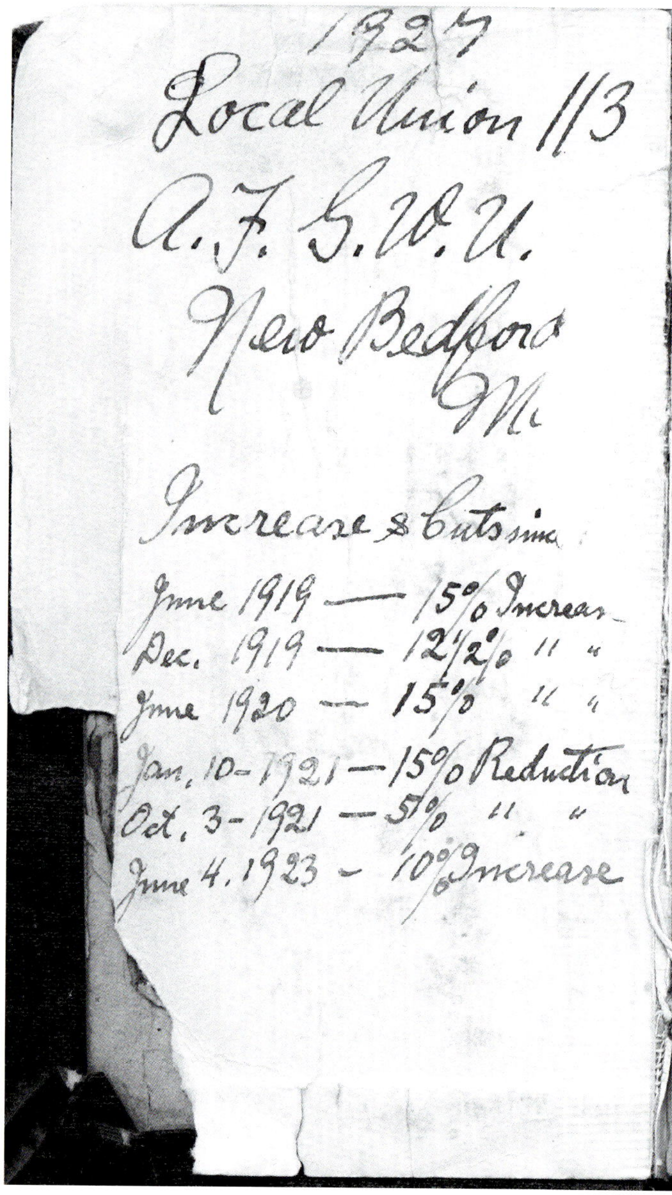
1927
Local Union 113
A. F. G. W. U.
New Bedford
Ma
Increase & Cuts since
June 1919 — 15% Increase
Dec. 1919 — 12½% " "
June 1920 — 15% " "
Jan. 10-1921 — 15% Reduction
Oct. 3-1921 — 5% " "
June 4. 1923 — 10% Increase

Page 1, Pairpoint Engraving Department Cost Book

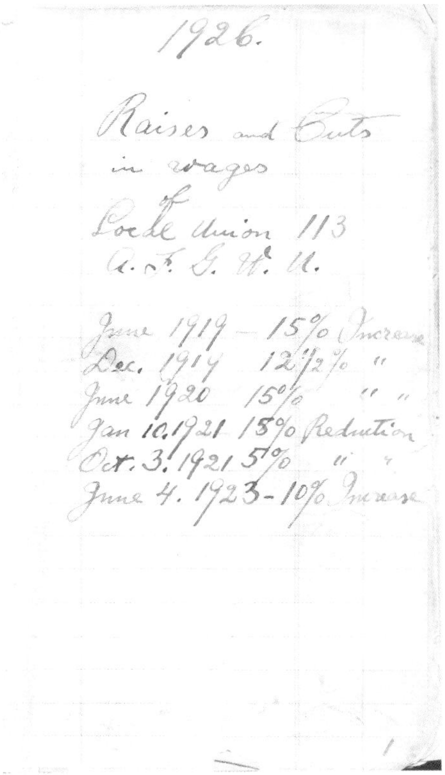
1926.

Raises and Cuts in wages of Local Union 113 A.F.G.W.U.

June 1919	15%	Increase
Dec. 1919	12½%	"
June 1920	15%	" "
Jan 10. 1921	18%	Reduction
Oct. 3. 1921	5%	" "
June 4. 1923	10%	Increase

Page 2, Pairpoint Engraving Department Cost Book

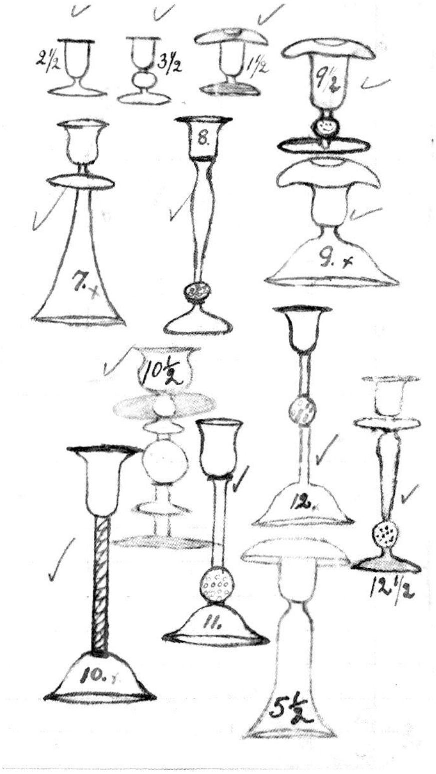

Page 4, Pairpoint Engraving Department Cost Book

Page 6, Pairpoint Engraving Department Cost Book

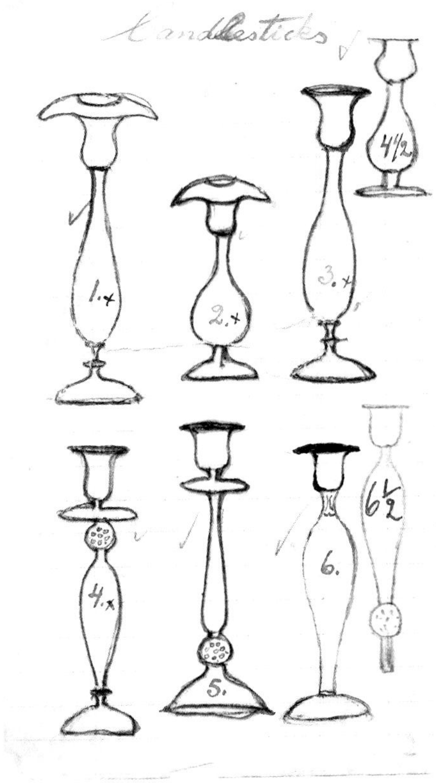

Page 3, Pairpoint Engraving Department Cost Book

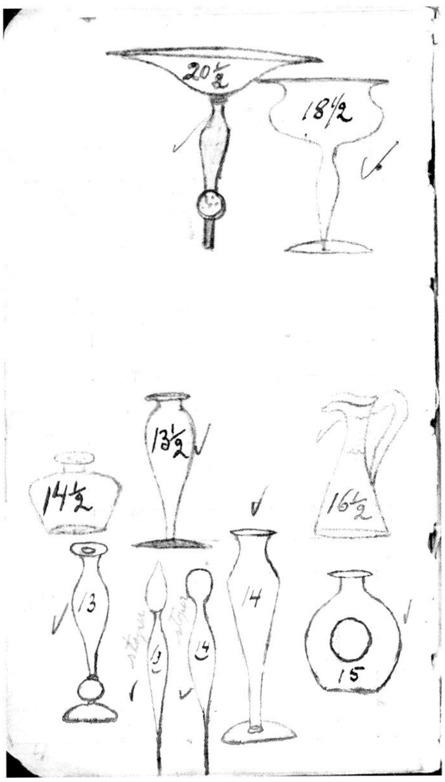

Page 5, Pairpoint Engraving Department Cost Book

Page 7, Pairpoint Engraving Department Cost Book

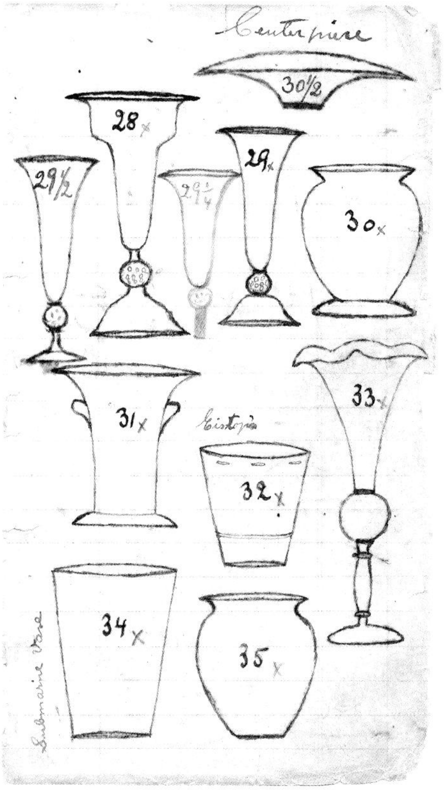

Page 8, Pairpoint Engraving Department Cost Book

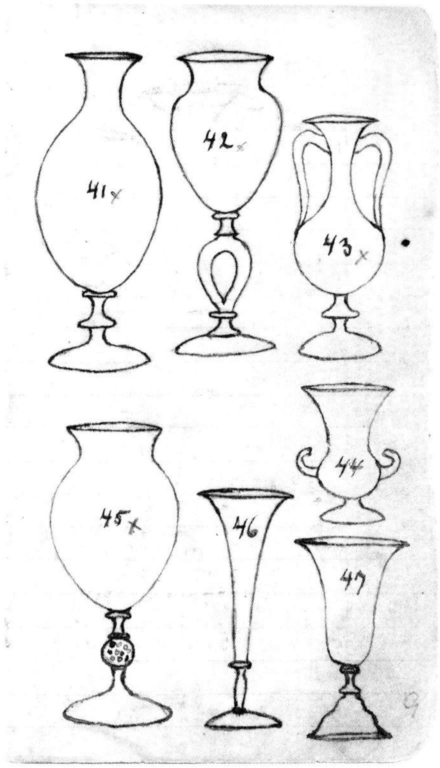

Page 10, Pairpoint Engraving Department Cost Book

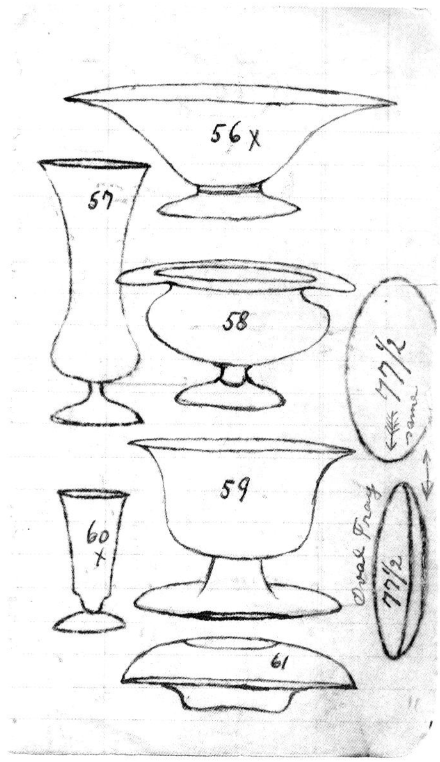

Page 12, Pairpoint Engraving Department Cost Book

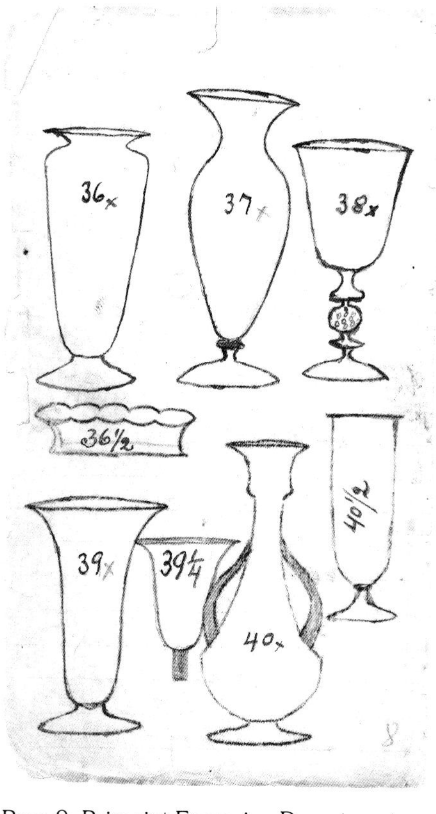

Page 9, Pairpoint Engraving Department Cost Book

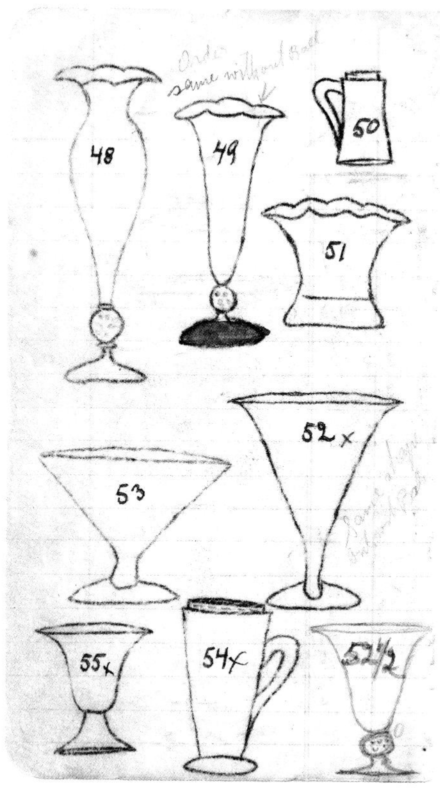

Page 11, Pairpoint Engraving Department Cost Book

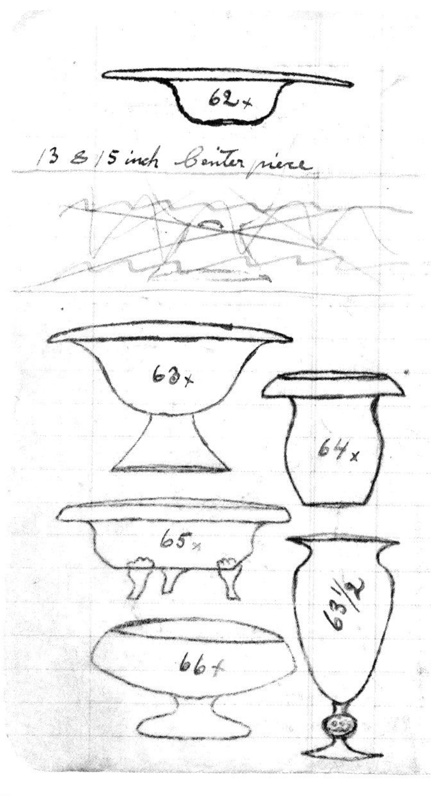

Page 13, Pairpoint Engraving Department Cost Book

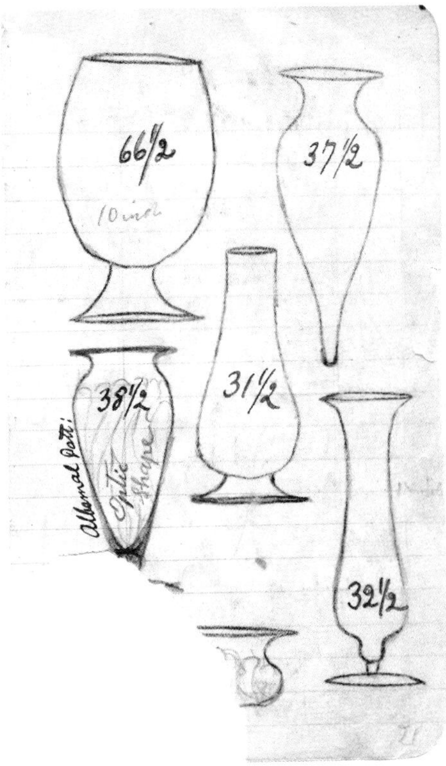

Page 14, Pairpoint Engraving Department Cost Book

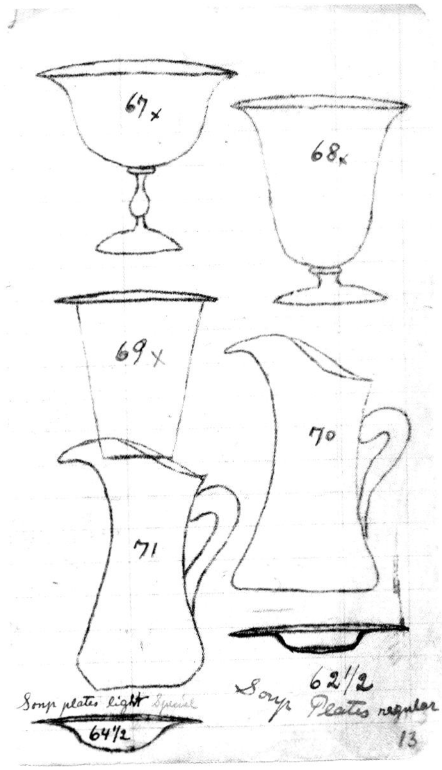

Page 16, Pairpoint Engraving Department Cost Book

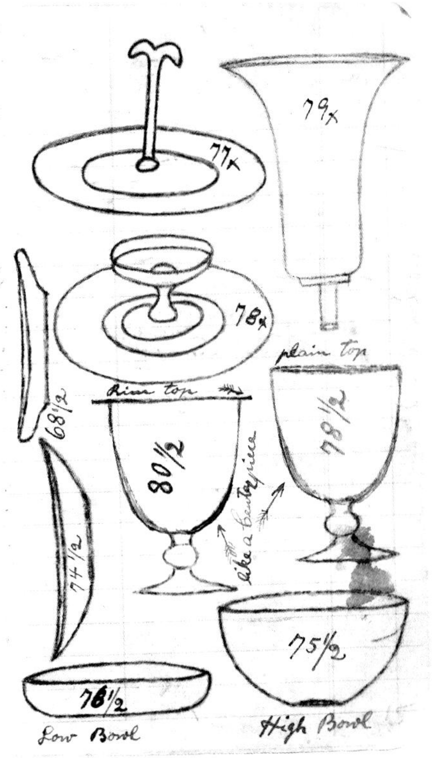

Page 18, Pairpoint Engraving Department Cost Book

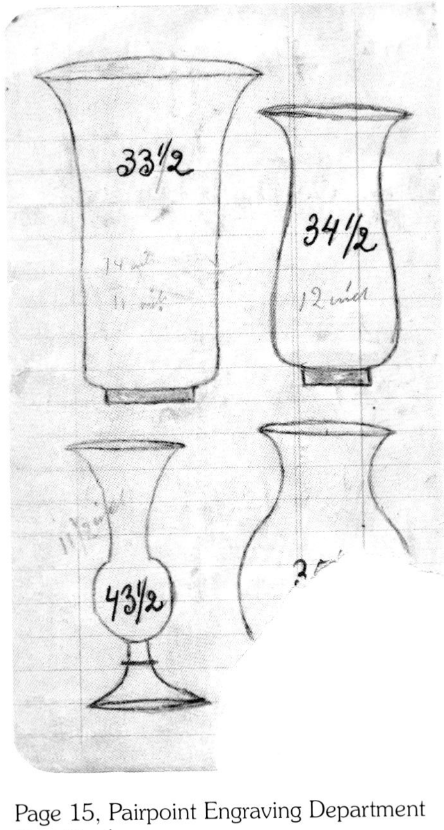

Page 15, Pairpoint Engraving Department Cost Book

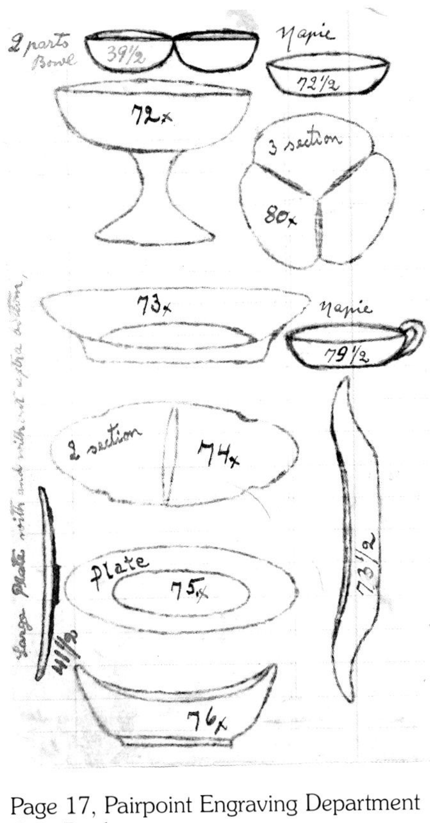

Page 17, Pairpoint Engraving Department Cost Book

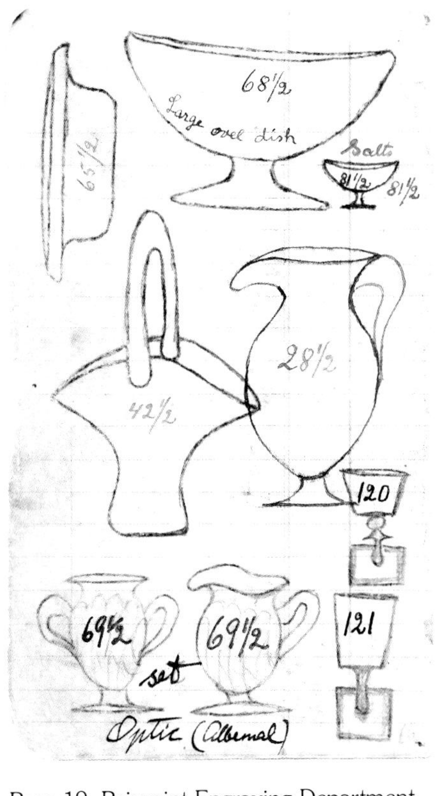

Page 19, Pairpoint Engraving Department Cost Book

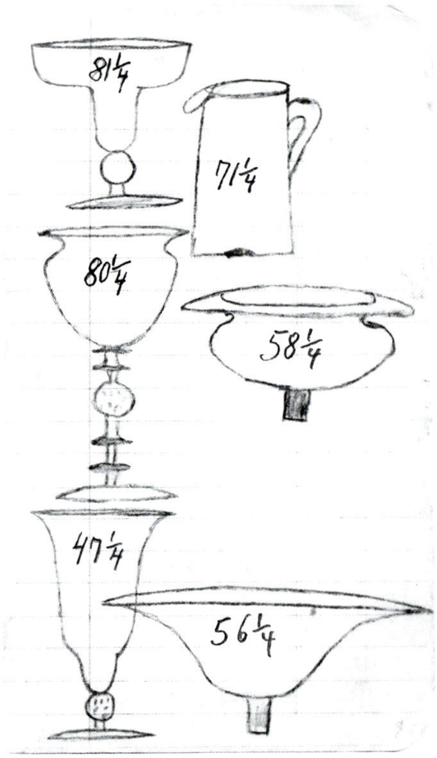

Page 20, Pairpoint Engraving Department Cost Book

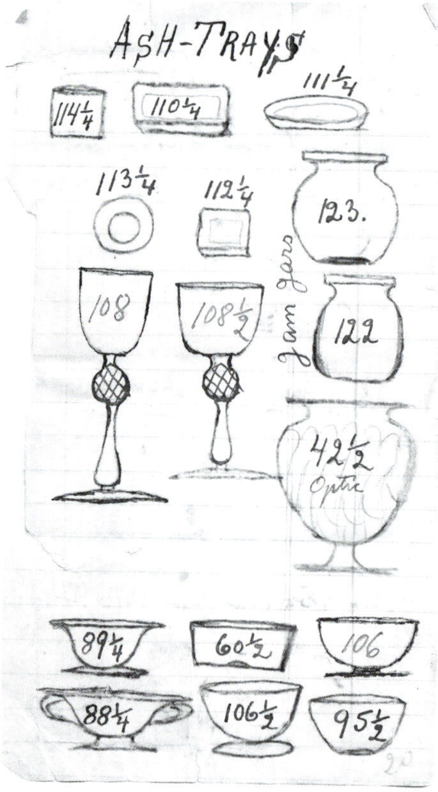

Page 21, Pairpoint Engraving Department Cost Book

Page 22, Pairpoint Engraving Department Cost Book

Engraver's Book Code #	Convert To Catalog #	Dimensions From Engraver's Book	Comments
1	1641	9.50	Candle
1-1/2	Unk 15		Candle
2	1635		Candle
2-1/2	Unk 101		Candle
3	1629	9.5, 10.75, 12, 14, 16	Candle
3-1/2	Unk 14		Candle
4	B-1628	12	Candle
4-1/2	Unk 100	8"	Candle with heavy optic
5	B-1811	12, 16	Candle
5-1/2	642		Candle
6	1600	10.75, 12, 14, 16	Candle
6-1/2			Component for Fine Arts Line Candlestick
7	1616		Candle
7-1/2			Cigarette Holder
8	B-1627	9, 10.75, 12	Candle
9	1640	Large, Small	Candle
9-1/2	Unk 10	Large, Small	Candle
10	F-1624	10	Candle
10-1/2	B-1634		Candle
11	B-1626	10, 12	Candle
12	F-1623	10	Candle
12-1/2	Unk 13		Candle

Cross-reference Chart, Page 1

Engraver's Book Code #	Convert To Catalog #	Dimensions From Engraver's Book	Comments
13	B-31		Cologne
13-1/2		4.50h, 6h, 7h	Cologne
14		5.50, 7	Cologne
14-1/2	14		Cologne
15	632		Donut Decanter
16	A-228	6, 7, 8, 9, 10, 12.50	Comport
16-1/2	544		Oil/Cruet
17	A-294	5.50, 6.50, 7.50, 8, 8.50, 9.50, 10.50	Comport
18	372	7, 7.50, 8.50	Comport
18-1/2	Unk 102	6d x 6.75h	Comport with heavy optic
19	B-228	6, 7, 8, 9	Comport
19-1/2		9.50	
20	B-366	6.50, 7.50, 8.50	Comport
20-1/2			Component for Fine Arts Line Comport
21	Unk 97	One Size	Comport
21-1/2	364		Comport
22	B-367		Comport
22-1/2			Comport
23	A-298	8, 11	Covered Urn
23-1/2	B-915	6.50, 8	Covered Candy Jar
24	B-382		Covered Comport
24-1/2	Unk 92	7.50	Covered Comport

Cross-reference Chart, Page 2

Engraver's Book Code #	Convert To Catalog #	Dimensions From Engraver's Book	Comments
25	Unk 23		Tall Covered Comport
25-1/2	A-295	6, 6.50, 8	Covered Urn
26	951	6, 6.50, 7.50, 8	Covered Box
26-1/2			
27	B-1612	12	Urn Vase
28	B-373	11, 12	Urn Vase
28-1/2			Jug (?)
29	B-959	10, 12	Vase
29-1/4			Component for Fine Arts Line Vase
29-1/2	B-961	10, 12	Vase
30	A-1073	9, 10	Vase
30-1/2	Unk 3	13, 15, 16	Centerpiece Bowl
31	A-1068	8, 10	Vase made with or without loop handles
31-1/2	Unk 106		Vase
32	1159	6.50, 7.50	Ice Pail to be finished with silver-plated rim, handle, and drainer
32-1/2	Unk 107	11, 14	Vase
33	A-1074	10.75, 14	Vase
33-1/2		11, 14	Component for Fine Arts Line Vase
34	1158	8.50, 9.50, 12	"Submarine Vase"
34-1/2		12	Component for Fine Arts Line Vase
35	A-1072	9, 9.50	Vase
35-1/2	A-1078		Vase

Cross-reference Chart, Page 3

Engraver's Book Code #	Convert To Catalog #	Dimensions From Engraver's Book	Comments
36	A-1099	10	Vase
36-1/2	A-1091	9, 12	Flower Holder
37	A-1063	12, 14	Vase
37-1/2			Component for Fine Arts Line Vase
38	B-1083	10	Vase-Available with or without cover
38-1/2			Vase with heavy optic
39	A-1062	6, 8, 8.50, 10, 12, 14, 16	Vase
39-1/4			Component for Fine Arts Line Vase
39-1/2	A-253		2-part tray
40	A-1069		Vase
40-1/2	Unk 42		Vase
41	1071		Vase
41-1/4		14, 16	
41-1/2	319	12, 13, 14, 15, 16	Deep Plate
42	1818		Venetti Design Vase
42-1/2 "A"	A-235	7	Basket (Duplicate numbering)
42-1/2 "B"			Vase with heavy optic (Duplicate numbering)
43	A-1070	7.50	Vase
43-1/2	Unk 108	11.50	Vase
44	A-1055	4.25 x 6	Vase
45	B-962	10	Vase
45-1/2			

Cross-reference Chart, Page 4

Engraver's Book Code #	Convert To Catalog #	Dimensions From Engraver's Book	Comments
46	A-1084	12	Vase
47	A-1164	12	Vase
47-1/4	B-1485		Vase
48	Unk 104		Vase
49	B-960	8, 9, 10, 10.50, 12	Vase
50		5	
51	Unk 87	5, 5.50, 7, 7.50	Flower Holder
52	A-1007	6, 8, 10	Vase
52-1/2	Unk 44	8	Vase
53	A-104	6, 8, 10	Comport
54	Unk 64		Mixer Base
54-1/2			
55	1174	4.50 (top?), 5.75 top x 5.50 h, 6 top x 5 h	Bowl
55-1/4			
56	A-194	9, 10, 12, 14, 16	Center Bowl
56-1/4		12	Component for Fine Arts Line Center Bowl
57	A-1005	10	Vase
57-1/2		10, 12, 14	
58	A-1065	10, 12, 14, 16	Center Bowl
58-1/4			Component for Fine Arts Line Center Bowl
58-1/2		10, 12, 14	
59	A-192	10	Centerpiece Bowl on Plate

Cross-reference Chart, Page 5

Engraver's Book Code #	Convert To Catalog #	Dimensions From Engraver's Book	Comments
60	Unk 105	3.25 top x 6 h	
60-1/2		4.50 top, 4.25 top	
61	Unk 2	13, 15	Center Bowl
62	324	10, 11, 13, 15	Centerpiece Bowl
62-1/2		6.50, 7.50, 8, 8.50, 9, 9.50	Soup Plates - Regular
63	A-145	8, 9, 10, 12, 14, 15	Pedestal Centerpiece Bowl
63-1/2	B-1107	10, 12, 14	Vase
64	A-1100		Vase
64-1/2		6.50, 8.50	Soup Plates - Light/Special
65	A-193	13	3-Footed Bowl
65-1/2			Bowl (Same as #65, but without feet)
66	A-1106	13	Pedestal Bowl
66-1/2	1474	10	Vase
67	A-299	10, 12	Comport
68	Unk 109	9	Vase
68-1/2 "A"		13	Tray (Duplicate numbering)
68-1/2 "B"	A-239		Oval Dish/Comport (Duplicate numbering)
69	Unk 88	10	Vase
69-1/2			Cream & Sugar set with heavy optic
70	3858		Jug
70-1/2			
71	459		Jug

Cross-reference Chart, Page 6

Engraver's Book Code #	Convert To Catalog #	Dimensions From Engraver's Book	Comments
71-1/4	400		Jug
72			
72-1/2	286	5, 6, 7, 8	Nappy
73		9 x 13	Bread Tray
73-1/2	815	13	Bread Tray
74	A-265	8.50	2-section tray
74-1/2			Celery Tray
75	329	6, 6.50, 6.75, 7, 7.50, 8, 8.50, 9, 10, 10.75, 12, 14, 16	Flat Plate Regular
75-1/2	111	8, 9, 10	High Bowl
76	317	11	Oval Bowl
76-1/2	210 - 210.5	7, 8, 9, 10	Low Bowl
77	336	10	Handled Plate
77-1/2	Unk 70	8, 8.50, 9, 10	Oval Tray
78	322	10	Cracker & Cheese Plate
78-1/2			Same as #80-1/2 but with plain top - no rim
79			Component for Fine Arts Line Vase
79-1/2	205	5, 6	Nappy
80		9 dia x 2 h	3-part nappy or dish
80-1/4	Unk 111		Vase
80-1/2			Same as #78-1/2 but with a rim top

Cross-reference Chart, Page 7

Engraver's Book Code #	Convert To Catalog #	Dimensions From Engraver's Book	Comments
81		2.25 top x 4.75 h, 2.50 top x 5.50 h, 2.875 top x 5.875 h, 3 top x 6 h, 3.75 top x 9.75 h	
81-1/4	Unk 110		Vase
81-1/2	A-239	3.50, 5.25, 5.50	Salt/Oval Comport
82		7.5	
82-1/4			
82-1/2			
83		4 top x 5.25 h, 4 top x 6.50 h, 4 top x 7 h	
83-1/2		1.75 top x 5.25, 2 top x 5.875, 2.25 top x 6.50, 2.50 top x 6.75, 2.75 top x 7.75, 3.25 top x ___, 3.50 top x 8.125	
84		3.25 top x 4.50, 3.50 top x 4.50, 3.75 top x 5.25	
84-1/2		3.25 top x 5.25 h	
85		3.375 x 7	
85-1/2		3.25 top x ___, 3.50 top x 8.125	
86		3.25 x 5.75, 4 x 6.25	Stems
86-1/2			
87		4 x 4.75, 4 x 5, 4 x 5.25	
87-1/2			
88-1/4			
88-1/2		4.50 top	
89			Clarets

Cross-reference Chart, Page 8

Engraver's Book Code #	Convert To Catalog #	Dimensions From Engraver's Book	Comments
89-1/4			
89-1/2			
90-1/2		5 top x 2.50 h	
91		3.125 top x 5.875 h	Tumbler
91-1/2			Tumbler
92		Small	Tumbler
92-1/2		3 top x 5.50 h	Tumbler
93			
93-1/2			
94			
94-1/2	5000		Goblet
95			Finger Bowl
95-1/2			
96			
97		5.25 top	Finger Bowl
97-1/2		4 - 3.75??	
98-1/2			
101		2.50 top x 4 h	Stems
101-1/2			
102		3 x 4, 3.50 x 4.50, 4 x 4	Stems
102-1/2			
103		2 top x 3.25 h, 3 top x 5.50 h, 3.75 top x 7 h	Stems

Cross-reference Chart, Page 9

Engraver's Book Code #	Convert To Catalog #	Dimensions From Engraver's Book	Comments
103-1/2			
104		3.50 top x 4.75 h	Stems
104-1/2		3 top x 4 h	Stems
105			
106		4.5 top x 2.50 h, 4.50 top x 2.75 h	
106-1/2		4.50 top x 2.75, 5.50 top x 2.75	
107			
108		3.375 x 8.25 h	
108-1/2			
109			
110-1/4			Ash Tray
111-1/4			Ash Tray
112-1/4			Ash Tray
113-1/4			Ash Tray
114-1/4			Ash Tray
116			
120			
121			
122			Jam Jar
123			Jam Jar

Cross-reference Chart, Page 10

Bibliography

Books

Avila, George C. *The Pairpoint Glass Story*. New Bedford, Massachusetts: George C. Avila and Reynolds-DeWalt Printing, Inc., 1968.

Frost, Marion and Sandra, *The Essence of Pairpoint*, Atglen, Pennsylvania: Schiffer Publishing, Ltd., 2001

Padgett, Leonard E. *Pairpoint Glass*. Des Moines, Iowa: Wallace-Homestead Book Co., 1979.

Index